World
HISTORY

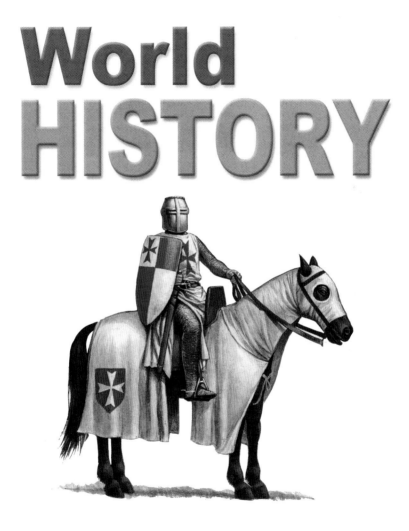

First published in 2004 by Miles Kelly Publishing Ltd
Harding's Barn, Bardfield End Green, Thaxted, Essex, CM6 3PX, UK

Copyright © Miles Kelly Publishing Ltd 2004

This edition updated and published 2010

2 4 6 8 10 9 7 5 3 1

Editorial Director Belinda Gallagher
Art Director Jo Brewer
Editor Stuart Cooper
Editorial Assistant Bethanie Bourne
Cover Designer Simon Lee
Designer Debbie Meekcoms
Indexer Charlotte Marshall
Production Manager Elizabeth Collins
Reprographics Anthony Cambray, Rick Caylor, Stephan Davis,
Liberty Newton, Ian Paulyn
Assets Manager Bethan Ellish

British Library Cataloguing-in-Publication Data
A catalogue record for this book is available from the British Library

ISBN 978-1-84810-357-3

Printed in China

Made with paper from a sustainable forest

www.mileskelly.net   info@mileskelly.net

www.factsforprojects.com

Self-publish your
children's book

buddingpress.co.uk

World HISTORY

John Farndon & Victoria Parker
Consultant: Richard Tames

Contents

ANCIENT HISTORY

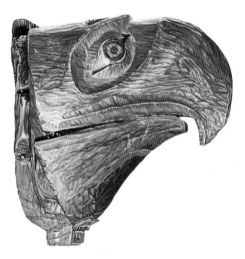

MODERN HISTORY

Origins of mankind

- **Humans and apes** have so many similarities – such as long arms and fingers, and a big brain – that most experts think they must have evolved from the same creature.

- **Our common ancestor** may be four-legged orang-utan-like creatures called dryopithecines that lived in trees from 22 to 10 million years ago, like 'Proconsul' from East Africa.

- **The break came when** 'hominids' (human-like apes) began to live on the ground and walk on two legs.

- **Footprints** of three bipedal (two-legged) creatures from 4 million years ago were found preserved in ash at Laetoli, Tanzania.

- **The oldest hominid** is called *Ardipithecus ramidus*, known from 4.4-million-years-old bone fragments found in Aramis, Ethiopia.

- **Many very early hominids** are australopiths ('southern apes'); for example, *Australopithecus anamensis* from 4.2 million years ago.

- **Australopiths** were one m tall and their brain was about the same size as an ape's, but they were bipedal.

- **The best known australopith** is 'Lucy', a skeleton of *Australopithecus afarensis* of 3 million years ago, found in Kenya in 1974.

1

2

14

- **Lucy's discoverers** – Don Johanson and Maurice Tieb – called her Lucy because they were listening to The Beatles' song 'Lucy in the Sky with Diamonds' at the time.

- **Many early hominid remains** are just skulls. Lucy was an almost complete skeleton. She showed that hominids learned to walk upright before their brains got bigger.

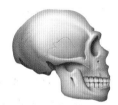

The Neanderthal skull (above) is smaller than a modern human skull (below). Brain size has increased over thousands of years.

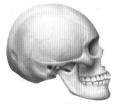

◀ *Experts once thought humans had evolved in a single line from australopiths, through* Homo habilis *(1),* Homo erectus *(2) and Neanderthal man (3) to humans (4). They now realize there were many branches.*

15

Handy man

- **The first really human-like hominids** appeared around 2.5–1.8 mya. These hominids are all given the genus (group) name *Homo*, and include us.

- **The best known** early examples are *Homo rudolfensis* and *Homo habilis.*

- **The first early humans** were taller than australopiths and had bigger brains.

- **Unlike australopiths**, these hominids ate meat. They may have been forced to eat meat when the climate warmed up, cutting the amount of plant food that was available.

- **Brains need** a lot of food, and eating meat gave the extra nourishment that is required for bigger brains.

▲ Homo habilis *was the first tool-making human. Flint was the most suitable material and flakes were chipped off using a bone hammer. The main piece of flint was shaped into a hand axe. The flakes of flint were used as cutting tools.*

- *Homo habilis* is known from pieces of hand bones, a jaw and a skull found in Tanzania's Olduvai Gorge in 1961.

- *Homo habilis* means 'Handy Man'. He gets his name because he has a good grip for wielding tools – with a thumb that can be rotated to meet the tip of a finger. This is called an 'opposable thumb'.

- **The first Homo species** used stones to break open bones for the nourishing marrow inside. Later they sharpened stones to cut meat for eating and hides for making clothing. Experts believe that they may even have built simple shelters to live in.

16

- **Some experts think** the bulge in 'Broca's area' of some *Homo habilis* skulls suggests that they could speak in a crude way. Most think they could not.
- **The first hominids in the genus *Homo* lived** for a million or more years alongside 'robust' (bigger) australopiths such as *Paranthropus boisei*.

◀ *Skulls that have been found show that the first Homos, like* Homo habilis, *had brains of 650 cubic cm (cc) – twice as big as australopiths. However, they had ape-like faces with protruding jaws and sloping foreheads. Today's human brains measure about 1400 cc.*

Man, the hunter

- **About 2 mya**, a much taller hominid called *Homo ergaster* appeared. Ergasters were the first creatures to have bodies much like ours, with long legs and straight backs.

- **Adult ergasters** were 1.6 m tall, weighed 65 kg and had brains of 850 cc, well over half as big as ours.

- **Ergasters did not just scavenge** for meat like *Homo habilis*. They went hunting for large animals.

- **For hunting** and cutting up meat, ergaster made double-edged blades or 'hand-axes' from pieces of stone, shaping them by chipping off flakes. Experts call this Acheulean tool-making.

- **To hunt effectively**, ergasters had to work together, so co-operation was the key to their success – and may have quickly led to the development of speech.

- **Ergasters may have painted** their bodies with red ochre (a mineral found in the ground).

- **Shortly after *Homo ergaster*** came *Homo erectus* ('Upright Man').

- **Remains of *Homo erectus*** are found as far from Africa as Java. Stone tools 700,000 years old were found on the Indonesian island of Flores and suggest they may have travelled by boat.

▲ *This teardrop-shaped stone tool is typical of ergaster and* H. erectus.

- ***Homo erectus* learned to light fires**, so they could live in colder places, and make a wider range of food, edible by cooking.

▼ *As he developed a greater variety of stone tools, early man was more successful at hunting and eating wild animals.*

...FASCINATING FACT...
Long legs and working in groups helped ergaster to spread beyond Africa into Asia and maybe Europe.

Later hunters

- **Hominids appeared in Europe** much later. The oldest, called *Homo antecessor*, dates from 800,000 years ago. This may have been a kind of erectus, or another species.

- **Later, around 800,000–600,000 years ago**, *Homo heidelbergensis* appeared in parts of Europe, Asia and Africa.

- **Heidelbergensis** may be a single species that came from Africa – or various species that evolved in different places.

- *Homo heidelbergensis* has many features in common with *Homo erectus*, but is a major step on the way to modern humans with, for the very first time, a brain as big as ours.

- **Using stone**, Heidelbergensis made good tools. They did this by making the core first, then shaping the blade with a single blow.

- **Heidelbergensis was ancestor** to Neanderthal Man, who lived in Europe from 250,000 to 30,000 years ago.

- **Neanderthals were named** after the Neander valley in Germany, where remains were found in 1856.

- **Although slightly shorter** than modern humans, Neanderthals were much stronger and with bigger brains.

- **Neanderthals buried** their dead, often with tributes of flowers.

- **Around 28,000 years ago** Neanderthals were living in Croatia – long after modern humans had appeared. No one knows why Neanderthal Man died out, leaving humans alone.

▼ *Most early hominid remains have been found in Africa. Many species – including modern humans – may have emerged first in Africa, then migrated elsewhere. These are sites where remains have been found.*

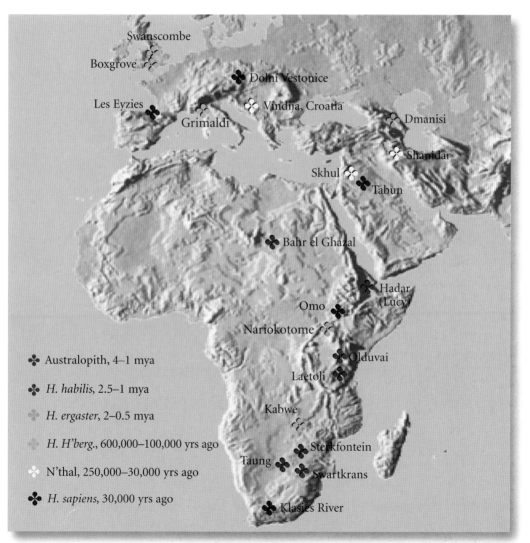

Swanscombe

Boxgrove

Dolni Vestonice

Les Eyzies

Vindija, Croatia

Grimaldi

Dmanisi

Shanidar

Skhul

Tabun

Bahr el Ghazal

Hadar (Lucy)

Omo

Nariokotome

Olduvai

Laetoli

Australopith, 4–1 mya

H. *habilis*, 2.5–1 mya

H. *ergaster*, 2–0.5 mya

H. *H'berg.*, 600,000–100,000 yrs ago

N'thal, 250,000–30,000 yrs ago

H. *sapiens*, 30,000 yrs ago

Kabwe

Sterkfontein

Taung

Swartkrans

Klasies River

Modern humans

- **The scientific name** for modern humans is *Homo sapiens sapiens*. The word *sapiens* is used twice to distinguish us from *Homo sapiens neanderthalis* (Neanderthal Man).

- **Unlike Neanderthals**, modern humans have a prominent chin and a flat face with a high forehead.

- **Some scientists think** that because we all share similar DNA, all humans are descended from a woman nicknamed 'Eve', who they calculate lived in Africa about 200,000 years ago. DNA is the special molecule in every body-cell that carries the body's instructions for life.

- **The oldest human skulls** are 130,000 years old and were found in the Omo Basin in Ethiopia and the Klasies River in South Africa.

  - **About 30,000 years ago**, modern humans began to spread out into Eurasia from Africa.

    - **The earliest modern Europeans** are called Cro-Magnon Man, after the caves in France's Dordogne valley where skeletons from 35,000 years ago were found in 1868.

- **About 50,000 years ago**, modern humans reached Australia by boat from Indonesia. They reached the Americas from Asia about the same time.

◄ *Both modern humans and Neanderthals used beautifully made spears for hunting.*

- **Modern humans lived** alongside Neanderthals for tens of thousands of years in the Middle East and Europe.

- **Modern humans** were probably the first creatures to speak what we would call language. Some scientists think language was a sudden genetic 'accident' that remained and developed because it gave humans a huge advantage.

- **With modern humans came rapid advances** in stone-tool technology, the building of wooden huts, a rise in population and a growing interest in art.

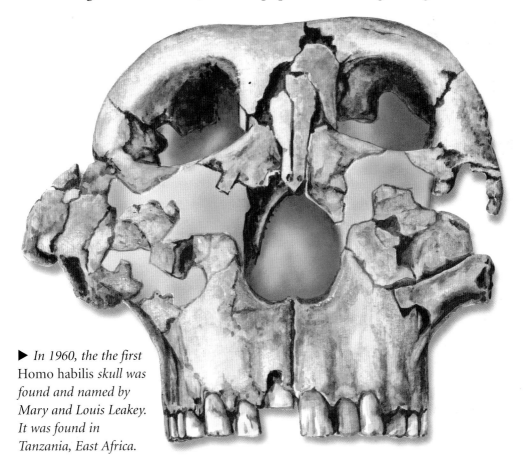

▶ *In 1960, the the first* Homo habilis *skull was found and named by Mary and Louis Leakey. It was found in Tanzania, East Africa.*

Cave painters

- **Prehistoric people** sometimes lived in caves, but more often they went into caves to paint and draw.

- **The world's most famous** cave paintings, at Lascaux in France and Altamira in Spain, were found by children.

- **Carbon dating shows** that the paintings in Lascaux are 31,000 years old. Those in Chauvet in the French Ardèche are nearly twice as old.

- **The pictures** at Cougnac, France, were painted over a period of 10,000 years.

- **Most paintings in caves** show large animals such as bison, deer, horses and mammoths.

- **Caves may have been the temples** of prehistoric times, and the paintings linked to religious rituals.

- **Cave artists often painted** by spitting paint, a practice also followed by the aboriginal people of Australia.

- **To reach the 14,000-year-old paintings** in France's Pergouset, you must crawl through 150 m of passages.

- **In the caves** at Nerja in Spain there are rock formations that prehistoric people played like a xylophone.

- **The aboriginal paintings** on rocks in Arnhemland, Northern Territory, Australia, may be over 50,000 years old.

▶ *The most famous cave paintings are those in the Hall of Bulls at Lascaux in France. These paintings show bison.*

The Stone Ages

- **The Stone Ages** were the periods of time before humans discovered metals and so used mainly stones for making tools.

- **Stone tools were made** by chipping away stones to make hammers, spear heads and arrow heads, knives and scrapers.

- **People usually used local stone**, but sometimes good stones were imported from a great distance.

- **Early Europeans** used mainly flint for their stone tools. Africans used quartz, chert, basalt and obsidian.

- **In Europe**, there were three Stone Ages – Old (Palaeolithic), Middle (Mesolithic) and New (Neolithic).

- **The Palaeolithic** began 2 million years ago, when various human ancestors gathered plants and hunted with stone weapons.

- **The Mesolithic** was the transition from the Old to the New Stone Age – after the last Ice Age ended around 12,000 years ago.

- **The Neolithic** was the time when people began to settle down and farm. This occurred first in the Near East, about 10,000 years ago.

◀ *A well-made, properly shaped stone tool could chop right through wood, meat, bone and animal skin.*

- **In 1981**, a pebble shaped into a female form, 500,000 years old was found at Berekhat Ram in Israel's Golan Heights.
- **Venus figurines** are plump stone female figures from *c.*25,000 years ago, found in Europe, e.g. the Czech Republic.

▶ *Mesolithic people hunted with bows and arrows and flint-tipped spears.*

27

The Bronze Age

- **The Bronze Age** is the period of prehistory when people first began to use the metal bronze.

- **Bronze is an alloy** (mix) of copper with about 10 percent tin.

- **The first metals** used were probably lumps of pure gold and copper, beaten into shape to make ornaments in Turkey and Iran about 6000 BC.

- **Metal ores** (metals mixed with other minerals) were probably discovered when certain stones were found to melt when heated in a kiln.

- **Around 4000** BC, metalsmiths in southeast Europe and Iran began making copper axeheads with a central hole to take a wooden shaft.

- **The Copper Age** is the period when people used copper before they learned to alloy it with tin to make bronze. Metalworking with copper was flourishing in the early cities of Mesopotamia, in the Middle East, about 3500 BC.

- **The Bronze Age** began several times between 3500 and 3000 BC in the Near East, Balkans and Southeast Asia, when smiths discovered that, by adding a small quantity of tin, they could make bronze. Bronze is harder than copper and easier to make into a sharp blade.

▶ *A Bronze Age axe, 1500–700 BC.*

▶ *By 1000 BC, beautiful metal swords and other weapons with sharp blades like this were being made all over Europe and western Asia.*

- **Knowledge of bronze** spread slowly across Eurasia, but by 1500 BC it was in use all the way from Europe to India.

- **The rarity of tin** spurred long-distance trade links – and the first mines, like the tin mines in Cornwall, England.

- **Bronze can be cast** – shaped by melting it into a clay mould (itself shaped with a wax model). For the first time people could make things any shape they wanted. Skilled smiths across Eurasia began to cast bronze to make everything from weapons to cooking utensils.

The Iron Age

- **The Iron Age** is the time in prehistory when iron replaced bronze as the main metal.

- **The use of iron** was discovered by the Hittites in Anatolia, Turkey, between 1500 and 1200 BC. This discovery helped to make the Hittites immensely powerful for a few centuries.

- **Around 1200 BC**, the Hittite Empire collapsed and the use of iron spread through Asia and central Europe. The Dorian Greeks became famous iron masters.

- **Tin is rare**, so bronze objects were made mostly for chieftains. Iron ore is common, so ordinary people could have metal objects such as cooking utensils.

- **Many ordinary farmers** could afford iron scythes and axes. With tough metal tools to clear fields and harvest crops quickly, farming developed much more rapidly.

- **Growth in population** put pressure on resources and warfare increased across Eurasia. Partly as a result, many northern European settlements developed into hillforts – hilltop sites protected by earth ramparts, ditches and stockades.

- **Around 650 BC**, peoples skilled in iron-working, called Celts, began to dominate northern Europe.

▶ The easy availability of iron in the Iron Age meant that even a fairly poor man might have his own sword.

> ...FASCINATING FACT...
> In 1950, an Iron Age man was found in a peatbog at Tollund in Jutland, Denmark, perfectly preserved over 2000 years.

- **Iron-working** reached China around 600 BC. The Chinese used large bellows to raise furnace temperatures enough to melt iron ore in large quantities.

- **Iron tools** appearing in West Africa around 400 BC were the basis of the Nok culture. Nok Farmers speaking Bantu languages spread south and east all over Africa.

Typical Iron Age round houses, built of wood and straw thatch

The hilltop village within the defences covered about 17 hectares

The inner rampart was 14 m high and topped by a fence of huge, upright timbers. It was faced with big limestone blocks, not grass

A series of ditches and banks were built up from clay

◀ *Maiden Castle in Dorset is the largest of around 1000 hillforts built in southern Britain in the Iron Age. This is how it might have looked in about 300 BC.*

The entrance through the inner ramparts had massive timber gates

The approach to the entrance wound between ramparts to make life hard for attackers

Megaliths

- *Megalith* means 'giant stone'.

- **Megaliths are monuments** such as tombs made from huge blocks of stone, built in western Europe in the Neolithic and Bronze Ages between 4000 and 1500 BC.

- **It was once thought** that megaliths began in one place. Now experts think they emerged in many areas.

- *Menhirs* are large standing stones. Sometimes they stand by themselves, sometimes in avenues or circles.

▼ *The most famous avenues of stone are at Carnac in Brittany, France, where thousands of stones stand in long lines.*

...FASCINATING FACT...
The Grand Menhir Brisé stone, near Carnac in France, is seven times as heavy as the biggest stones at Stonehenge, UK.

▶ *It took about 1400 years to construct Stonehenge. The people of Stone Age Britain first built a ring of ditches, and giant stones from as far away as 350 km were slowly added. The biggest upright stones are 9 m high and weigh 50 tonnes. Stonehenge may have been a temple or astronomical observatory.*

- **The largest known** existing menhir is the Grand Menhir Brisé at Locmariaquer, near Carnac in France. This single stone once stood 20 m tall and weighed 280 tonnes.

- **The largest stone circle** is at Avebury in Wiltshire, southern England.

- **The most famous stone circle** is Stonehenge on Salisbury Plain, Wiltshire, built between 2950 and 1600 BC.

- **Some megaliths align** with amazing accuracy with astronomical events, such as sunrise at the summer solstice (midsummer day) and may have acted as calendars.

- **Erecting such stones** took huge teams of men working with enormous wooden rollers, levers and ropes.

Archaeology

- **Archaeology is** the scientific study of relics left by humans in the past, from old bones to ancient temples.

- **Most archaeological relics** are buried beneath the ground or sunk beneath the sea.

- **Aerial photographs** often reveal where archaeologists should dig. Crops and grass will grow differently if the soil is affected by a buried wall or filled-in ditch.

▲ *Archaeological digging is a very painstaking process. Diggers work with immense care to avoid overlooking or breaking tiny, fragile relics.*

- **Geophysical surveys** involve using metal detectors and other electronic probes to pick up features underground.

- **Field walking** involves walking over the site, carefully scanning the ground by eye for tiny relics.

- **During a dig**, archaeologists dig carefully down through the layers. They note exactly where every relic was found, in case its position helps to reveal the story behind the site.

Pottery   Statue   Lamps   Jewellery

◀ *Archaeologists have found many remains of Roman life. Roman pottery was beautifully made and designed, while statues give an idea of how Romans looked. Oil-burning lamps have been unearthed, and we know that the Romans loved beautiful jewellery.*

- **Archaeologists** call on many different kinds of expert to help them to interpret finds. Forensic scientists may help to tell how a skeleton died, for instance.

- **The deeper a relic is buried**, the older it is likely to be.

- **Radio carbon dating** is a way of dating the remains of once-living things from their carbon content. This is accurate up to 50,000 years ago.

- **Potassium argon dating** helps to date the rocks in which relics were found from their potassium and argon content. Human remains in Africa were dated in this way.

▶ *An archaelogist's dig uncovers remains from the Roman period. We can gain greater understanding of Roman life from the evidence unearthed.*

The first farms

- **Starch marks** on stone implements found in Papua New Guinea suggest yams may have been grown there at least 30,000 years ago.

- **Water chestnuts** and beans may have been farmed near Spirit Cave in north Vietnam from 11,000 to 7500 BC.

- **About 9000** BC, some people abandoned the old way of life, hunting animals and gathering fruit, and settled down to farm. Experts call this great change the Neolithic Revolution.

- **Farming began** as people planted grasses for their seed (or grain) in the Near East, in Guangdong in China and in Latin America – and perhaps planted root vegetables in Peru and Indonesia, too.

- **Emmer wheat** and barley were grown in the Near East *c.*8000 BC. Sheep and goats were tamed here soon after.

- **The ox-drawn plough** was used from *c.*5000 BC. The Chinese used hand ploughs even earlier.

- **Crop irrigation canals** were dug at Choya Mami, near Mandali in Iraq, between 5500 and 4750 BC.

- **China, the Indus**, Egypt and Babylonia all had extensive irrigation systems in place by 3000 BC.

- **The first farmers** reaped their grain with sickles of flint.

- **Farmers soon learned** to store food. Underground granaries at Ban-Po, Shansi, China, date from *c.*4800 BC.

▲ *Farming began about 11,000 years ago, as people began saving grass seed to grow so that they could grind new seed into flour.*

The first cities

- **The walls of the city of Jericho** on the river Jordan, in the Near East, are 11,000 years old, and the city has been continuously occupied longer than anywhere else in the world.

- **People began to live** in towns when farming produced enough extra food for people to specialize in crafts such as basket-making and for people to begin to trade with each other.

- **Villages and towns** probably first developed in the Near East in the Neolithic period, about 8000 BC.

- **Tells are mounds** that have built up at ancient settlement sites (in the Near and Middle East) from mud-brick houses that have crumbled.

- **The most famous ancient town** is Catal Hüyük in Anatolia, Turkey, which was occupied from 7000 to 5500 BC. Ten thousand people may have lived here.

- **The houses** in Catal Hüyük were made from mud bricks covered with fine plaster. Some rooms were shrines, with bulls' heads and mother goddesses.

- **Asikli Hüyük** is a nearby forerunner of Catal Hüyük, dating from over a thousand years earlier.

- **The first big city** was Eridu in Mesopotamia (modern Iraq's Abu Shahrain Tell), which has a temple dating from 4900 BC.

- **In 3500 BC,** 50,000 people were living in Sumerian Uruk (modern Warka) on the banks of the Euphrates River in Iraq.

- **Sumerian Ur** was the first city to have a population of a quarter of a million, by about 2500 BC.

▲ *Houses in Catal Hüyük were so tightly packed that people had to walk over flat roofs to get to their home, and then climb down a ladder to enter through an opening.*

'Between rivers'

- **Mesopotamia lies between** the Tigris and Euphrates rivers in Turkey, Syria and Iraq. *Mesopotamia* is Greek for 'between rivers'.

- **Mesopotamia is called** the 'cradle of civilization' because many ancient civilizations arose here, including the Sumerian, Babylonian and Assyrian.

- **The first great civilization** was that of the Sumerians, who farmed irrigated land by the Euphrates River *c.*5000 BC and lived in mud-brick houses.

- **By 4000** BC, the settlements of Eridu, Uruk and Ur had grown into towns with water supplies and drainage systems, as well as palaces and mountain-shaped temple-mounds called *ziggurats*.

- **Sumerians devised** the first writing system (cuneiform), made with wedge-shaped marks on clay tablets.

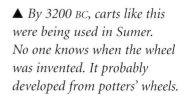

▲ *By 3200 BC, carts like this were being used in Sumer. No one knows when the wheel was invented. It probably developed from potters' wheels.*

- **Sumerians cast** all kinds of beautiful objects – first in copper, then, from 3500 BC, in bronze.

- **The Sumerian tale** *Epic of Gilgamesh* tells of a flood similar to that in the biblical story of Noah's Ark.

- **In 2350** BC, Sumer was overrun by Sargon of Akkad, but Sumerian power was re-established at Ur in 2150 BC.

- **The Sumerians developed** the first known elaborate systems of law and government.

- **At first**, each city or 'city-state' was run by a council of elders, but in wartime a *lugal* (leader) took charge. By 2900 BC, the lugals had become kings and ruled all the time.

▶ *The* Epic of Gilgamesh *was composed around 2000 BC. It tells the tale of Gilgamesh (right), a powerful and oppressive king in ancient Sumeria. When his people pray for help, the gods create Enkidu, who meets Gilgamesh in battle. But the two become friends and share many adventures. The poem concludes with a great flood, which has been likened to the Bible story of Noah.*

41

Indus civilization

- **About 3000** BC, a civilization developed from small farming communities in the Indus valley in Pakistan.

- **The remains** of over 100 towns of the Indus civilization have been found. The main sites are Mohenjo-Daro, Harappa, Kalibangan and Lothal.

- **Indus cities** were carefully planned, with straight streets, bath-houses and big granaries (grain stores).

- **At the centre** was a fortified citadel, built on a platform of bricks. The rulers probably lived here.

- **Indus houses** were built of brick around a central courtyard. They had several rooms, a toilet and a well.

▼ *Seals like this were used by Indus merchants to stamp bales of goods.*

- **The Indus civilization** had its own system of writing, which appears on objects such as carved seals – but no one has yet been able to decipher it.

- **Single-room huts** at all intersections are thought to be police-posts.

- **Mohenjo-Daro** and Harappa had 35,000 inhabitants each by about 2500 BC.

● **By 1750 BC**, the Indus civilization had declined, perhaps because floods changed the course of the Indus River. War may also have played a part. It finally vanished with the arrival of the Aryans in India about 1500 BC.

▲ *The people of Mohenjo-Daro used ox-drawn carts. However, this form of transport would have been very slow and they probably relied on the river as their main source of transportation.*

. . . FASCINATING FACT . . .
Soapstone trading seals from the Indus civilization have been found as far away as Bahrain and Ur.

Great migrations

- **The first migrations** occurred when human-like *Homo ergaster* walked out of Africa 750,000 years ago.

- **Experts once thought** that oceans had blocked migrations but it now seems that boats have been used since the earliest days.

- **Humans moved out** of Africa into the Near East around 100,000 years ago.

- **Around 50,000 years ago**, humans began the great expansion that took them to every continent except Antarctica within 20,000 years – and replaced Neanderthal Man.

- **Humans spread across Asia** and Australasia 50,000–40,000 years ago. Next, 40,000–35,000 years ago, they moved into Europe. Then, 30,000–25,000 years ago, they trekked out of northeast Asia and crossed into the Americas.

- **Early humans** were mainly nomadic hunters, always on the move, following animals into empty lands.

- **Changes in climate** triggered many migrations. People moved north in warm times and retreated in Ice Ages. When the last Ice Age ended, 10,000 years ago, hunters moved north through Europe as the weather warmed. Those left behind in the Middle East settled down to farm.

▶ *Just like American pioneers in the 1800s, Aryans living 4000 years ago moved their families and possessions in covered wagons, probably pulled by oxen.*

▲ *During the Ice Age, people used spears made from bone, antler or flint to bring down animals such as huge woolly mammoths.*

● **From 9000 to 7000 years ago**, farming spread northwest across Europe – partly through people actually moving, partly by word of mouth.

● **Around 4000 years ago**, Indo-Europeans spread out from their home in southern Russia. They went south into Iran (as Mittanians) and India (Aryans), south-west into Turkey (Hittites) and Greece (Mycenaeans) and into the west (Celts).

● **About 3000 years ago**, the Sahara area began to dry up, and people living there moved to the fringes. Bantu-speaking people from Nigeria and the Congo spread south through Africa.

45

Ancient Egypt

- **While dozens of cities** were developing in Mesopotamia, in Egypt the foundations were being laid for the first great nation.

- **From 5000 to 3300** BC, farmers by the river Nile banded together to dig canals to control the Nile's annual flooding and to water their crops.

- **By 3300** BC, Nile farming villages had grown into towns. Rich and powerful kings were buried in big, boxlike mud-brick tombs called *mastabas.*

- **Egyptian townspeople** began to work copper and stone, paint vases, weave baskets and use potter's wheels.

- **Early Egypt was divided** into two kingdoms – Upper Egypt, and Lower Egypt on the Nile delta. In 3100 BC, King Menes of Upper Egypt conquered Lower Egypt to unite the two kingdoms, but a king of Egypt was always called King of Upper and Lower Egypt.

▶ *The ancient Egyptians built great cities and monuments along the Nile valley during the days of the Old Kingdom.*

▶ *The principal sites and cities of ancient Egyptian civilization.*

- **Menes founded** a capital for a united Egypt at Memphis.

- **With Menes**, Egypt's Dynasty I – the first family of kings – began. The time of Dynasties I and II, which lasted until 2649 BC, is known by historians as the Archaic Period.

- **After the Archaic Period** came the Old Kingdom (2649–2134 BC), perhaps the greatest era of Egyptian culture.

- **Craftsmen** made fine things, scholars developed writing and the calendar and studied astronomy and maths.

- **The greatest scholar** and priest was Imhotep, minister to King Zoser (2630–2611 BC). Imhotep was architect of the first of the great pyramids, the Step Pyramid at Sakkara.

47

The gods of Egypt

- **The mighty sun god**, Ra-Atum, was called many different names by ancient Egyptians.

- **The sun god** was sometimes pictured as a scarab beetle. This is because a scarab beetle rolls a ball of dung before it, as the ball of the sun rolls across the sky.

- **Myths say** that the sun god has a secret name, known only to himself, which was the key to all his power.

▲ *The blue scarab beetle Khephri is one of the many forms of the sun god. This amulet was made over 3000 years ago.*

- **The ancient Egyptians** believed that part of the spirit of a god could live on Earth in the body of an animal. This is why their gods are pictured as humans with animal heads.

- **Hathor** or Sekhmet was the daughter and wife of Ra-Atum. She could take on the form of a terrifying lioness or cobra to attack and punish enemies of the sun god.

- **Osiris** was the son of Ra-Atum. He became king of Egypt and later, ruler of the underworld Kingdom of the Dead.

- **Osiris's brother**, Seth, represented evil in the universe. He hatched a wicked plot to murder Osiris and take the crown of Egypt for himself.

- **Osiris's sister and wife** was called Isis. She was a powerful mother goddess of fertility.

- **Horus** was Osiris's son. He inherited the throne of Egypt. Ancient Egyptians believed that all pharaohs were descended from Horus, and therefore they were gods.

- **An amulet** is a piece of jewellery with magical powers. Many amulets were in the shape of an eye – either the sun god's or Horus's. The sacred eye was thought to have healing powers and to ward off evil.

◀ *This picture shows the god Osiris on his throne. He wears the crown of Egypt, as does his son, Horus, who faces him. The goddess Isis is standing behind Osiris.*

Babylon

- **Babylon was one of the greatest** cities of the ancient world. It stood on the banks of the Euphrates River, near what is now Al Hillah in Iraq.

- **The city reached its peak** in two phases: the Old Babylonian Empire (1792–1234 BC) and the New Babylonian Empire (626–539 BC).

- **Babylon first grew as a city** from 2200 BC, but only when Hammurabi became king in 1792 BC did it become powerful. In his 42-year reign, Hammurabi's conquests gave Babylon a huge empire in Mesopotamia.

- **Hammurabi** was a great law-maker, and some of his laws were enscribed on a stone pillar, or stele, now in the Louvre in Paris. One of his main laws was that 'the strong shall not oppress the weak'. There were also laws to punish crimes and protect people from poor workmanship by builders and doctors.

▼ *The Greeks described the Hanging Gardens of Babylon as one of the Seven Wonders of the Ancient World. Nebuchadnezzar II is said to have had them built for his wife, who missed the greenery of her mountain home.*

Gardens of lush trees and flowers filled rising brick terraces

The gardens were on a huge pyramid of brick and tar, 25 m high

Water for the plants was continually raised from the river by screw pumps wound by slaves

- **After Hammurabi died**, Babylonian power declined and the Assyrians gained the upper hand. After long Babylonian resistance, the Assyrians destroyed the city in 689 BC, only to rebuild it 11 years later.

- **Just 60 years later**, Babylonian king Nabopolassar and his son Nebuchadnezzar II crushed the Assyrians and built the new Babylonian Empire.

- **Under Nebuchadnezzar II**, Babylon became a vast, magnificent city of 250,000 people, with grand palaces, temples and houses.

▲ *Under Nebuchadnezzar II (630–562 BC), Babylon achieved its greatest fame. He is known for conquering Jerusalem and for his great building projects.*

- **The city was surrounded by walls** 26 m thick – glazed with blue bricks, decorated with dragons, lions and bulls and pierced by eight huge bronze gates. The grandest gate was the Ishtar Gate, which opened on to a paved avenue called the Processional Street.

- **Babylonians were so sure** of their power that King Belshazzar was having a party when the Persians, led by Cyrus, attacked. Cyrus's men dug canals to divert the Euphrates River, then slipped into the city along the riverbed.

...FASCINATING FACT...
Dying of a fever, Macedonian king Alexander the Great found cool relief in Babylon's Hanging Gardens.

Mesopotamia

- **Myths from the Middle East** are the oldest recorded mythology in the world, dating from 2500 BC.

- **The Babylonian creation** myth grew from the Sumerian creation myth. It is called the Enuma Elish.

- **The Enuma Elish was found** written in a language called cuneiform on seven clay tablets by archaeologists excavating Nineveh in AD 1845.

- **The Enuma Elish says** that in the beginning the universe was made of salt waters (Mother Tiamat), sweet waters (Father Apsu), and a mist (their son Mummu).

- **The waters gave birth** to new young rebellious gods who overthrew Apsu and Mummu.

- **Tiamat and her followers** (led by a god called Kingu) were conquered by a male Babylonian god, Marduk, in a battle of powerful magic.

- **The Babylonians pictured Marduk** with four eyes and four ears, so he could see and hear everything. Fire spurted from his mouth and haloes blazed from his head.

- **Marduk became** the new ruler. He made Tiamat's body into the earth and sky. He appointed gods to rule the heavens, the earth and the air in between.

- **Humans** were created out of Kingu's blood. Marduk made them build a temple to himself and the other gods at Babylon.

● **Every spring**, Babylon was in danger of devastating flooding from the mighty rivers, Tigris and Euphrates. Historians believe that the Enuma Elish might have been acted out as a pantomime to please Marduk so he kept order and prevented the flooding.

▼ *Around 2100 BC, the Sumerians of Mesopotamia built massive stepped temples of mud-bricks called ziggurats.*

Early China

● **In China**, farming communities known as the Yanshao culture developed by the Huang He (Yellow River) 7000 years ago. By 5000 BC, the region was ruled by emperors.

● **Early Chinese** emperors are known of only by legend. Huang-Ti, the Yellow Emperor, was said to have become emperor in 2697 BC.

● **In about 2690** BC, Huang-Ti's wife, Hsi-Ling Shi, discovered how to use the cocoon of the silkworm (the caterpillar of the *Bombyx mori* moth) to make silk. Hsi-Ling was afterwards known as Seine-Than (the Silk Goddess).

● **By 2000** BC, the Chinese were making beautiful jade carvings.

● **The Hsias family** were said to be one of the earliest dynasties of Chinese emperors, ruling from 2000 to 1750 BC.

◀ *The Shang emperors were warriors. Their soldiers fought in padded bamboo armour.*

- **The Shangs** were the first known dynasty of emperors. They came to power in 1750 BC.

- **Shang emperors** had their fortune told every few days from cracks on heated animal bones. Marks on these 'oracle' bones are the oldest examples of Chinese writing.

- **Under the Shangs**, the Chinese became skilled bronze-casters.

- **In the Shang** cities of Anyang and Zengzhou, thick-walled palace temples were surrounded at a distance by villages of artisans.

- **Shang emperors** went to their tombs along with their servants and captives, as well as entire chariots with their horses and drivers.

▲ *Silkworms (the larvae, or young, of the* Bombyx mori *moth) feed on mulberry leaves. Silk was invented in China, and for many years the method of making it was a closely guarded secret.*

The Han dynasty

- **In 210 BC**, the small Han kingdom was ruled over by Liu Bang. Liu Bang was a poor villager who had come to power as the Qin Empire broke down.

- **In 206 BC**, Liu Bang led an army on the Qin capital, Xiangyang. He looted Shi Huangdi's tomb, and burned the city and the library containing the books Shi Huangdi had banned – the only existing copies.

- **In 202 BC**, Liu Bang proclaimed himself to be the first Han emperor and took the name Gaozu.

- **Under the Han**, China became as large and powerful as the Roman Empire; art and science thrived. Chinese people still sometimes call themselves Han.

- **Under Wudi** (141–87 BC), Han China reached its peak.

- **Han cities were huge**, crowded and beautiful, and craftsmen made many exquisite things from wood, paint and silk. Sadly, many of these lovely objects were destroyed when Han rule ended.

- **Silk, jade and horses** were traded along the Silk Route, which wound through Asia as far as the Roman Empire.

- **Han emperors** tried to recover the lost writings and revive the teachings of Confucius. Public officials became scholars and in 165 BC the first exams for entry into public service were held.

▼ *Richly coloured silks were bought from Chinese merchants by traders from ancient Persia (modern-day Iran). Silk was also transported from China by camel trains to Damascus, the gateway between the East and West.*

◀ *Beautiful objects like this bronze urn were traded between China and Europe along the famous Silk Route for thousands of years.*

● **About AD 50,** Buddhist missionaries reached China.

● **By AD 200,** the Han emperors were weakened by their ambitious wives and eunuchs (guardians). Rebellions by a group called the Yellow Turbans, combined with attacks by warriors from the north, brought the empire down.

Chinese myths

- **The Chinese myths we know** may not be the oldest Chinese stories. Certain emperors in the past burned many ancient books and also ordered traditional tales to be rewritten in line with their own religious beliefs.

- **There are many Chinese creation myths.** The most common story says that in the beginning, the universe was an egg containing a mass of chaos.

- **Most myths say** that the first being was a dwarf-like creature called Panku, who pushed open the egg. The chaos separated into a heavy mass of Earth and a light mass of sky.

- **Many Chinese people today** believe that everything in the universe has the force of one of these first two masses: Yin (the female, negative force of the Earth) and Yang (the male, positive force of the sky).

- **Myths say that Panku** grew and grew every day for 18,000 years, pushing the sky and Earth apart.

- **Some stories say that Panku** then fell asleep and died. Everything in the world was born from his body.

- **Other stories say that Panku** remained alive and carved everything in the world, with the help of a tortoise, phoenix, unicorn and dragon.

- **According to an ancient writing** called the Shu Ching, eight rulers created the universe together. These were the Three Sovereigns and the Five Emperors.

- **Many legends explain** that it is the duty of the ruler of China to keep order and balance in the universe by establishing systems of government in heaven as well as on Earth.

▶ *According to many Chinese creation myths, a creature called Panku played a vital role in shaping the world.*

. . . FASCINATING FACT . . .
Certain myths tell that the first people were created
from wet clay by a mother goddess called Nugua.

Chinese divinities

- **For thousands of years**, the Chinese have worshipped the spirits of dead ancestors, believing they can help the living.

- **The first emperors** in China ruled over warrior tribes and belonged to a family called the Shang dynasty (around 1500–1050 BC). They were believed to be gods, as were all following emperors.

- **According to many myths**, the first Shang emperor is the most powerful of all Chinese gods. He is known as the Jade Emperor.

- **The Jade emperor's wife** was a goddess who grew Peaches of Immortality in her palace gardens. They only ripened once every 6000 years.

- **The first Chinese man to die** and find his way to the Underworld became the chief god of the dead, Yen-Lo Wang.

- **The Chinese believe** that their homes are guarded by special spirits. Tsao Chun is the god of the kitchen. He reports back to heaven on each family.

▲ *Chinese emperors kept the vast country cut off from the rest of the world until the 19th century.*

- **As in other civilizations**, through the centuries many real Chinese heroes have been turned into the larger-than-life characters of myths and legends. The heroes were often appointed to be gods, thousands of years after their deaths.

▲ *The Ming dynasty of emperors (1368–1644) built a huge palace in Beijing that ordinary Chinese people were not allowed to enter. It became known as the Forbidden City.*

- **Kuan Ti** lived in the 3rd century AD and became famous as one of China's finest warriors. He was made a war god, to defend China from enemies.

- **Wen Chang** was an outstanding student who lived in the 3rd or 4th century AD. He was made god of literature.

- **Wen Chang has an assistant god**, Kuei Hsing, whom people pray to for help in exams. Stories say that he was a very gifted scholar, but incredibly ugly!

61

Egyptian writing

- **Ancient Egyptian writing** developed between 3300 and 3100 BC – perhaps inspired by Sumerian scripts.

- **Egyptian writing** is called *hieroglyphic* (Greek for 'holy writing'). The Egyptians called it the 'words of the gods', because they believed writing was given by the god Thoth.

- **The last known hieroglyphs** were written in AD 394, long after most people knew how to read them.

- **In AD 1799,** the French soldiers of Napoleon's army found a stone slab at Rosetta in Egypt. It was covered in three identical texts.

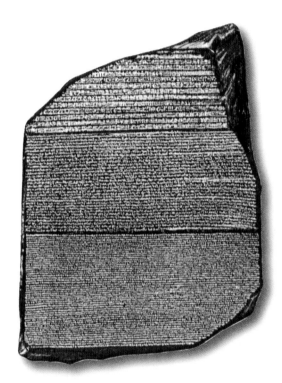

▲ *When Frenchman Jean-François Champollion translated the Greek text on the Rosetta Stone, he was able to crack the code to its passage of hieroglyphs.*

- **In AD 1822,** Jean-François Champollion deciphered the Rosetta Stone, realizing that hieroglyphs are pictures that stand for sounds and letters, and not just for objects.

- **There were 700 hieroglyphs** in common use. Most are pictures and can be written from left to right, right to left or downwards.

▲ *The walls of Egyptian tombs are covered in hieroglyphs.*

- **Words inside an oval shape** called a *cartouche* are the names of pharaohs.

- **There were two** shorthand versions of hieroglyphs for everyday use – early hieratic script and later demotic script.

- **Egyptians not only wrote** on tomb walls but wrote everyday things with ink and brushes on papyrus (paper made from papyrus reeds) or on *ostraca* (pottery fragments).

- **Only highly trained scribes** could write. Scribes were very well paid and often exempt from taxes.

▲ *Papyrus was made by taking wet strips of the pithy stems of papyrus plants and pressing them, side by side.*

Egyptian life

- **Egyptians washed every day** in the river or with a jug and basin. The rich were given showers by their servants.

- **Instead of soap** they used a cleansing cream made from oil, lime and perfume. They also rubbed themselves all over with moisturizing oil.

- **Egyptian women** painted their nails with henna and reddened their lips and cheeks with red ochre paste.

- **Egyptian fashions** changed little over thousands of years, and their clothes were usually white linen.

▲ *Egyptian women were highly conscious of their looks, wearing make-up and jewellery and dressing their hair with great care.*

- **Men wrapped linen** around themselves in a kilt. Women wore long, light dresses. Children ran around naked during the summer.

- **Every Egyptian wore jewellery**. The rich wore gold inlaid with gems, the poor wore copper or faience (made by heating powdered quartz).

- **Egyptians loved to play board games**. Their favourites were 'senet' and 'hounds and jackals'.

- **Rich Egyptians** held lavish parties with food and drink, singers, musicians, acrobats and dancers.

- **The pastimes of rich Egyptians** often included fishing or boating.

▶ *In ancient Egypt, a man provided for his family, and his wife ran the home and was held in great respect. Some couples lived with the parents of the husband or wife.*

...FASCINATING FACT...
Egyptian men and women wore kohl eyeliner, made from the minerals malachite and galena.

65

Egyptian mythology

- **The mythology** of ancient Egypt may go back to 4000 BC, when the land was populated by farming peoples.

  - **People in each area of Egypt** originally worshipped their own gods. Their stories spread and merged, so there are many versions and some gods are known in different forms.

    - **Egyptian myths** say that in the beginning the universe was filled with dark waters.

    - **The first god** was Ra-Atum. He appeared from the waters as the land of Egypt appears every year out of the flood waters of the Nile.

    - **Ra-Atum** spat and the spittle turned into the gods Shu (air) and Tefnut (moisture).

    - **Humans were created** one day when Shu and Tefnut wandered into the dark wastes and got lost. Ra-Atum sent his eye to find them. When they were reunited, Ra-Atum's tears of joy turned into people.

    - **The world was created** when Shu and Tefnut gave birth to two children: Nut – the sky, and Geb – the Earth.

◀ *Here the sun god is holding an ankh in his right hand. This is the sign of life and the key to the Underworld.*

● **Ancient Egyptians believed** that Ra-Atum originally lived in the world with humans. When he grew old, humans tried to rebel against him. Ra then went to live in the sky.

● **Egyptian myths** were written down in hieroglyphic writing. This was invented around 3000 BC, when Upper Egypt and Lower Egypt united into one kingdom.

● **It was not until** the 1820s that experts worked out what hieroglyphs meant. Before that, we knew about ancient Egyptian mythology from old writings in other languages.

◀ ▶ *Hieroglyph means 'sacred carving'. Each picture stands for an object, an idea or a sound.*

67

Ancient Crete

- **The Minoan civilization** of Crete – an island south of Greece – was the first civilization in Europe.

- **Minoan civilization began** about 3000 BC, reached its height from 2200 to 1450 BC, then mysteriously vanished – perhaps after the volcano on the nearby island of Santorini erupted.

- **The name *Minoan*** comes from the Greek legend of King Minos. Minos was the son of Europa, the princess seduced by the god Zeus in the shape of a bull.

- **Greek stories** tell how Minos built a labyrinth (maze) in which he kept the Minotaur, a monster with a man's body and a bull's head.

- **Catching a bull** by the horns and leaping over it (bull-leaping) was an important Minoan religious rite.

- **Experts now think** Minos was a title, so every Cretan king was called Minos.

- **The Minoans were great** seafarers and traded all over the eastern Mediterranean.

▲ *The minotaur of Greek myth.*

- **At the centre of each Minoan town** was a palace, such as those found at Knossos, Zakro, Phaestos and Mallia.
- **The largest Minoan palace** is at Knossos. It covered 20,000 square metres and housed over 30,000 people.
- **The walls of the palace** are decorated with frescoes (paintings), which reveal a great deal about the Minoans.

▼ *The famous Minoan palace at Knossos.*

The pharaohs

- **Pharaohs were the kings** of ancient Egypt. They were also High Priest, head judge and commander of the army.

- **Egyptians thought** of the pharaoh as both the god Horus and the son of the sun god Re. When he died he was transformed into the god Osiris, father of Horus. Since he was a god, anyone approaching him had to crawl.

- **The pharaoh** was thought to be so holy that he could not be addressed directly. Instead, people referred to him indirectly by talking of the pharaoh, which is Egyptian for 'great house'. Only after about 945 BC was he addressed directly.

- **In official documents** the pharaoh had five titles: Horus, Two Ladies, Golden Horus, King of Upper and Lower Egypt and Lord of the Double Land (Upper and Lower Egypt), and Son of Re and Lord of the Diadems.

- **The pharaoh's godlike status** gave him magical powers. His *uraeus* (the snake on his crown) was supposed to spit flames at his enemies and the pharaoh was said to be able to trample thousands.

- **There were 31 dynasties** (families) of pharaohs, beginning with Menes in *c.*3100 BC and ending with the Persian kings in 323 BC. Each dynasty is identified in order by a Roman numeral. So the fifth dynasty is Dynasty V.

- **A pharaoh usually married** his eldest sister to keep the royal blood pure. She became queen and was known as the Royal Heiress, but the pharaoh had many other wives. If the pharaoh died while his eldest son was still a child, his queen became regent and ruled on his behalf.

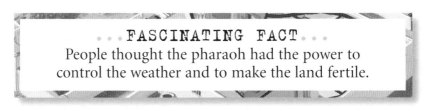

> ...FASCINATING FACT...
> People thought the pharaoh had the power to
> control the weather and to make the land fertile.

- **To preserve their bodies** forever, pharaohs were buried inside massive tombs. The first pharaohs were buried in huge pyramids. Because these were often robbed, later pharaohs were buried in tombs cut deep into cliffs.

- **One of the greatest pharaohs** was Ramses II, who ruled from 1290 to 1224 BC. He left a legacy of many huge buildings, including the rock temple of Abu Simbel.

▼ *The pharaohs' prestigious officials were building great houses like this around 1200 BC.*

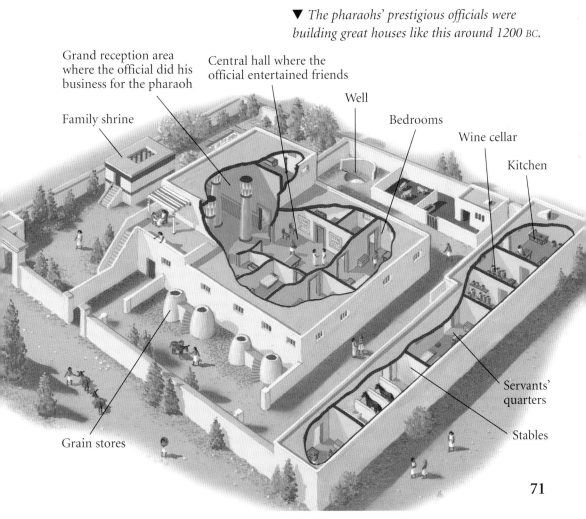

Grand reception area where the official did his business for the pharaoh

Central hall where the official entertained friends

Well

Bedrooms

Wine cellar

Kitchen

Family shrine

Servants' quarters

Stables

Grain stores

71

Pharaohs and pyramids

▼ *The ancient Egyptians believed that the jackal-headed god, Anubis, brought the souls of the dead into an underworld courtroom to be judged as good or bad.*

- **The ancient Egyptians believed** that people could enjoy life after death by preserving the body through mummification, putting food and personal possessions in their tomb and following elaborate funeral rites.

- **Part of mummification** involved removing the internal organs into pots called canopic jars.

- **Each mummy** had a mask, so every spirit could recognize its body.

- **People believed** that they would work in the afterlife, so models of their tools were buried with them. Pharaohs were buried with model servants called ushabtis, to work for them.

- **The ancient Egyptians copied** their funeral rites from the funeral the god Horus gave to his father, Osiris. These were written in a work called *The Book of the Dead.*

- **One important funeral rite** was called the Opening of the Mouth ceremony.

- **Egyptian myth** says that the dead person's soul, or 'ka' was brought to an underworld Hall of Judgement.

- **First, a jackal-headed god** called Anubis weighed their heart against a feather of truth and justice. If the heart was heavier than the feather, it was devoured by a crocodile-headed god called Ammit.

- **If the heart was lighter** than the feather, the god Horus led the 'ka' to be welcomed into the Underworld by the god Osiris.

- **People used to think** that the pharaohs enlisted slaves to build their pyramid tombs. Today, many historians think the ancient Egyptians did this willingly, to please the gods and better their chances for life after death.

▼ *How the blocks reached their final destination is a puzzle. Historians agree that they were dragged up ramps – but disagree about what shape the ramps were. One idea says there was one ramp that wrapped around the pyramid in a spiral shape. Another says that there were four ramps, one on each side of the pyramid.*

The afterlife

- **Egyptians saw death as a step** on the way to a fuller life in the Next World.

- **Everyone was thought to have three souls:** the *ka*, *ba* and *akh*. For these to flourish, the body must survive intact, so the ancient Egyptians tried to preserve their dead bodies as well as they could.

- **Gradually, the Egyptians developed** embalming techniques to preserve the bodies of kings and rich people who could afford it.

- **The organs** were cut out and stored in *canopic* jars and the body was dried with *natron* (a naturally occurring compound of salts).

- **The dried body** was filled with sawdust, resin and a naturally occurring salt called natron, which acted as a preservative, then wrapped in bandages. The embalmed body is called a 'mummy'.

- **A portrait mask** was put over the mummy's head, and it was then put into a coffin.

- **Anthropoid (human-shaped) coffins** were used from about 2000 BC onwards. Often, the mummy was put inside a nest of two or three coffins, each carved and painted and perhaps decorated with gold and gems.

- **The wooden coffin** was laid inside a stone coffin, or sarcophagus, inside the burial chamber.

▲ *Egyptians carried amulets (charms) to ward off bad spirits. This one shows the eye of the all-powerful Egyptian god, Horus.*

74

- **At first, the prayers said** for a dead ruler were carved on pyramid walls as 'Pyramid Texts'. Later, they were put on coffins as 'Coffin Texts'. From 1500 BC, they were written on papyrus in *The Book of the Dead*.

- **To help him overcome** various tests and make it to the Next World, a dead man needed amulets and *The Book of the Dead*, containing magic spells and a map.

▼ *When placing the mask over a mummy, the chief embalmer himself wore a mask, representing the jackal god, Anubis.*

75

Olmecs and Chavins

- **People began farming** in Meso America (Mexico and Central America) 9000 years ago, almost as long ago as in the Middle East.

- **By 2000** BC, there were permanent villages and extensive farms growing corn, beans, squash and other crops.

- **Between 1200 and 400** BC, a remarkable culture was developed by the Olmecs in western Mexico.

- **The Olmecs had a counting system** and calendar, but no writing system, so little is known about them.

▲ *The Olmec heads were carved from huge blocks of volcanic rock weighing up to 14 tonnes. No one knows how they were moved.*

- **The ruins of a huge** Olmec pyramid have been discovered at La Venta in Tabasco, Mexico.

- **The Olmecs carved** huge 'baby-face' heads from basalt with enormous skill – apparently with only stone chisels, since they had no metal.

- **By 2000** BC, huge religious sites were being built all over what is now Peru, in South America.

- **From 800 to 400** BC, the Chavin civilization spread from the religious centre of Chavin de Huantar in the Peruvian mountains.

- **From AD 100 to 700**, America's first true city developed at Teotihuacán, with vast pyramids and palaces.

- **Teotihuacán** may have been the world's biggest city in AD 300, with a population of over 250,000.

▼ *The main street at Teotihuacán, near Mexico City, is known as The Avenue of the Dead. It was originally 2.5 km long.*

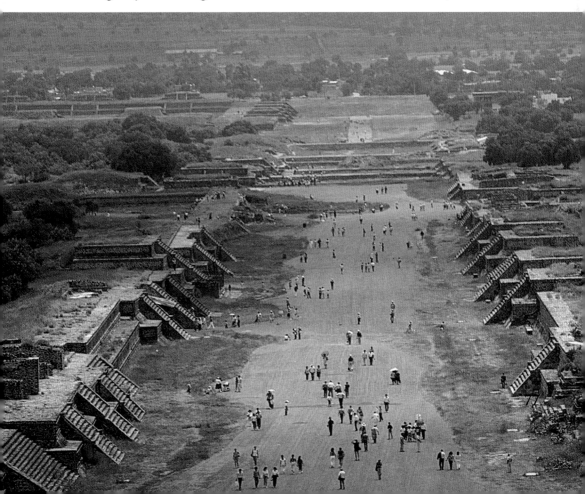

South American stories

- **Most South American myths** we know come from the Inca race, who built a great empire in Peru from the 13th century AD until they were conquered by Spanish invaders in 1532.

- **Inca means 'children of the sun'.** Some South American myths say that the sun was created on an island in Lake Titicaca.

- **Inca mythology** grew from ancient tales told by tribal peoples who had lived in Peru from around 2500 BC.

- **A pre-Inca Tiahuanaco myth** tells that in the beginning a god called Con Ticci Viracocha emerged out of nothingness and created everything.

- **Con Ticci Viracocha** is said to have later returned to earth out of Lake Titicaca, destroyed his world in a huge flood, and created everything again.

- **Another myth** tells how the first humans were created by a boneless man called Con, who was the son of the sun. He was later overthrown by another child of the sun, Pachacamac, who created a new race of people.

◀ *This statue was created by the Tiahuanaco people of Peru. This important civilization lived in the highlands around Lake Titicaca before the Incas invaded.*

- **An ancient coastal tribe in Peru** believed in a creator god called Coniraya. They believed he had filled the sea with fish and taught them how to farm the land.

- **The Canaris tribe** believed they were descended from an ancient parrot or macaw, who had bred with the few survivors of a terrible flood.

- **The Inca believe** they magically appeared one day from a place called Paccaritambo, which means 'inn of origin'.

- **Myths say that the first Incas** were led by eight royal gods: four brothers and four sisters.

▼ *These modern-day Peruvians are fishing on Lake Titicaca – an important site in Inca myth.*

Aryan India

- **The Aryans** were a lighter-skinned herding people from southern Russia, ancestors to both Greeks and Indians.

- **About 2000** BC, the Aryan people began to sweep through Persia and on into India, where they destroyed the existing Indus civilization.

- **Tough warriors**, the Aryans loved music, dancing and chariot racing, but they slowly adopted Dravidian gods and settled in villages as farmers.

▶ *The dark-skinned Dravidian people who were living in India when the Aryans arrived became the servant class.*

- **Aryan people** were originally split into three categories: *Brahmins* (priests) at the top, *Kshatriya* (warriors) in the middle and *Vaisyas* (merchants and farmers) at the bottom.

- **When they settled** in India, the Aryans added a fourth category – the conquered, dark-skinned Dravidians, who became their servants.

- **The Aryans gave India** the language of Sanskrit.

- **From the four Aryan classes**, the elaborate system of castes (classes) in today's India developed.

- **Ancient Sanskrit** is closely related to European languages such as Latin, English and German.

- **The Aryans had no form of writing**, but they passed on history and religion by word of mouth in spoken *Books of Knowledge*, or *Vedas*.

- **The Brahmins created** the first Hindu scriptures as *Vedas*, including the *Rig-Veda*, the *Sama-Veda* and *Yajur-Veda*.

धेनुः ग्राम्यः पशुः।

▲ *Sanskrit is the oldest literary language of India, and simply translated it means 'refined' or 'polished'. It forms the basis of many modern Indian languages such as Hindi and Urdu. Urdu is also the national language of Pakistan.*

Indian myths

▲ *The beliefs and myths that the Aryans brought to India formed the basis of an early form of Hinduism. One of the three main deities in Hindu mythology is Shiva (shown above).*

- **People have lived in India** for thousands of years. Myths are still an important part of their culture and religions today.

- **The earliest Indians** were farmers who thought that Prithivi, the Earth, and Dyaus, the sky, were the parents of all gods and humans.

- **A warrior race** called the Aryans then invaded India. They believed a god called Varuna created the world by picturing everything in his eye, the Sun.

- **Aryans believed** that the storm god Indra later took over as chief god, supported by human beings. He rearranged the universe by organizing the heavens and the seasons.

▲ *The creator god Brahma is shown looking in all directions with four heads, to show that he has knowledge of all things.*

- **The Hindu religion** grew from Aryan beliefs. Hindus believe that one great spirit, Brahman, is in everything. They worship this spirit as thousands of different gods.

- **The god who creates the world** is Brahma. He emerges from a lotus flower, floating on the floodwaters of chaos and thinks everything into being.

- **The god Vishnu** preserves the balance of good and evil in the universe by being born on earth as a human from time to time, to help men and women.

- **The god Shiva** is the destroyer god. He combats demons and keeps the universe moving by dancing.

- **After each 1000 Great Ages**, Shiva destroys the world by fire and flood. He preserves the seeds of all life in a golden egg, which Brahma breaks open to begin the rebirth of creation.

...FASCINATING FACT...
Hindu mythology says the world is created, destroyed and re-created in cycles that go on for ever.

Hindu deities

- **According to Hindu belief**, one day in the life of the supreme spirit, Brahman, is equivalent to 4320 million years on earth.

- **Hindus believe** that there is a set, correct way for everyone to behave, according to their role in society. Myths say that the god Vishnu established this code of good behaviour on earth, known as 'dharma'.

- **The wife of the mighty destroyer god**, Shiva, is a very important goddess. She has three forms: the gentle Parvati, the brave demon-fighter Durga and bloodthirsty Kali.

- **Ganesha** is the popular Hindu god of wisdom. He is pictured with an elephant's head.

- **The Hindu word for temple** is 'mandir'. Worship is 'puja'.

- **Hindus believe that gods and goddesses** are actually present in their shrines and temples. The picture or statue that represents the god or goddess living there is known as a murti.

▶ *Hindu temples are ornately decorated with statues and carvings of the gods.*

- **When Hindus worship** at a shrine or temple, they leave the god or goddess a small offering of food or flowers.

- **In Hindu art**, gods and goddesses are often painted blue, which is the Hindu colour of holiness.

- **Hindu gods and goddesses** are often pictured with several heads or arms, to show their special characteristics. For instance, Vishnu has four arms, two holding objects to show his holiness, and two holding weapons to show his power.

- **In 1995, thousands of people** in India reported that statues of Hindu gods were drinking milk. Some believed this was a miracle. Others said that the statues were made of porous stone, which was soaking up the liquid.

▲ *The magnificent Hindu temple of Angkor Wat was built in Cambodia in the 12th century, by the then-ruler of the Khmer empire, King Suryavarman II.*

The Ramayana

◀ Hindus believe that the hero Rama was one of the ten human forms of the god Vishnu.

- **The Indian epic poem** the *Ramayana* focuses on the battle between the forces of good and evil in the universe.

- **Historians believe** that it was largely composed between 200 BC and AD 200. The poet is believed to be called Valmiki, but little is known about him.

- **Like the Greek epic the *Iliad*,** the *Ramayana* involves the rescue of a stolen queen (called Sita).

- **Like the Greek epic the *Odyssey*,** the *Ramayana* follows a hero (Prince Rama) on a long and difficult journey.

- **Prince Rama's enemy** is the mighty demon, Ravana. He can work powerful magic, but is not immortal and can be killed.

- **The demon Ravana's followers** are known as Rakshasas. They can shape-shift and disguise themselves so they do not appear evil. This way, they can tempt good people to do the wrong thing.

- **The poem** demonstrates that it is important to respect animals. Rama needs the help of the hero Hanuman and his army of monkeys to rescue Sita.

- **The story says** that Rama and Sita are earthly forms of the great god Vishnu and his wife, Lakshmi.

- **Hindus see the** *Ramayana* as a book of religious teaching because Rama and Sita are models of good behaviour.

- **The legend ends** when Rama has ruled as king for 10,000 years and is taken up to heaven with his brothers.

▶ *The monkey god Hanuman was the son of the wind and a great hero who helped Prince Rama.*

Semites

- **Jewish people** and Arabs are Semitic people.

- **In 2500 BC**, the Semites were farming peoples such as the Akkadians, Canaanites and Amorites, who lived in what is now Israel, Jordan and Syria.

- **In 2371 BC**, an Akkadian called Sargon seized the throne of the Sumerian city of Kish. He conquered all Sumer and Akkad and created a great empire.

- **The Akkadian Empire** collapsed c.2230 BC, under attacks from tribes of Gutians from the mountains.

- **From 3000 to 1500 BC**, Canaanite Byblos was one of the world's great trading ports, famous for its purple cloth.

- **About 2000 BC**, Amorites conquered Sumer, Akkad and Canaan. In 1792 BC, the Amorite Hammurabi was ruler of Babylon.

- **The first Hebrews** were a Semitic tribe from southern Mesopotamia. Their name meant 'people of the other side' – of the Euphrates River.

- **According to the Bible**, the first Hebrew was Abraham, a shepherd who lived in the Sumerian city of Ur, 4000 years ago. He led his family first to Syria, then to Canaan (now Palestine), where he settled.

- **Abraham's grandson Jacob** was also called Israel and the Hebrews were afterwards called Israelites.

- **About 1000 BC**, the Israelite people prospered under three kings – Saul, David and Solomon.

▶ *The* Dead Sea Scrolls *are ancient Hebrew manuscripts found by shepherds in 1947 in a cave near the Dead Sea. They include the oldest known texts of the Bible's Old Testament. Today the Scrolls are housed in a museum in Israel.*

The Assyrians

- **The Assyrians** came originally from the upper Tigris valley around the cities of Ashur, Nineveh and Arbela.

- **About 2000** BC, Assyria was invaded by Amorites. Under a line of Amorite kings, Assyria built up a huge empire. King Adadnirari I called himself 'King of Everything'.

- **The Old Assyrian Empire** lasted six centuries, until it was broken by attacks by Mitannian horsemen.

- **From 1114 to 1076** BC, King Tiglath Pileser I rebuilt Assyrian power by conquest, creating the New Assyrian Empire.

◄ *Assyrian stone carvings were skilfully done. Many, such as this one showing a genie, decorated palace walls.*

. . . **FASCINATING FACT** . . .
King Assurbanipal's (668–627 BC) palace was filled with books and plants from all over the world.

- **The New Assyrian Empire** reached its peak under Tiglath-Pileser III (744–727 BC) and was finally overthrown by the Medes and Babylonians in 612 BC.

- **Ruthless warriors**, the Assyrians grew beards and fought with bows, iron swords, spears and chariots.

- **The Assyrians** built good roads all over their empire, so that the army could move fast to quell trouble.

- **They also built** magnificent palaces and cities such as Khorsabad and Nimrud.

- **Arab warriors** rode camels into battle for the Assyrians.

▶ *Wealthy Assyrians strove to outdo each other with elaborate clothing and luxurious houses.*

Oceania

- **The people of the Pacific** – Oceania – may have been the greatest seafarers of the ancient world.

- **Up until 5000 years ago**, the sea level was lower and Tasmania, Australia and New Guinea were all part of one big continent.

- **About 50,000 years ago**, bold, seafaring people crossed the ocean from Southeast Asia and settled in Australia.

- **Most early sites** are now lost offshore under the sea, which rose to cut off New Guinea and Australia around 5000 BC.

- **The Australian aboriginals** are descendants of these original inhabitants.

- **The oldest settlement** in New Guinea is 40,000 years old.

- **About 4000 BC**, domesticated plants and animals reached New Guinea from Asia, and farmers drained fields around an area called Kuk Swamp. Many people, however, remained hunters.

- **About 2000 BC**, people sailed in canoes from Indonesia to colonize Melanesia and Micronesia – the islands of the western Pacific, such as Vanuatu.

- **Early Melanesians** are known by their 'Lapita' pottery, which originated in the Molucca Islands of Indonesia.

- **Rowing canoes** shown in a 50,000-year-old cave painting in Australia match those that can be seen all over the Pacific region, and in caves in South America's Amazon jungle.

▶ *The people of Oceania crossed the oceans in canoes like these tens of thousands of years before the great European explorers.*

Aboriginal beliefs

● **Aborigines from central Australia** believed that their ancestors slept beneath the Earth, with the Sun, the Moon and the stars. Eventually the ancestors woke up and wandered about the Earth in the shapes of humans, animals and plants, shaping the landscape.

● **The mythology** of Australia comes from wandering tribes of people collectively called Aborigines. Historians believe that they are descended from survivors of the Stone Age.

● **Most Dreamtime mythology** says that in the beginning, the Earth was just a dark plain.

● **There are various** Dreamtime stories, which came from different tribes.

● **The creation mythology** of the Aborigines is called the Dreamtime.

● **Aborigines from** south eastern Australia believed heroes from the sky shaped the world and created people.

◄ *Aborigines believe that their ancestors had magical powers of creation.*

- **Myths from central Australia** say that people were carved out of animals and plants by their ancestors who then went back to sleep in rocks, trees or underground – where they are to this day.

- **Tribes from the northeast** believed that everything was created by two female ancestors who came across the sea from the Land of the Dead.

- **A wise rainbow snake** plays an important part in many Dreamtime myths.

- **Aborigines believe** that even the harshest, most barren landscape is sacred because the life of the ancestors runs through it.

▶ *This Aboriginal artwork shows a monster called a Bunyip, much feared by children.*

Polynesians

▲ *Outriggers are traditional boats of Polynesia, and are named after rigging that sticks out to the sides to aid stability. Easy to pull ashore, and perfect for shallow waters, they are ideal for island life.*

- **Polynesians are the peoples** who live on the many islands in the middle of the Pacific Ocean, from Hawaii to Easter Island and New Zealand.

- **There are 10,000 islands** in Polynesia and the rest of the eastern Pacific, with hundreds of different cultures and languages, each with its own history.

- **Many Polynesian islands** may well have been first settled 40,000 years ago by people from Southeast Asia.

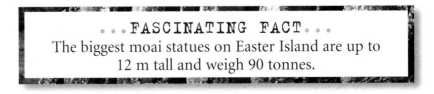

....FASCINATING FACT...
The biggest moai statues on Easter Island are up to
12 m tall and weigh 90 tonnes.

- **A second wave of migrants** moved east from Fiji, Samoa and Tonga to the Marquesas Islands 2000 years ago.

- **In their canoes** the settlers took crops (coconuts, yams, taros and breadfruit) and livestock (pigs and chickens).

- **Every island** developed its own style of woodcarving.

- **About** AD **400,** the new Polynesians moved on to Hawaii and Easter Island.

- **Easter Islanders** created strange stone statues called *moais*, carved with stone tools because they had no metal.

- **The settlers crossed the ocean** in small double canoes and boats called outriggers.

▶ *There are about 600 huge stone* moai *statues on Easter Island, on platforms called* ahus. *No one knows what they were used for.*

South Pacific stories

- **The remote islands of the South Pacific,** such as Polynesia, Hawaii and Tahiti, were untouched by the rest of the world for thousands of years. Mythological beliefs remain strong there to this day.

- **European explorers** took over many islands in the 19th century. Some islanders believed that this was because they had failed to keep myths and rituals alive properly, so they started to write them down for future generations.

  - **Myths from west Polynesia** say that in the beginning, the creator god Tangaroa lived in a dark emptiness known as Po.

  - **Some stories say that Tangaroa** formed the world by throwing down rocks into the watery wastes.

  - **Some myths say that Tangaroa** created humans when he made a leafy vine to give his messenger bird, Tuli, some shade – the leaves were people.

  - **Other Polynesian myths** say that the world was created by the joining of Ao (light) and Po (darkness).

  - **In New Zealand,** the two forces who joined together in creation were Earth Mother and Sky Father – Papa and Rangi.

◄ *The powerful god Tangaroa is an important figure in the mythologies of many South Pacific islands.*

▲ *The beautiful island of French Polynesia. The South Pacific islands cover*
an area over twice the size of the United Kingdom.

- **According to stories from New Zealand**, Tangaroa was the father of fish and reptiles.

- **Other gods in myths from New Zealand include** Haumia father of plants, Rongo father of crops, Tane father of forests, Tawhiri god of storms, and Tu father of humans.

- **Myths say that certain gods** were more important than others. These 'chief gods' vary from island to island, according to who the islanders believe they were descended from.

Persia

- **Iran is named after** the Aryan people who began settling there *c*.15,000 BC. Two Aryan tribes – the Medes and Persians – soon became dominant.

- **In 670 BC**, the Medes under King Cyaxeres joined forces with the Babylonians and finally overthrew the Assyrians.

- **In 550 BC**, the Medes themselves were overthrown by the Persians. The Persian king, Cyrus II, was the grandson of the king of the Medes, Astyages.

- **Cyrus II had an army** of horsemen and very skilled archers. He went on to establish a great Persian empire after conquering Lydia and Babylon.

- **The Persian Empire** was ruled by the Achaemenid family until it was destroyed by Alexander the Great in 330 BC.

- **Under the rule of Darius I**, the Persian Empire reached its greatest extent. Darius who called himself Shahanshah ('King of kings') introduced gold and silver coins, and also brought chickens to the Middle East.

▲ *Darius the Great ruled Persia from 521 to 486 BC.*

- **Darius built a famous road system** and split his empire into 20 *satrapies* (regions), each ruled by a *satrap*.

- **'King's Ears' were officials** who travelled around the empire and reported any trouble back to the king.

- **The Persians built** luxurious cities and palaces – first at Susa, then in Darius's reign, at Persepolis.

● **Persian priests**, or *magi*, were known for their magic skills, and gave us the word 'magic'. A famous magus called Zarathustra, unusually, worshipped a single god – Ahuru Mazda. His god's evil enemy was Angra Mainyu.

◄ *Rich carvings adorned the walls at Persepolis – the great city and palace of Darius's reign.*

Beliefs from Persia

- **We know many of Persia's myths** and legends from a document called the Book of Kings. This was written by a poet called Firdausi around AD 1000.

- **An ancient Persian myth** says that in the beginning there was only a flat mass of earth and water. Then evil came crashing through the sky, stirring up the landscape.

- **According to early myth**, Persia was at the centre of the world. The mighty Mount Alburz grew for 800 years until its peak touched the heavens. At its base was a gateway to hell.

- **The earliest Persian gods** were good and evil forces of nature, such as Vayu (the wind god who brought life-giving rain) and Apaosha (the demon of drought).

- **Much of Persia's mythology** comes from a religion founded by a prophet called Zoroaster in the 6th century BC. The chief god was called Ahura Mazda. His most beautiful form was the sun.

- **According to Zoroastrianism**, the world began when Ahura Mazda created time. He gave birth to everything that is good: light, love, justice and peace.

- **The first human** was a man known as Gayomart. Ahura Mazda created him from light.

- **Evil entered the universe** when Ahura Mazda's jealous twin, Ahriman, attacked the world and set free hunger, pain, disease and death to spoil creation.

> ....FASCINATING FACT....
> Persia is the ancient name for modern-day Iran.

● **Ahriman killed Gayomart**, but Ahura Mazda created a new human couple, Mashya and Mashyoi. Ahura Mazda left them free to worship either himself or the wicked Ahriman as humans have been free to do ever since.

◀ *The people of Persia followed the teachings of the prophet Zoroaster, shown in the top right of this painting, from the 6th century* BC *until the country became Muslim in the 7th century* BC.

103

The Persian pantheon

- **The earliest Persians** worshipped nature deities such as Tishtrya, god of fertility, and Anahita, goddess of the lakes and oceans.

- **Three famous priests** of the nature god cult were the Magi – the three wise men or kings who visited baby Jesus.

- **In ancient times**, the god of victory, Verethragna, was worshipped widely through the Persian empire by soldiers. Like the Hindu god Vishnu, he was born ten times on Earth to fight demons. He took different animal and human forms.

▶ *One Persian myth says that the god Mithras brought fertility to the world by killing a bull, which contained all the strength of the Earth, and sprinkling its blood over the land.*

- **The human heroes** of Persian myths and legends were also worshipped as god-like rulers. One was the hero Faridun, who battled a monster of evil and imprisoned him at the ends of the Earth.

- **In the 1st and 2nd centuries**, the god of light, Mithras, became an important deity. He was another warrior hero who protected creation by killing the forces of evil.

- **From the 6th century**, the beliefs of a prophet called Zoroaster spread through Persia. In this religion, Zoroastrianism, the ancient gods became saints called Yazatas.

- **The chief god in Zoroastrianism**, Ahura Mazda, was later known as Ohrmazd.

- **Ahura Mazda was said to be** Zoroaster's father. Zoroaster's mother was believed to be a virgin, like Jesus's mother, Mary.

▶ *The tomb of Cyrus the Great, the founder of the Persian Empire, who ruled from 549–529 BC.*

- **According to Zoroaster**, creation is protected by seven spirit guardians known as Amesha Spentas.

- **Zoroastrians believe that everyone** is looked after by a guardian spirit, or Fravashi. These spirits represent the good in people and help those who ask.

Weapons of war

- **Early stone axes and spears** may have been used both for hunting and as weapons. Remains of a wooden spear from half a million years ago were found at Boxgrove, England.

- **A spear-thrower** was a stick with a notch in one end to take the end of a spear. With it, hunters (or fighters) could hurl a spear with tremendous force. Spear-throwers were the first ever machines made by humans, c.35,000 BC.

- **The first pictures of bows** come from North Africa, c.30,000–15,000 BC. Bows could be devastatingly effective and were the main weapons of the earliest civilizations.

- **The invention of bronze**, c.3000 BC, meant that people could make metal swords, daggers, axes and spears.

- **A tiny bronze statue** of a chariot found at Tell Agrab, Iraq, dates from 3000 BC. This is the first image of a chariot.

▲ *Legendary warrior Alexander the Great, king of Macedonia, led vast numbers of soldiers who used artillery crossbows to fire huge arrows.*

- **The Persian emperor Cyrus** (559–529 BC) added scythes (long, sharp blades) poking out sideways from chariot wheels to slice through the legs of enemy soldiers and horses.

- **The oldest helmet** (*c.*2500 BC), made of a gold and silver alloy (mix) called electrum, was found in the royal tombs of Ur.

- **The crossbow was invented** in the Greek colony of Syracuse, about 400 BC.

- **Alexander the Great** used crossbows, firing 5-m arrows, to win his empire between 340 and 323 BC.

- **Around AD 100**, Dionysius of Alexander in Egypt invented a rapid-firing crossbow, able to fire dozens of bolts a minute.

▼ *The chariot was the air force of the ancient civilizations, carrying archers and spear-throwers across the battlefield. Egyptians, Hittites and Assyrians fought huge battles with thousands of chariots.*

Tutankhamun

▶ *A fabulous gold mask was found in Tutankhamun's innermost coffin, over the young king's decaying remains. His skull showed signs of hammer blows.*

- **The pharaoh (king) of ancient Egypt** from 1347 to 1339 BC was Tutankhamun. He was a boy when he became pharaoh and only 18 when he died.

- **Tutankhamun was the last** of the great 18th dynasty (family) of pharaohs who ruled Egypt 1567–1339 BC. They included the warrior queen Hatshepsut, and Thutmose III, who led Egypt to the peak of its power, around 1400 BC.

- **The father of Tutankhamun** was Akhenaten, who, with his queen Nefertiti, created a revolution in Egypt. Akhenaten replaced worship of the old Egyptian gods with worship of a single god, and moved the capital city to Armarna.

- **Tutankhamun's wife** was his half-sister Ankhesenamun. When he died – perhaps murdered – Ankhesenamun was at the mercy of his enemies, Ay and General Horemheb. She wrote to the Hittite king asking for his son to marry, but the Hittite prince was murdered on the way to Egypt.

- **The Valley of the Kings**, near Luxor on the river Nile in Egypt, is the world's greatest archaeological site. It was the special burial place of the 18th dynasty pharaohs and contains the tombs of 62 pharaohs, and high officials.

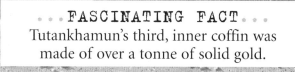

... FASCINATING FACT ...
Tutankhamun's third, inner coffin was
made of over a tonne of solid gold.

- **Tutankhamun's tomb** was the only tomb in the Valley of the Kings not plundered over the centuries. When opened, it contained 5000 items, including many fabulous carved and gold items.

- **English archaeologist** Howard Carter discovered Tutankhamun's tomb in 1922.

- **Rumours of a curse** on those who disturb the tomb began when Carter's pet canary was eaten by a cobra – the symbol of the pharaoh – at the moment the tomb was first opened.

- **Experts worked out** the dates of Tutankhamun's reign from the date labels on wine-jars left in the tomb.

▼ When Carter opened Tutankhamun's tomb, he came first to an anteroom. It took him three years to clear this room and enter the burial chamber, with its huge gold shrines containing the coffins.

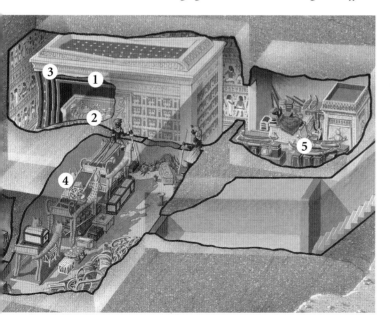

1. Inside the shrines, there was a red sandstone sarcophagus (coffin)

2. Inside the sarcophagus were three gold coffins, one inside the other

3. In the burial chamber were four shrines of gilded wood, one inside the other

4. Fabulous beds, chests, gold chariot wheels and carved animals in the anteroom were just a taste of the riches to come

5. Beyond the burial chamber was a treasury full of gold and other treasures

The Trojan Wars

- **From 1600 to 1100** BC, mainland Greece was dominated by tough warrior people called the Mycenaeans.

- **The Mycenaeans fought** with long bronze swords, long leather shields and bronze armour.

- **Mycenaeans lived in small kingdoms**, each with its own fortified hilltop city – called an *acropolis*.

- **A typical Mycenaean noble** was like a Viking chieftain. In the middle of his palace was a great hall with a central fireplace where warriors would sit around, telling tales of heroic deeds.

- **After 1500** BC, Mycenaean kings were buried in a beehive-shaped tomb called a *tholos*, with a long, corridor-shaped entrance.

- **The Greek poet Homer** tells how a city called Troy was destroyed by the Mycenaeans after a ten-year siege. Historians once thought this was just a story, but now that Troy's remains have been discovered, they think there may be some truth in it.

▶ *Troy fell when the Greeks pretended to give up and go home, leaving behind a huge wooden horse. The jubilant Trojans dragged this into the city – only to discover Greeks hiding inside it.*

▶ *The Trojan War lasted for ten bloody years. Many lives were lost during battles, even though the soldiers wore protective armour. Achilles and Hector would have worn crested helmets like those shown here, to make them look more frightening and impressive. A bronze breast plate would have protected the upper body while bronze leg guards were worn to protect the lower legs.*

- **The Trojan War** in Homer's tale is caused by the beautiful Helen of Sparta. She married Menalaus, brother of King Agamemnon of Mycenae, but she fell in love with Prince Paris of Troy.

- **Helen and Paris** eloped to Troy and Agamemnon and other Greeks laid siege to Troy to take her back.

- **The battle featured** many heroes – such as Hector, Achilles and Odysseus.

- **The Greeks finally captured** Troy when Greek soldiers hidden inside a wooden horse found their way into the city.

Odysseus and The Odyssey

- ***The Odyssey* is an adventure story** that follows the Greek hero, Odysseus, after the Trojan War, on his long and difficult sea voyage home.

- **Odysseus** and his men have to face many magical dangers on their journey, including ferocious monsters and terrifying giants.

- **On one occasion**, some of Odysseus's sailors eat lotus fruit, which makes them forget all about returning to their families and homes.

▲ *One Greek legend says that the Sirens were so furious when Odysseus escaped their clutches that they drowned themselves.*

- **Odysseus has to sail** safely past the Sirens. These are half-woman, half-bird creatures who live on a craggy seashore. They sing a magical song that lures sailors to steer their ships onto the rocks to their deaths.

- **The goddess of war**, Athena, acts as Odysseus's patron, giving him special help and guidance.

- **The sea god Poseidon** hates Odysseus and seeks to shipwreck him.

- **By the time Odysseus** finally reaches his palace in Ithaca, he has been away for 20 years. Disguised as a beggar, only his faithful old dog recognizes him.

- **Once home, Odysseus's troubles** are not over. Powerful suitors are pressurizing his faithful wife, Penelope, for her hand in marriage, so they can seize Odysseus's crown.

- **Women often hold positions** of great power in the poem. For instance, Circe is a very powerful sorceress who turns some of Odysseus's sailors into pigs. The goddess Calypso keeps Odysseus captive on her island for seven years.

...FASCINATING FACT...
Unlike its companion poem, the *Iliad*,
the *Odyssey* has a happy ending.

The Aeneid

- **The *Aeneid* is an epic poem** that follows the adventures of a Trojan prince, Aeneas, after the end of the Trojan War.

- **The *Aeneid* was not composed** in the oral tradition. The Roman author, Virgil, wrote it down in Latin.

- **The son of a farmer**, Virgil was well educated. The Roman Emperor, Augustus Caesar, recognized his talent for writing and became his patron (provided him with money).

- **Virgil based the legends** in his poem and its structure on the epics the *Iliad* and the *Odyssey*.

- **In the *Iliad***, Aeneas fights many times against the Greeks, but is always saved by the gods because he has another destiny.

- **It was popular in the 6th century** BC to illustrate part of the legend of Aeneas on vases – how Aeneas carried his father to safety out of the smoking ruins of Troy.

- **Virgil designed the *Aeneid*** to give Augustus and the Roman empire a glorious history. It explains that the gods themselves instructed Aeneas to travel to Italy, to be the ancestor of a great race – the Romans. It shows how Augustus Caesar was directly descended from the mighty hero.

- **In the *Aeneid***, Aeneas falls in love with Queen Dido of Carthage and then abandons her, sailing for Italy. Virgil probably made up this myth to explain the hatred that existed between Rome and Carthage in the 3rd century BC.

- **In 29 BC**, Virgil began writing the *Aeneid* and worked on it for the last ten years of his life. As he lay dying of a fever, he asked for the poem to be burnt. However, Augustus Caesar overruled his wishes.

● **A great Italian poet** called Dante Alighieri (1265–1321) used Virgil's style and legends of the *Aeneid* as the basis for his poem, the *Divine Comedy.*

▶ *According to one ancient source, the poet Virgil was tall and dark with the appearance of a countryman.*

Early Greece

- **Around 1200 BC**, the Mycenaeans began to abandon their cities, and a people called the Dorians took over Greece.

- **Many Mycenaeans fled overseas** in a large battle fleet, and the Egyptians called them the Sea Peoples. Some ended up in Italy and may have been the ancestors of the Etruscan people there.

- **With the end of Mycenaean civilization**, Greece entered its Dark Ages as the art of writing was lost.

- **About 800 BC**, the Greeks began to emerge from their Dark Ages as they relearned writing from the Phoenicians, a people who traded in the eastern Mediterranean.

- **The period of Greek** history from 800 to 500 BC is called the Archaic (ancient) Period.

- **In the Archaic Period**, the Greek population grew rapidly. States were governed by wealthy aristocrats.

◄ *Greek cargo ships carried oil, wheat and wine for trading. The sailors painted eyes on either side of the prow in the hope they would scare away evil spirits.*

▲ *A Greek house may have looked like this 2600 years ago, with first-floor bedrooms overlooking a central courtyard.*

- **The early Greeks loved athletics** and held four major events. They were called the Panhellenic Games and drew competitors from all over the Greek world.

- **The four Panhellenic Games** were the Olympic, Pythian, Isthmian and Nemean Games.

- **The Olympic Games** started in 776 BC and were the most important. They were held every four years, at Olympia.

- **The Greek poet Homer** wrote his famous poems about the Trojan Wars around 700 BC.

117

The Maya

- **The Maya were a people** who dominated Central America from 500 BC to AD 1524 (when they were conquered by Spanish invaders).

- **The Maya began building** large pyramids with small temples on top between 600 BC and AD 250.

- **Mayan civilization peaked** between AD 250 and 900. This has become known as the Classic Period.

- **During the Classic Period**, Mayan civilization centred on great cities such as Tikal in the Guatemalan lowlands. They traded extensively – on foot and in dug-out canoes.

▶ *The Mayan pyramid at Chichén Itzá, in the Yucatán.*

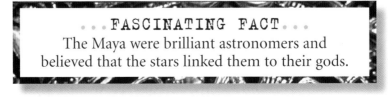

. . . FASCINATING FACT . . .
The Maya were brilliant astronomers and believed that the stars linked them to their gods.

- **Mayan people** in the Classic Period developed a clever form of writing in symbols representing sounds or ideas. They recorded their history on stone monuments called *stelae*.

- **Mysteriously, around** AD **800,** the Maya stopped making *stelae* and the Guatemalan cities were abandoned.

- **From** AD **800 to 1200**, the most powerful Mayan city was Chichén Itzá, in the Yucatán region of modern-day Mexico. From AD 1200 to 1440 another city, Mayapán, came to the fore. After 1440, Mayan civilization rapidly broke up, following revolts by the leaders of some Mayan cities against Mayapán, and the division of Yucatán into separate warring states.

- **The Maya were very religious**. Deer, dogs, turkeys and even humans were often sacrificed to the gods in the temples on top of the pyramids.

- **Mayan farmers** grew mainly corn, beans and squash. From the corn, women made flat pancakes that are now called tortillas, and an alcoholic drink known as *balche*.

▶ *The Maya created complex calendars based on their detailed observation of the stars.*

119

Mayan mythology

- **The Mayan creation story** is written in an ancient document known as the Popol Vuh.

- **The Maya believed** that in the beginning there was nothing but darkness, with sky above and sea below.

- **Myths say** that a group of gods together shaped the landscape and formed animals and birds.

- **The Popol Vuh** explains that the first two human races made by the Creators were not good enough and had to be destroyed. The first people were mindless, made from clay. The second people were soulless, made from wood.

- **The first successful people** were made out of corn, at the suggestion of a jaguar, a coyote, a crow and a parrot.

- **The Maya believed** that the third race of humans were so perfect, they were almost as good as the Creators themselves. So the Creators clouded the intelligence of the humans so they could no longer see the gods.

- **The Popol Vuh** says that women were created after men, as in the Christian creation story in the Bible.

- **By taking certain** mind-altering drugs, the Maya believed that they could get back in touch with the gods.

- **The Maya believed** that when human beings were created all the world was still in darkness. People begged for some light, so that is why the Creators made the Sun, Moon and stars.

...FASCINATING FACT...
One Mayan manuscript mentions more than
160 different gods and goddesses.

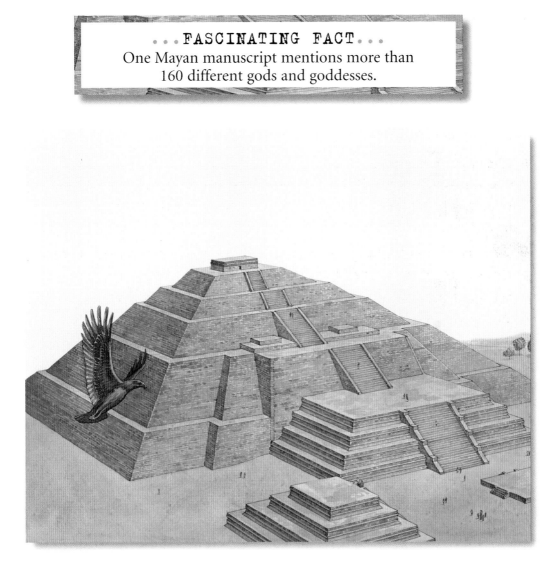

▲ *The Maya built huge stone temples and palaces in the shape of pyramids,*
like this one at Teotihuacán.

Confucius

- **Confucius** (say: *con-few-shuss*) is the most famous thinker and teacher in Chinese history.

- **Chinese people called him** Kongzi or K'ung-Fu-Tzu, but Confucius is the name used by Europeans.

- **Confucius was born** in Lu, now Shantung Province, in 551 BC, traditionally on September 28th, and died in 479 BC.

- **After mastering the six Chinese arts** – ritual, music, archery, charioteering, calligraphy (writing) and arithmetic – Confucius went on to become a brilliant teacher.

- **He was the first person** in China to argue that all men should be educated in order to make the world a better place, and that teaching could become a way of life.

- **In middle age**, Confucius served as a minister for the King of Lu. He had a highly moral approach to public service. He told statesmen this golden rule: 'Do not do to others what you would not have them do to you.'

- **The King of Lu** was not interested in Confucius' ideas, so Confucius went into exile, followed by his students.

- **After his death**, Confucius' ideas were developed by teachers like Mencius (390–305 BC) and Xunzi (*c.*250 BC) into a way of life called Confucianism. Until recently, this dominated Chinese life.

- **Living at the same time as Confucius** may have been a man called Lao-Tse. Lao-Tse wrote the *Tao Te Ching*, the basis of Taoist religion.

- **The *Tao Te Ching*** tells of the Tao (Way) – the underlying unity of nature that makes everything what it is.

◀ *Little is known about Lao-Tse, the founder of Taoism. Legend has it that while travelling on an ox one day, he was stopped at a border post. There he wrote down his teachings. He then vanished and was never seen again.*

▶ *Confucius' belief was that court officials should not plot for power but study music, poetry and the history of their ancestors.*

123

Chinese technology

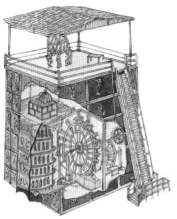

▲ The Chinese invented mechanical clocks in AD 723 – 600 years earlier than Europe. This is Su Sung's 'Cosmic Engine', an amazing 10-m high clock built in AD 1090.

● **Western experts** have only recently realized that ancient Chinese technology was very advanced, and many of their early inventions only reached Europe thousands of years later.

● **In the early AD 1600s,** the English thinker Francis Bacon said that three recent inventions had changed the world – printing, gunpowder and the ship's magnetic compass. In fact, all of these had been invented in China a thousand years earlier.

● **One of the oldest surviving printed books** is the *Diamond Sutra*, printed in China *c.*AD 868. However, printing in China goes back to the 7th century AD.

● **The world's first robot** was an amazing ancient Chinese cart. Gears from the wheels turned a statue on top so that its finger always pointed south.

▲ A compass called a sinan was made by the Chinese over 2000 years ago. A ladle made of magnetic lodestone spins on a bronze plate to point south.

▲ The Chinese discovered gunpowder and made the first guns about 1100 years ago. They also became famous for their fireworks.

▲ In AD 132, Chang Heng made the world's first earthquake detector. When even a faint, distant quake occurred, a metal ball fell from the dragon's mouth at the top of a jar into a toad's mouth.

The tomb of Emperor Shih Huangdi, who died in 210 BC, had huge magnetic security doors.

- **The Chinese had alcoholic spirits** 2000 years ago, over a thousand years before they came to Europe.

- **The horse stirrup** was probably invented in China in the 3rd century BC. This gave horse-soldiers a platform to fight from and allowed them to wear armour.

- **The wheelbarrow** was invented by the Chinese in about 100 BC.

- **Cast-iron ploughs** were made in China *c.*200 BC.

- **Football was invented** in China. About 200 BC, they were playing a game called *t'su chu*. It involved kicking an inflated leather ball through a hole in a silk net.

▲ *Water-powered machines for spinning cloth are often thought of as inventions of the English Industrial Revolution in the AD 1700s. In fact, the Chinese were building them at least 500 years earlier, to spin a cloth called ramie.*

▲ *Acupuncture involves sticking pins in certain points on the body to treat illness. The Chinese used it 1800 years ago – but it may have been used earlier in Europe.*

▲ *One particularly nasty Chinese invention was the 'Heaven-Rumbling Thunderclap Fierce Fire Erupter'. This was a gunpowder-fired device that shot out shells of poisonous gas.*

125

The search for Troy

- **Troy is the city** in the ancient Greek poet Homer's famous epic, the *Iliad*. It was once thought to be entirely mythical.

- **In 1822**, British scholar Charles McClaren suggested that Homer's Troy might be in Turkey. He pinpointed a mound called Hisarlik near the Dardanelles – a narrow sea linking the Black Sea and the Aegean.

- **German archaeologist** Heinrich Schliemann began digging at Hisarlik mound in 1871.

- **In 1873**, Schliemann uncovered fortifications and remains of a very ancient city, which he believed to be Troy.

- **Schliemann also found** a treasure of gold and silver, which he called Priam's treasure after the Trojan king Priam, mentioned in the *Iliad*. He smuggled this out of Turkey to take to Europe.

- **In 1876**, Schliemann was digging at Mycenae in Greece. He came across what he thought was the tomb of Agamemnon – king of the Trojans' enemies in Homer's *Iliad*.

- **In the 1890s**, Wilhelm Dorpfield showed that Hisarlik mound is made of nine layers of city remains. This is because the city was destroyed by fire or earthquake nine times. Each time the survivors built on the rubble.

- **Schliemann thought Homer's Troy** was Troy II, second layer from the bottom. Dorpfield thought it was Troy VI.

- **Troy I to V** are now thought to date from the early Bronze Age (*c.*3000 to 1900 BC).

- **Experts now think** Homer's Troy may be Troy VIIa, a layer of the seventh city, dating from about 1250 BC.

▲ *When Schliemann found this gold mask at Mycenae, in 1876, he thought it must be Agamemnon's. In fact, it dates from 300 years earlier.*

Greek city-states

- **Ancient Greece was not a single country** in its early days, but a collection of independent cities or city-states.

- **A Greek city-state** was called a *polis* (plural *poleis*).

- *Polis* gives us the words politics, police and polite.

- **There were several hundred *poleis*** in ancient Greece. The largest were Athens and Sparta.

- **Each city** typically had a mound called an *acropolis* with a temple on top, and a market place called an *agora*.

- **To start with** (from about 800 to 600 BC), city-states were governed by oligarchs (a few powerful men) or a tyrant, but other people gradually got more say in how things were run.

- **People in Greek city-states** were either free or slaves. Free men (not women) were split into citizens (born in the city itself) and *metics* (immigrants).

- **In 508 BC**, a man called Cleisthenes gave Athens a new system of government called democracy.

- **The word democracy** comes from the Greek terms *demos* ('people') and *kratos* ('rule'). The idea was that every citizen (except metics and slaves) had the right to speak and vote in the Assembly, held every ten days on a hill called the Pnyx.

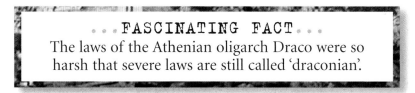

...FASCINATING FACT...
The laws of the Athenian oligarch Draco were so harsh that severe laws are still called 'draconian'.

▼ *The most famous acropolis is the Acropolis in Athens with the Parthenon temple on top.*

The Zhou and Qin

- **About 100 BC**, the Shang in China were conquered by a people called the Zhou.

- **The Zhou extended** the Shang's territory far across China, but the kingdom was divided into large estates, each with its own ruler.

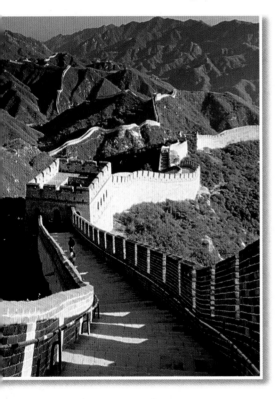

▲ *Although today's brick and stone wall dates from the AD 1400s, the Great Wall of China was first built of earth bricks in 214 BC, under Shi Huangdi.*

- **At this time**, the Chinese began using iron for ploughs and weapons, and made advances in technology.

- **Great thinkers** such as Laozi and Confucius came to the fore.

- **Confucius believed** morals were vital in government, but a minister called Shang Yang thought that the law must be strengthened by any means. This is called Legalism.

- **Shang Yang's family** – the Qin – overthrew the Zhou in 312 BC.

- **In 246 BC**, Qin emperor Zheng expanded the empire and called himself Shi Huangdi, First Emperor. He had the 4000-km-long Great Wall built to protect his empire from nomads from the north.

- **Shi Huangdi banned books** and buried 460 Confucian scholars alive. When his eldest son Fu Su objected, he was banished.

● **When Shi Huangdi died**, in 210 BC, his body was taken secretly to the capital by minister Li Si with a fish cart to hide the smell of rotting flesh. Li Si sent a letter to Fu Su, pretending it was from his father, telling him to commit suicide. Fu Su did and so Li Si came to power.

● **Shi Huangdi was buried** with an army of 6000 life-size clay soldiers, called the Terracotta Army when found in 1974. Certain parts of the tomb are said to be booby-trapped.

▼ *The great tomb of the Terracotta Army (or Warriors) is located near Xi'an, central China. In their underground chambers, the life-size figures are arranged in precise military formation.*

Famous generals

- **In 2300 BC**, King Sargon of Akkadia led his soldiers to victory over much larger armies by using especially far-shooting bows.

- **Thutmose III** (1479–1425 BC) was perhaps the greatest warrior-pharaoh, fighting 17 campaigns and taking Egypt's empire to its greatest extent.

- **Assurbanipal** (669–627 BC) was the great Assyrian leader whose chariots gave him a powerful empire from the Nile to the Caucasus Mountains.

- **Sun-Tzu** was the Chinese military genius who, in 500 BC, wrote the first manual on the art of war.

- **Alexander the Great** (356–323 BC) was the Macedonian whose army of 35,000 was the most efficient yet seen. He perfected the phalanx (soldiers arranged in very close formation), which proved highly effective in battle.

- **Hannibal** (247–182 BC) was the greatest general of the powerful city of Carthage (now near Tunis in Africa).

- **Scipio** (237–183 BC) was the Roman general who conquered Spain and broke Carthaginian power in Africa.

- **Julius Caesar** (*c.*100–44 BC) was the greatest Roman general.

- **Belisarius** (AD 505–565) and Narses (AD 478–573) were generals for Byzantine Emperor Justinian. Their mounted archers defeated the Vandals and Goths.

- **Charles Martel** (AD 688–741), 'the Hammer', was the Frankish king who defeated the Moors at Tours in France in AD 732 and turned back the Arab conquest of Europe.

▼ *Hannibal's greatest feat was leading an army – with elephants – through Spain and then the Alps, in winter, to attack Rome from the north.*

Buddha

- **Buddha was the founder** of the Buddhist religion, who was living in India about 563–483 BC.

- **Buddha is not a name** but a title (like 'the Messiah') meaning 'enlightened one', so you should really say 'the Buddha'.

- **The Buddha's real name** was Siddhartha Gautama.

- **Archaeological excavations** finished in 1995 suggest that a man who may have been Siddhartha lived in the palace of his father Suddodhana on what is now the border of Nepal and India.

- **As a young prince**, Siddhartha lived a life of luxury. When he was 16 years old, he married his cousin the Princess Yasodhara, who was also 16 years old.

▼ *Young Buddhist monks in traditional orange robes. They are taught to follow eight steps towards truth and wisdom.*

- **The turning point** was when Siddhartha was 29 and he saw four visions: an old man, a sick man, a corpse and a wandering holy man.

- **The first three visions** told Siddhartha that life involved ageing, sickness and death. The fourth told him he must leave his wife and become a holy man.

- **After six years** of self-denial, Siddhartha sat down under a shady 'bo' tree to think – and after several hours great wisdom came to him.

- **The Buddha** spent the rest of his life preaching his message around India.

- **At the age of 80**, the Buddha died. His bones became sacred relics.

▶ *Most statues of the Buddha show him sitting cross-legged, in deep meditation (thought).*

Greek thinkers

- **The great thinkers** of ancient Greece were called philosophers. Philosophy is Greek for 'love of wisdom'.

  - **The key philosophers** were Socrates, Plato and Aristotle.

    - **Socrates** (466–399 BC) believed people would behave well if they knew what good behaviour was and challenged people to think about truth, good and evil.

    - **Plato** (427–348 BC) argued that behind the messy chaos of everyday experience there is a perfect and beautiful Idea or Form. He also tried to find the ideal way of governing a state.

  - **Aristotle** (384–322 BC) argued that for true knowledge you must find the 'final cause' – why something happens.

  - **Aristotle was the first** great scientist, stressing the need to collect data, sort the results and interpret them.

▲ *Euclid, the great Greek mathematician and author of the 13-volume work* Elements, *was teaching in Alexandria around 300 BC.*

- **Many of the basic ideas** in philosophy, even today, come from Socrates, Plato and Aristotle, and other Greek philosophers such as Epicurus and Diogenes.

- **Greek mathematicians** such as Euclid, Appolonius, Pythagoras and Archimedes worked out many of our basic rules of maths. Most school geometry still depends on the system devised by Euclid.

- **Greek astronomers** like Aristarchus and Anaxagoras made many brilliant deductions – but many of these were forgotten. Aristarchus realized that the Earth turned on its axis and circled the Sun. Yet it was almost 2000 years before this idea was generally accepted.

▲ *Aristotle, the brilliant tutor to Alexander the Great, was thought of as the ultimate authority on every subject for over 2000 years.*

...FASCINATING FACT...
Archimedes showed how the effect of a lever could be worked out by maths.

137

Homer

- **Homer is the ancient Greek poet** said to have written the ancient world's two greatest poems: the *Iliad* and the *Odyssey*.

- **Homer probably lived** in the 9th century BC in Ionia, on what is now the Aegean coast of Turkey, or on the island of Chios.

- **No one knows for certain** if Homer actually existed, or if he composed all of both poems. Most current experts think that he did.

- **In Homer's time** there was a great tradition of bards. These were poets who recited aloud great tales of heroic deeds. They knew the poems by heart and so never wrote them down.

- **The *Iliad*** and the *Odyssey* are the only poems from the times of the bards that were written down and so survive. They may have been written down at the time, or later.

- **After Homer's time**, the two great poems were used in religious festivals in Greece.

- **For centuries after Homer's time**, Greek children learned to read, and learned about the legends of the past, by studying Homer's two great poems.

- **In the 2nd century** BC, scholars at the Alexandrian Library in Egypt studied the poems. A few scholars came to the conclusion that they were so different in style they must have been written by two different poets.

◀ *Nothing is known for certain about Homer, but legend says that he was blind.*

138

- The *Iliad* is a long poem in lofty language about the Trojan Wars, in which the Greeks besiege the city of Troy to take back the kidnapped Helen.

- The *Odyssey* tells of a great journey made by hero Odysseus, and his adventures along the way.

▶ The Odyssey recounts the adventures of Odysseus on his 10-year journey home after the war against Troy. In one tragic scene, Odysseus's faithful old dog Argus dies as his master reaches his home town.

139

Early Americans

- **The Americas were the last** continents that humans occupied.

- **The first Americans** may have been Australian aboriginals who arrived by boat 50,000 years ago.

- **Ancestors of today's Native Americans** probably came to the Americas 20,000–35,000 years ago, from Asia. They are thought to have walked across the strip of land that once joined Asia and North America across the Bering Strait.

- **By 6000 BC**, the first Native Americans had spread south from Alaska and far down into South America.

- **There is evidence** that humans were living in Mexico over 20,000 years ago. At El Jobo in Colombia, South America, pendants that date back to 14,920 BC have been found.

- **Ten thousand years ago**, groups of 'Paleo-Indians' on North America's Great Plains hunted now-extinct animals such as camels and mammoths. In the dry western mountains, desert peoples planted wild grass-seed.

▲ *Large woolly mammoths originated in Africa and were related to elephants. Native Americans hunted them for their hide and flesh.*

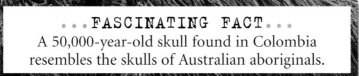

...FASCINATING FACT...
A 50,000-year-old skull found in Colombia
resembles the skulls of Australian aboriginals.

- **In Mexico**, people began to grow squash, peppers and beans at least 8500 years ago.

- **Corn** (maize) was probably first grown in Mexico, about 7000 years ago.

- **Corn, beans and squash** provided food for early American civilizations such as the Olmecs and Mayans.

▲ *The name 'squash' comes from the Indian word 'kutasquash', which means raw or uncooked. Squash is still a widely grown vegetable today.*

◀ *Carving wooden duck decoys for hunting is a North American tradition dating back thousands of years.*

Native Americans

- **Native American myths** come from the first people to live in North America. They walked there from Asia around 15,000 years ago when the two continents were linked by ice.

- **Native Americans settled** in many different tribes. Each tribe had its own myths and legends, although they shared many beliefs. The stories were passed down through generations by word of mouth.

- **Most tribes believed** that everything is part of one harmonious creation. Harming anything upsets the balance of the world.

- **The Iroquois** believed that Mother Earth fell into a lake from a land beyond the sky. The animals helped create the Sun, the Moon and stars.

- **According to the Algonquian**, the Earth was created by Michabo the Great Hare, from a grain of sand from the bottom of the ocean.

- **The Maidu tribe** believed that the gods Kodoyanpe and Coyote floated on the surface of a vast expanse of water and one day decided to create the world.

- **The Navajo people** believed that the first man and woman were created when four gods ordered the winds to blow life into two ears of corn.

◄ *Mythologies from all over the world have stories that explain the weather. Several Native American tribes told tales about a monster called the Thunderbird, who caused storms.*

▲ *The Iroquois tribe lived in an eastern area of North America now known as New York State.*

● **Many Native American** myths say that when the world was created, humans and animals lived together.

● **Some Native American** tribes believed that all creation is ruled over by a supreme spirit.

● **In 1855**, Henry Wadsworth Longfellow wrote an epic poem called *The Song of Hiawatha*, about a real Native American hero. Many aspects of his myth differ from reality. For instance, in the poem, Hiawatha is Iroquois, when in reality he was Algonquian.

Greek art

- **In the heyday of ancient Greece**, thousands of sculptors, architects, painters, dramatists and poets were creating a fantastic wealth of beautiful works of art.

- **The Greeks made** graceful statues and friezes to decorate temples and homes. They were carved mostly from marble and limestone and then painted, though in surviving statues the paint has worn away.

- **The most famous sculptors** were Phidias (*c.*490–420 BC), Praxiteles (*c.*330 BC), Lysippus (*c.*380–306 BC) and Myron (*c.*500–440 BC). Phidias's huge gold and ivory statue of the god Zeus was famed throughout the ancient world.

- **Greek architects** such as Ictinus and Callicrates created beautiful marble and limestone temples fronted by graceful columns and elegant triangular friezes. The most famous is the Parthenon in Athens.

- **The Greeks had three styles** for columns: the simple Doric, the slender Ionic, topped by scrolls, and the ornate Corinthian, topped by sculpted acanthus leaves.

- **The style created** by the Greek temples is now called Classical and has influenced architects ever since.

- **The Greeks believed** that different arts (such as dance or poetry) were inspired by one of nine goddesses, who were known as the Muses.

- **Ancient Greek writers** include the poets Homer, Sappho and Pindar. They created styles of writing that included epic poetry – long, dramatic tales of heroic deeds.

▲ *The famous Venus de Milo was found on the Aegean island of Milos in AD 1820. It was carved in Greek Antioch (now in Turkey) around 150 BC and shows the goddess of love, Aphrodite (Roman goddess Venus). The statue originally had arms.*

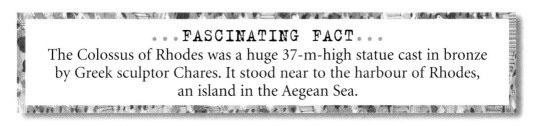

● **A tragedy is a grand drama** doomed to end unhappily for the hero. Tragedy was created by Greek dramatists such as Aeschylus, Euripides and Sophocles, who wrote the tragedy *King Oedipus.*

1. Audiences took cushions to sit on and picnics to sustain them through very long plays

2. A typical theatre, like the Theatre of Dionysus in Athens, seated 14,000 in stadium-like rows

3. A 'chorus' of actors linked the scenes with verse and songs

4. The circular acting area was called the *orchestra*

5. Scenes were played by just two or three actors, each wearing a mask

6. Behind the *orchestra* was a house or *skene*, where the actors changed. Later, this became a backdrop

7. In later Greek theatres, the *skene* developed side wings here called *paraskinia*

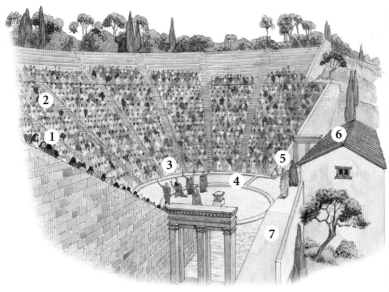

▲ *Formal drama was developed in ancient Greece in the 5th and 6th centuries* BC. *Huge audiences watched plays in open-air arenas.*

145

What people ate

- **People learned how to use fire** to cook food 1.5 million years ago. The oldest known cooking fire is at Swartkrans, South Africa.

- **The first ovens** were pits for hot coals, first used in the Ukraine about 20,000 years ago. The first real ovens were from Sumer and Egypt, *c.*2600 BC.

- **Grain seeds** were cooked and mixed with water to make gruel (porridge). Around 20,000 years ago, people learned to bake gruel on a hot stone to make flat bread, like pitta.

- **The development of pottery** meant that liquids could be heated to make stews. The oldest pottery is 13,000-year-old pots from Odai-Yamomoto in Japan. The first pots from the Near East, from Iran, date back 11,000 years.

◀ *Romans used to go to cheap eating houses called 'popinae' for their main meals. Here they could buy bread, cheese, fruit and cheap cuts of meat. Only the rich could afford to employ a chef to prepare meals.*

- **Around 12,000 years ago**, people found how to make food last by letting it ferment, making cheese from milk and wine from grapes.

- **Around 8000 BC**, people began to farm animals such as sheep and grow plants such as cereals for food. Diets became less varied than when people gathered wild food, but more reliable.

▶ Bread was the first processed food, made by baking ground-up grass seeds mixed with water.

- **Farmers in Palestine** were growing oil-rich olives to squeeze and make olive oil in huge amounts, around 4000 BC. Romans consumed it in vast quantities.

▶ The earliest people simply ate what food they could find – either by hunting animals or gathering fruits.

- **About 2600 BC**, the Egyptians found that by leaving gruel to ferment, they could make a dough. They baked this in ovens to make the first raised bread.

- **Honey** was the main sweetener. Egyptians kept bees for honey and also made sweet syrups from fruits.

- **The oldest recipe book** is an Assyrian stone tablet dating from 1700 BC. It features 25 recipes, including a bird called a tarru cooked in onion, garlic, milk and spices.

147

The Phoenicians

- **From about 3000 BC**, Semitic peoples such as Canaanites lived on the eastern Mediterranean coast and built the great city of Byblos.

- **From about 1100 BC**, the people living here became known as Phoenicians.

- **The word 'phoenicians'** comes from *phoinix*, the Greek word for a purple dye made famous by these people.

- **The Phoenicians** were great sea traders. Their ports, of Tyre and Sidon, bustled with ships carrying goods from all over the known world.

- **Using wool from Mesopotamia** and flax and linen from Egypt, the Phonicians made cloth. They also made jewellery from imported gems, metals and ivory.

- **The Phoenicians** invented the alphabet and gave us the word 'too'. The Phoenician words *aleph* ('ox') and *beth* ('house') became the Greek letters alpha and beta. The word 'bible' and the prefix 'bibli-' (meaning 'books') come from the city of Byblos.

- **The dye** for which the Phoenicians were famous was made from the shells of Murex snails.

- **About 600 BC,** Phoenician sailors sailed from the Red Sea right around Africa and back into the Mediterranean.

● **As far west as Gades** (now Cadiz, in Spain), the Phoenicians set up colonies across the Mediterranean.

   ● **The greatest Phoenician colony** was the city of Carthage in what is now Tunisia.

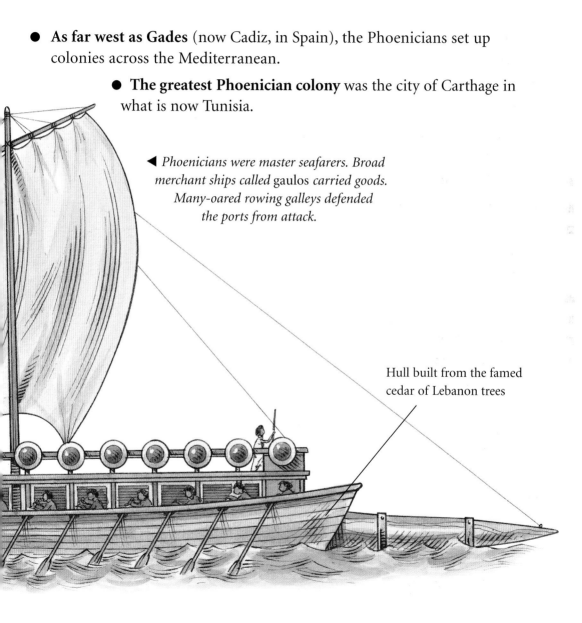

◄ *Phoenicians were master seafarers. Broad merchant ships called* gaulos *carried goods. Many-oared rowing galleys defended the ports from attack.*

Hull built from the famed cedar of Lebanon trees

Greek mythology

- **The Greeks had a wealth of myths** – stories about their gods, goddesses, heroes and villains.

- **We know about the myths** mainly from Homer's poems and Hesiod's book *Theogeny*, both from about 700 BC.

- *Theogeny* **tells how the Earth began**, with the earth goddess Gaia emerging from chaos and giving birth to Uranus, the king of the sky.

- **The many children** of Gaia and Uranus were called the Titans, led by Cronos.

- **Cronos married his sister** Rhea. Their children, led by Zeus, rebelled against the Titans to become the new top gods, called the Olympians.

- **The Olympians** were said to live on Mount Olympus, and include the most famous Greek gods, such as Apollo the god of light, Demeter the goddess of crops, Artemis the goddess of the Moon and Dionysius the wine god.

◀ ▲ *Many Greek gods were adopted by the Romans. The winged messenger Hermes* (above) *became Mercury in ancient Rome, while Aphrodite, the goddess of love* (left), *became Venus.*

- **Greek heroes** were mostly those who had performed great deeds during the times of the Trojan Wars or earlier.

- **Early heroes** include Jason, who led his Argonauts (his crew) in search of the fabulous Golden Fleece, and Theseus, who killed the Minotaur.

- **Trojan war heroes** included Achilles and Odysseus.

- **The greatest hero** was super-strong Heracles, who the Romans would later call Hercules.

▶ *King of the Greek gods was Zeus. He ruled from his home on Mount Olympus and headed a group of Greek gods called the Olympians. Zeus is the weather and sky god and is especially associated with thunder and lightning. The Roman god Jupiter is the equivalent to Zeus.*

151

Greek and Roman pantheons

- **The Greek gods and goddesses** have human qualities. They act because of love, hate and jealousy.

- **Myths say** that giants called the Cyclops gave Zeus the gift of thunder and lightning, and Poseidon the gift of a fishing spear called a trident, with which he could stir up sea-storms, tidal waves and earthquakes.

- **The gods were believed** to have taught humans life-skills: Zeus – justice, Poseidon – ship-building, Hestia – home-making, and Demeter – farming.

- **The gods** (except for Artemis, the hunter goddess) opposed human sacrifice and cannibalism. Zeus once punished King Lycaon for eating human flesh by turning him into a wolf.

▶ *The most famous Cyclops was named Geryon. He and his giant friends liked to feast on human flesh.*

- **The Greek gods and goddesses** sometimes fell in love with humans. Their children were heroes, such as Heracles and Perseus.

- **The gods and goddesses** of ancient Greece were adopted by the Romans, under new names. Hence Zeus became Jove, Hera became Juno, Poseidon became Neptune, and so on.

- **The stories about Greek** and Roman gods, spirits and heroes are known as Classical mythology.

- **The ancient Greeks and Romans** believed that spirits called dryads lived inside trees.

- **In Latin**, the language of the Romans, 'templum' means the space where a shrine to a god was erected. This is where we get our word temple from.

- **Greeks and Romans** would sometimes leave small offerings at the shrine of a god. These could be food, flowers, money or sweet-smelling incense.

▶ *The Greek sea god Poseidon, whose Roman name is Neptune, held a trident with which he could stir up waves into terrible sea-storms.*

153

The Titans

- **The Titans were 12 immortals** in Greek and Roman mythology.

- **The strongest of the Titans** was Atlas – he held up the sky. The cleverest was Prometheus.

- **A Titan called Epimetheus** is said to have married the first mortal woman, Pandora.

- **The Titan Helios became god of the Sun**. Selene became goddess of the Moon.

- **Oceanus became god of the river** that the Greeks believed surrounded the Earth.

- **Themis became goddess** of prophecies at a city called Delphi.

- **Rhea became** an earth goddess.

- **A prophecy said** that the youngest Titan, Cronus, would be overthrown by his own son. So when Cronus's children were born, he ate them. However, his wife hid one child away – this was Zeus.

◄ *The wise Titan Prometheus helped the human race by teaching mortals special skills.*

154

- **When Zeus was older,** he fed Cronus a cup of poison which caused him to vomit up all the other children he had swallowed. These emerged as the fully grown gods and goddesses: Poseidon, Hades, Hera, Demeter and Hestia.

- **Zeus and his brothers** and sisters fought against the Titans for ten years. The Titans were finally overthrown when the gods and goddesses secured the help of the Hundred-handed Giants and Cyclopes.

- **The Titans were hurled** into an underworld realm of punishment called Tartarus. There, they were bound in chains forever.

▶ *After the war between the gods and the Titans, the god Zeus punished the Titan Atlas by commanding him to hold up the skies on his shoulders.*

155

Alexander the Great

- **Alexander the Great** was a young Macedonian king who was one of the greatest generals in history. He built an empire stretching from Greece to India.

- **Alexander was born** in 356 BC in Pella, capital of Macedonia. His father, King Phillip II, was a tough fighter who conquered neighbouring Greece. His mother was the fiery Olympias, who told him that he was descended from Achilles, the hero of the *Iliad*.

Alexander the Great

- **As a boy**, he was tutored by the famous philosopher Aristotle. A story tells how he tamed the unridable horse Bucephalus, which afterwards carried him as far as India.

- **When Alexander was 20**, his father was murdered by a bodyguard and he became king. Alexander quickly stamped out rebellion.

- In 334 BC, Alexander crossed the narrow neck of sea separating Europe from Asia with his army. Within a year, he had conquered the Persian Empire.

- In 331 BC, Alexander led his army into Egypt, where he was made pharaoh and founded the city of Alexandria. He trekked to the desert oasis of Siwah, where legend says an oracle proclaimed him son of the Greek god Zeus.

◄ *The key to Macedonian success was the phalanx – armoured soldiers standing in tightly packed rows bristling with long spears. Such a formation could withstand a cavalry attack, yet still move swiftly.*

...FASCINATING FACT...
An old legend said that anyone who untied a tricky knot in a town
called Gordium would conquer Asia. Alexander instantly sliced
through this Gordian knot with his sword.

- **In 327 BC**, he married the lovely Bactrian princess, Roxane.

- **After capturing the city of Babylon** and finishing off the Persian king,
  Darius, Alexander led his conquering army into India. Here his homesick
  troops finally asked to go home.

- **In 325 BC**, Alexander had ships built and carried his army down the Indus
  River and returned to Babylon. Within a year, he fell ill and died.

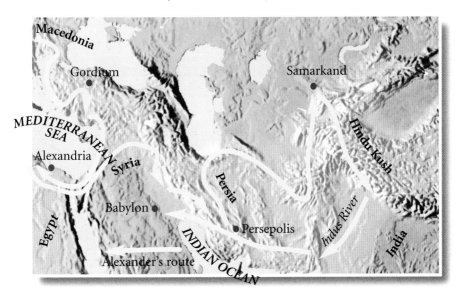

▲ *In just nine years and a series of brilliant campaigns, Alexander created a vast empire.*
No one knows exactly what his plans were. However, the teachings of his tutor Aristotle were
important to him, and he had his own vision of different peoples living together in friendship.

157

Romulus and Remus

- **The story of Romulus and Remus** tells how twin boys grew up to build the foundations of the mighty city of Rome.

- **Versions of the myth** were written by many of the greatest Roman writers, such as Livy, Plutarch and Virgil.

- **According to the legend**, Romulus and Remus were descendants of the hero Aeneas. They were the sons of a princess and the war god, Mars.

- **As babies**, the twin boys were cast out by their evil great-uncle, who had stolen the king's crown from their grandfather. They survived because a she-wolf found them and let them drink her milk. A bird also fed them by placing crumbs in their mouths.

▶ *The Roman legend of Romulus and Remus may have been the inspiration for the Tarzan story. In both cases, abandoned infants were brought up by animals.*

- **When the twins grew** up they overthrew their wicked uncle, restoring their father to his rightful throne.

- **The twins built a new city** on the spot where they had been rescued by the she-wolf. However, they quarrelled about who should be ruler of the city, and Romulus killed Remus.

- **Romulus became king** of the new city and named it Rome, after himself.

- **The new city had too many men** and not enough women. Romulus hatched a plot whereby he held a great celebration and invited neighbouring communities – then captured all their women!

- **Romulus built a strong army**, to defend Rome from attacks by local tribes. He brought about a 40-year period of peace.

- **One day, Romulus was surrounded** by a storm cloud and taken up to heaven, where he became a god.

▼ *You can still see the ruins of the mighty ancient city of Rome in the modern-day Italian capital. The huge round amphitheatre called the Colosseum overshadows the impressive central square, or Forum.*

The birth of Rome

- **People were living in Italy** long before Rome was founded, and a people called the Etruscans created an advanced civilization in the northwest of the country between 800 and 400 BC.

- **According to legend**, Rome was founded in 753 BC by the twins Romulus and Remus, who were said to have been brought up by a she-wolf.

- **By 550 BC**, Rome was a big city ruled by Etruscan kings.

- **In 509 BC**, the Roman people drove out the kings and formed themselves into an independent republic.

▲ *Senators were men from leading citizen familes who had served the Roman republic as judges or state officials. They made new laws and discussed government plans.*

▲ *The first rules of the Roman legal system were recorded in 450 BC in a document called the* Twelve Tables. *The Roman system forms the basis of many legal systems today.*

160

▶ *Legend has it that after founding the city of Rome, Romulus and Remus quarrelled and Romulus killed his brother.*

- **Republican Rome** was ruled by the Senate, an assembly made up of 100 patricians (men from leading families).

- **In theory**, Rome was governed by the people. However, real power was in the hands of patricians; plebeians (ordinary citizens) had little. Slaves had no power or rights at all.

- **Plebeians fought for power** and, by 287 BC, gained the right to stand as consuls, the highest official posts.

- **In the 400s and 300s** BC, Rome extended its power all over Italy, by both brute force and alliances.

- **By 264 BC**, Rome rivalled Carthage, the North African city that dominated the western Mediterranean. In 164 BC, Rome destroyed Carthage totally after the Punic Wars.

- **By 130 BC**, Rome had built a mighty empire stretching from Spain to Turkey and along the North African coast.

161

Cleopatra

- **Cleopatra** (69–30 BC) was the last Macedonian queen of Egypt. She was descended from Ptolemy, a general of Alexander the Great who made himself king after Alexander died.

- **Cleopatra may have been beautiful**. She was certainly intelligent, charming and highly determined.

- **In 51 BC**, Cleopatra became queen when her father died. Her ten-year-old brother Ptolemy became king.

- **Ptolemy's** guardians seized power and drove Cleopatra out. She was restored to the throne by the Roman armies of Julius Caesar.

▲ *Octavian described Cleopatra as a wicked temptress – and the idea has stuck. Her people in Egypt, however, thought of her as a great, just and much-loved queen.*

- **Legend has it** that Cleopatra had herself delivered to Caesar rolled up in a carpet. Whatever the truth, Caesar fell in love with her, and she had a son, Caesarion, by him.

- **Caesar invited Cleopatra** and Caesarion to Rome, where she stayed until 44 BC, when Caesar was brutally assassinated.

- **The Roman general Mark Antony** went to Cleopatra for her support in his bid for power in Rome. He too fell in love with her. They later married and had three children.

- **Mark Antony returned to Rome** to make a political marriage to Octavia, sister of Octavian. However, he soon returned to Cleopatra.

- **Mark Antony and Cleopatra** were ambitious and strove to take over the eastern Roman Empire. Their armies, however, were defeated at the Battle of Actium, off Greece, in 31 BC by the forces of Octavian (later known as Augustus Caesar).

- **As Octavian chased them both** to Alexandria, Cleopatra spread rumours that she was dead. In despair, Mark Antony stabbed himself. He died in her arms. Cleopatra tried to make peace with Octavian but failed. She took her own life by placing an asp, a poisonous snake, on her breast.

▼ *Much has been made of Mark Antony and Cleopatra's romantic relationship, but theirs was also a strong political alliance.*

Rome on the rise

- **As Rome's empire spread**, the creation of plantations worked by slaves put small farmers out of work. The gap between rich and poor widened.

- **Many joined the army** to escape poverty and became more loyal to their generals than to the Senate (the government's ruling body).

- **Two popular generals**, Pompey and Julius Caesar, used their armies to take over Rome and suspend the Republic.

- **Caesar and Pompey argued**, and after battles right across the empire, Caesar gained the upper hand.

- **Once in power**, Caesar restored order and passed laws to reduce people's debts.

- **Caesar was made dictator** and ruled Rome without the Senate.

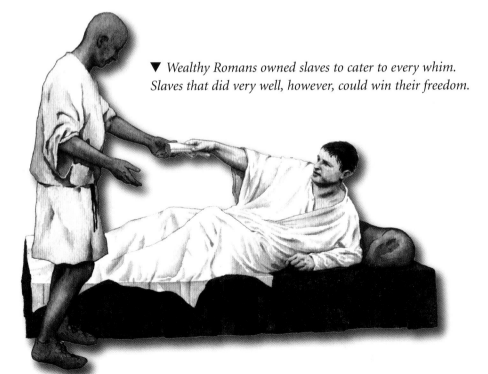

▼ *Wealthy Romans owned slaves to cater to every whim. Slaves that did very well, however, could win their freedom.*

- **In 44 BC**, a man called Brutus killed Caesar to restore the Republic – but Caesar's place was taken by another general, Octavian, Caesar's adopted son.

- **By 27 BC**, Octavian was so powerful he declared himself the first Roman emperor and took the name Augustus.

- **Under Augustus**, rebellious parts of Spain and the Alps were brought under control and the empire was expanded along the Rhine and Danube Rivers.

- **By 1 BC**, the days of strife were over and Rome presided over a vast, stable, prosperous empire.

▲ *Many Romans lived in comfortable two-storey townhouses* (domi), *with heated pools and underfloor heating.*

165

Jesus Christ

- **Jesus Christ was** one of the world's great religious leaders. The religion of Christianity is based on his teachings.

- **Our knowledge of Jesus's life** comes almost entirely from four short books in the Bible's New Testament: the gospels of Matthew, Mark, Luke and John.

- **Roman writers** such as Pliny mention Jesus briefly.

- **Jesus was born** in Bethlehem, Palestine, between 4 and 1 BC.

▼ *The site of Jesus's birth, now called the Church of the Nativity, can be found in the heart of Bethlehem. A silver star marks the exact place where Jesus was born.*

- **The Bible tells** how his poor young virgin mother, Mary, became miraculously pregnant after a visit by the archangel Gabriel, and that Jesus is the only Son of God.

- **Little is known** of Jesus's childhood. His teaching began after he was baptized by John the Baptist at the age of 30.

- **Jesus's mission** was to announce that the Kingdom of God was coming. From his many followers, he chose 12 'apostles' to help him spread the word.

- **Jesus is said to have performed** all kinds of miracles to convince people of the truth of his teachings.

- **Many Jews felt Jesus was a troublemaker**, especially after a triumphal entry into Jerusalem. They had the Roman governor, Pontius Pilate, put him to death by crucifixion (nailing to a cross).

▶ *The word 'Christ' is actually a title. It comes from the Greek word* christos, *which means 'anointed one'.*

.. . FASCINATING FACT . . .
After his death, Jesus was said to have been resurrected – brought to life again.

167

The Roman Empire

- **For 200 years** after Augustus became emperor in 27 BC, Roman emperors ruled over an empire so large and secure that citizens could talk of the *Pax Romana* (Roman Peace).

- **The Romans built straight roads** to move their troops about quickly. On the whole, they governed peacefully and also built hundreds of towns in the Roman manner.

- **After Augustus died**, in AD 14, his stepson Tiberius succeeded him. Then came a succession of Augustus's descendants, including Gaius, Claudius and Nero.

- **Gaius** (AD 37–41) was known as Caligula ('little boots') because of the soldiers' boots he wore as a child.

  - **Soon after Caligula** became emperor, an illness left him mad. He spent wildly, had people whipped and killed, married and murdered his sister and elected his horse as a minister. Eventually he was murdered by soldiers.

    - **Claudius** (AD 41–54) replaced Caligula. People thought he was stupid because he stuttered and was physically disabled. However, he proved the wisest and most humane of all emperors.

◀ *Gladiators were prisoners and criminals who were made to fight in big arenas called amphitheatres to entertain people.*

168

▶ *The orange area of this map shows the empire at its peak under the Emperor Trajan (AD 98–117). It was divided into areas called provinces, such as Britannia (England and Wales) and Gallia (northern France). Each had its own Roman governor.*

▼ *Leading imperial officials wore flowing robes called togas.*

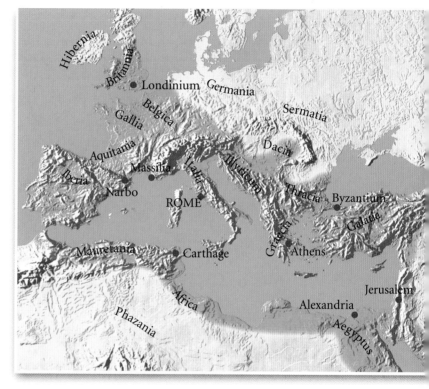

- **Claudius** was probably poisoned by his fourth wife Agrippina, who wanted power for her son Nero.

- **The power of Roman emperors** reached a peak under the 'Antonines' – Nerva, Trajan, Hadrian, Antoninus and Marcus Aurelius. They ruled AD 96–180.

- **The Roman Empire** grew only a little after Augustus's death. Britain was conquered in AD 43, and Emperor Trajan took Dacia (now Hungary and Romania).

169

Roman towns

- **Roman towns** were the biggest and most sophisticated the world had ever seen. They were not built on rigid grids like Greek cities, but they all had certain features in common.

- **A Roman town had** two main streets and many side streets with spaces in between called *insulae* (islands).

▲ *The remains of the Forum in Rome give a glimpse of just how magnificent Roman cities must have been.*

- **The *insulae*** were tightly packed with private houses – houses of the rich, called *domi*, and apartment blocks (also called *insulae*). The bigger Roman houses had courtyards.

- **Traffic jams** were so common that many towns banned wheeled traffic from the streets during daylight.

- **Most towns** had numerous shops, inns (*tabernae*), cafés (*thermopilia*) and bakeries (*pistrina*).

- **The forum** was a large open market and meeting place that was surrounded on three sides by a covered walkway. On the fourth side was the law courts and the town hall (*basilica*).

- **Most towns** had many grand temples to Roman gods.

- **There was a large open-air theatre** in most towns. There was also a games arena, or stadium, where warriors called gladiators fought and chariot races were held.

- **The bath houses** (*thermae*) were places where people came to sit around and dip into hot and cold baths in magnificent surroundings.

- **Towns had** highly sophisticated water supplies and sewage systems.

▼ *The Roman town of Ostia had blocks of flats called* insulae. *A typical block was three or four storeys high, with up to 100 small, dirty, crowded rooms.*

171

The Roman army

- **Rome owed its power** to its highly efficient army.

- **In a crisis**, Rome could raise an army of 800,000 men.

- **The Roman** army fought mainly on foot, advancing in tight squares bristling with spears and protected by large shields called *scutari*. They often put shields over their heads to protect them from arrows. This formation was called a *testudo* – or 'tortoise'.

- **Under the Republic**, the army was divided into legions of 5000 soldiers. Legions were made up of ten cohorts. Cohorts, in turn, consisted of centuries containing 80 to 100 soldiers.

- **Each legion** was led by a *legatus*. A cohort was led by a *tribunus militum*. A century was led by a *centurion*.

- **All Roman soldiers** had a short sword (60 cm long) and carried two throwing spears. They also wore armour – first, vests of chain mail and a leather helmet; later, metal strips on a leather tunic and a metal helmet.

- **Roman armies** built huge siege engines and catapults when they had to capture a town.

- **After 100** BC, most Roman soldiers were professionals, who joined the army for life. Food accounted for about a third of their wages.

- **In training**, soldiers went on forced 30-km marches three times a month. They moved at 8 km per hour, carrying very heavy packs.

- **Soldiers were flogged** for misbehaviour. Mutiny was punished by executing one in ten suspects. This was called *decimation*.

▼ *Roman soldiers had to be tough – while on the march they carried all their weapons and armour, plus a pack full of clothes, food and tools for digging and building.*

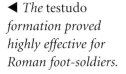

◀ *The* testudo *formation proved highly effective for Roman foot-soldiers.*

173

How Romans lived

- **In the big cities**, rich Romans had a comfortable way of life.

- **For breakfast**, Romans typically ate bread or wheat biscuits with honey, dates or olives, and water or wine.

- **A Roman lunch** (*prandium*) consisted of much the same things as breakfast.

- **Romans had *cena*** (the main meal) in the afternoon, typically after a visit to the baths. This became a very lavish affair with three main courses, and each course had many dishes.

- **Rich Romans** had a lot of free time, since slaves did all the work. Leisure activities included gambling by tossing coins (*capita et navia*) and knucklebones (*tali*).

- **Public entertainments** were called *ludi* (games). They included theatre, chariot races, and fights with gladiators (trained fighters) and animals.

- **The Emperor Trajan** went to a gladiator contest that lasted 117 days and involved 10,000 gladiators.

- **Romans had more slaves** than any empire in history. Many were treated cruelly, but some lived quite well.

- **Between 73 and 71** BC, a man called Spartacus led a revolt of slaves that lasted two years, until it was crushed by Roman armies.

> ...FASCINATING FACT...
> The Circus Maximus chariot racetrack
> in Rome held up to 250,000 spectators.

▲ *Romans were very clean and spent many hours at public baths or bathing at home.*
These are the Roman baths at Bath, England.

Gilgamesh

- **This epic poem** is from Sumeria – one of the earliest civilizations to have city states, laws and irrigation.

- **Gilgamesh was a real king** of the Sumerian city Uruk, around 2700–2500 BC.

- **In the poem**, King Gilgamesh is a man of mighty strength who is loved dearly by the gods.

- **When the nobles of Uruk** complain to the gods that King Gilgamesh is a tyrant, the Mother Goddess makes a hero called Enkidu to challenge him. Gilgamesh meets his match in Enkidu, and the two become firm friends.

- **When Enkidu dies**, Gilgamesh begins to fear his own death. He embarks on a quest to find out how to become immortal.

- **He does not win eternal life**, but Gilgamesh is rewarded with a plant that will keep him young and strong for the rest of his days. When a watersnake steals it from him, he nearly despairs.

- **Gilgamesh finally realizes** that the only type of immortality humans can achieve is fame through performing great deeds and building lasting monuments.

- **The poem was discovered** in 1845, when archaeologists were excavating at the ancient city of Nineveh.

- **Experts think that** *Gilgamesh* was first written down on clay tablets in an ancient language called cuneiform. It is the earliest recorded major work of literature.

- **Fragments of** *Gilgamesh* have been found by archaeologists in ancient sites throughout many countries of the Middle East.

▲ *This ancient Sumerian stone relief shows the hero Gilgamesh as the central figure.*

Yamato

- **The oldest signs** of farming in Japan date back to 300 BC, but Japan was inhabited long before that.

- **The first known** inhabitants of Japan were the Ainu or Ezo, who were short, hairy, fair-skinned people. Some Ainu people still survive in northern Japan.

- **About 250** BC, the Yayoi people became dominant in Japan. They used objects made of iron and bronze.

- **Around 660** BC, Jimmu Tenno, the legendary first emperor of Japan, established power in Yamato.

- **Jimmu Tenno** is said to be the descendent of the sun goddess Amaterasu.

- **From** AD **200 to 645**, the Yamato dynasty dominated Japan.

- **Right up to today**, Japanese emperors claim to be descended from the Yamato. The Yamato, in turn, claimed to be descended from the Shinto sun-goddess, Amaterasu.

- **Shotoku Taishi** (AD 574–622) was a young regent for old Empress Suiko. He gave Japan organized, Chinese-style government and promoted both Buddhism and Confucianism.

- **Shinto** or 'way of the gods' has been Japan's main religion since prehistoric times. It gained its name during the 6th century AD, to distinguish it from Buddhism and Confucianism.

.....FASCINATING FACT.....
In 2000, the postholes of a round hut half a
million years old, were found in Japan.

◄ *Shinto priests
believe that all
things that inspire
awe – from twisted
trees to dead
warriors – can have*
kami *(spirits).*

Early Japanese myths

- **The earliest people** to live in Japan were called the Ainu. They believed that in the beginning the world was a swampy mixture of water and earth where nothing lived.

- **According to Ainu myth**, a creator god called Kamui sent a water wagtail to the swamp. This fluttered its wings and tail, and islands appeared from the water.

- **During the 1st and 2nd centuries** BC people from Asia arrived in Japan. They brought a nature religion called Shinto with them.

- **According to Shinto myths**, the world was originally an ocean of chaos, which gradually divided into the light heavens above and the heavy Earth below.

- **Shinto mythology says** that the first god was like a reed shoot that grew in the space between heaven and Earth.

- **Shinto beliefs say that a female god** called Izanami and a male god called Izanagi gave shape to the world. They stood on the rainbow and Izanagi stirred the ocean with a spear. An island formed, and the two gods left heaven to go and live on it.

- **The Ainu believed that** people and animals were created by Kamui to live on the islands.

- **Izanami and Izanagi** had many other children. These were the gods that shaped and then lived in every aspect of nature: the winds, seas, rivers, trees and mountains.

- **The ruler of the universe** is the sun goddess, known as Amaterasu. She was born from Izanagi's left eye.

...FASCINATING FACT...
The Shinto creation myth says that Japan was
formed when the goddess Izanami gave birth to
eight children who became islands.

◀ *The Shinto religion has traditional
dances that date from AD 400. They are
performed to religious chanting and
accompanied by the rhythmic
beating of huge drums.*

181

Immortals of Japan

- **The myths of the early Japanese** do not tell of a supreme spirit. Instead, they suggest that a divine force flows through all nature in the form of millions of gods.

- **The storm god Raiden** got his name from two Japanese words: 'rai' for thunder and 'den' for lightning.

- **Susano** was the god of seas and oceans. He was banished from heaven and sent to live in the Underworld.

- **Inari** was the god of crops. He is pictured as a bearded man holding sheaves of rice and riding on a fox – his servant and messenger.

▲ *Masks of spirits, demons and gods are used in a form of Japanese theatre called Noh. It is influenced by traditional stories from the Buddhist and Shinto religions.*

▶ *The religion of Buddhism spread to Japan from India. Worshippers follow the teachings of the Buddha, or 'enlightened one'.*

● **Over the centuries**, the number of nature gods increased as warrior heroes, religious leaders and emperors became gods, too.

● **In the 6th century**, a religion called Buddhism was introduced into Japan and a pantheon of Japanese Buddhist gods and goddesses developed.

● **In Japanese Buddhism**, Amida is the god of a paradise for the dead. He has two helpers, Kwannon, the goddess of mercy, and Shishi, the lord of might.

● **Japanese myth** says that there are about 500 immortal men and women called Sennin who live in the mountains. They can fly and work powerful magic.

● **A Shishi is a spirit** pictured as a cross between a dog and a lion (a character that came originally from Chinese mythology). It is believed to ward off evil demons, and Shishi statues are sometimes found at the entrance to temples and houses.

● **There are seven Japanese gods of luck**, called Shichi Fukujin, which means 'seven happiness beings'.

The Mauryan Empire

- **In 321 BC**, the first great Indian empire was created by Chandragupta Maurya (*c.*325–297 BC). Its capital was Pataliputra.

- **The Mauryan Empire** at its peak included most of modern Pakistan, Bangladesh and all but the southernmost tip of India.

- **The most famous** of the Mauryan emperors was Chandragupta's grandson, Asoka (*c.*265–238 BC).

- **After witnessing** an horrific battle, Asoka was so appalled by the suffering that he resolved never to go to war. Instead, Asoka devoted himself to improving the lot of his people.

- **Asoka became a Buddhist** and his government promoted the Dharma, or 'Universal Law'.

▲ *Banyan trees have many trunks, each originating from its branches. They were planted to provide shade for travellers along newly built roads.*

184

- **The Universal Law** preached religious tolerance, non-violence and respect for the dignity of every single person.

- **Asoka's men dug wells** and built reservoirs all over India to help the poor. They also provided comfortable rest-houses and planted shady banyan trees for travellers along the new roads.

- **Asoka said** 'all men are my children', and sent officials out to deal with local problems.

- **A vast secret police force** and an army of 700,000 helped Asoka to run his empire.

- **Asoka's Sarnath lion** insignia is now the national emblem of India.

◀ *During Asoka's reign, stupas – domed shrines said to contain relics of the Buddha – were built all over India.*

Early North America

- **Maize** (sweetcorn) was grown in southwestern USA, around 2000–1000 BC.

- **The first farming villages** in the southwest were those of the Anasazi, Mogollon and Hohokam peoples and dated from AD 100. They lived either in caves or in underground 'pit houses' carved into the desert rock.

- *Anasazi* is Navajo Indian for 'Ancient Ones'.

- **The first Anasazi** are also known as Basket-Makers because of their skill in weaving baskets.

- **About AD 700**, the Anasazi began to build large stone villages known as *pueblos*, which is why from this time they are also called Pueblo Indians.

- **In the 'Classic' Pueblo period**, from AD 1050 to 1300, the Anasazi lived in huge apartments carved out of cliffs, like Pueblo Bonito. Pueblo culture began to fade about AD 1300.

- **In the east**, the first farming villages were those of the Hopewell peoples of the Illinois and Ohio valleys, between 100 BC and AD 200.

- **The Hopewell peoples** are known for their burial mounds. Things found in these mounds show they traded all over America.

- **About AD 700**, farming villages with temple mounds developed near St Louis on the Mississippi River.

⋯FASCINATING FACT⋯
Cliff Palace in Mesa Verde (Colorado) had
space for 250 people in its 217 rooms.

▲ *The most famous cliff pueblos are in Mesa Verde, Colorado.*

187

The early Irish

- **Ireland** was settled late. The earliest proof of settlers are 8000-year-old flints left on beaches in the northeast, near the modern Irish town of Larne.

- **The New Stone Age** (Neolithic) began when the first farms and permanent homes appeared, 5000 years ago.

- **Neolithic people** honoured their dead with long mounds or barrows – called 'court graves' because they have a courtyard at the entrance. They also built barrows called portal graves with three huge stones set like a door.

- **The most dramatic remains** from earliest times are 'passage' graves, in which a passage leads to a stone chamber. The most famous is Newgrange, near Dublin.

- **The Celts invaded** Ireland in the Iron Age, about 400 BC, and many of Ireland's rich collection of heroic myths are probably based in this time.

- **Celtic Ireland** was split into 150 kingdoms or clans called *tuatha* and later into five provinces – Ulster, Meath, Leinster, Munster and Connaught. After AD 500, there was a high king (*ard-ri*) ruling Ireland from Tara in Leinster.

- **Irish Celts** were both warriors and herdsmen who valued cows highly. They also revered poets (*file*), and their metalwork, revealed in items such as the Tara brooch and the Ardagh chalice, is extraordinarily beautiful.

- **Early Celtic priests** were druids, but legend says that in AD 432, St Patrick came to convert Ireland to Christianity.

- **Irish monasteries** became havens of art and learning in the Dark Ages, creating the famous *Book of Kells*.

▼ ▶ The huge burial mound at Newgrange, near Dublin, was built around 3100 BC. A long, narrow passage leads to a burial chamber deep inside the mound. Above the entrance is an unusual 'roof-box' – a special slot through which the midwinter sun shines into the chamber.

Every year, at exactly 8.58 a.m. on 21 December (the winter solstice), the rising sun shines through this roof-box and down the passage to light up the burial chamber

One of Newgrange's most distinctive features is the ornamentation – especially the carved spirals, which had a ritual significance

Julius Caesar

- **Julius Caesar** (*c.*100–44 BC) was Rome's most famous general and leader. He was also a great speaker who had the power to excite huge crowds.

- **Caesar's individuality** was clear from the start. At 17, he defied Sulla, the dictator of Rome and married Cornelia, the daughter of the rebel leader Cinna. Cornelia died when Caesar was about 30.

- **Caesar began** as a politician and made himself popular by spending his own money on public entertainments.

- **In 60 BC**, he formed a powerful triumvirate (group of three people) with Crassus and Pompey, which dominated Rome.

- **In 58 BC**, Caesar led a brilliantly organized campaign to conquer Gaul (now northern France), and also invaded Britain.

- **Caesar wrote** an account of his campaigns in Gaul that is a classic of historical writing.

- **Pompey was alarmed** by the fame that Caesar's conquests brought him. The two began a war that lasted five years, ending in Egypt in 48 BC, where Caesar met and fell in love with Cleopatra.

◀ *Caesar was not only a brilliant general, but a great statesman who brought in many reforms and tried to stamp out corruption.*

- **By 45 BC**, Caesar had become the undisputed master of the Roman Empire. The people elected him dictator for life.

- **Caesar was asked** to become king, but he refused.

- **On March 15, 44 BC** – a date known as 'the Ides of March' – Caesar was stabbed to death as he entered the Senate. His assassins were a group led by Brutus and Cassius, who felt that Caesar's ambitions posed a threat to Rome.

▶ *Caesar planned all kinds of bold economic, social and government reforms – but had been unable to carry many of them out by the time he was assassinated.*

191

The Guptas

- **The Guptas** were a family of rulers who reigned in northern India from AD 320 to *c*.500. This was one of India's golden ages, when literature, sculpture and other arts were at their peak.

- **The Guptas** were originally a family of rich landowners, who took over control of the small kingdom of Magadha in the Ganges valley.

- **Chandragupta I** came to the throne in AD 320. He extended his lands by marrying the right women.

- **Chandragupta's son**, Samudragupta, and his grandson, Chandragupta II, gained control over much of northern India by military conquests.

- **The Hindu and Buddhist** religions both began to develop and flourish during the great Gupta period.

- **Beautiful temples** and religious sculptures were created across northern India.

- **About AD 450**, Kalidása, India's greatest poet and dramatist, wrote his famous play *Sákuntala*, filled with romance and adventure.

- **Music and dance** developed their highest classical form.

- **Hindu mathematicians** developed the decimal system (counting in tens) that we still use today.

- **The Guptas' power** collapsed by about AD 500, under repeated attacks by Hun people from the north.

▲ *The Hindu and Buddhist sculpture and painting of the Gupta period has been the model for Indian art down the centuries.*

Rivers, lakes and the sea

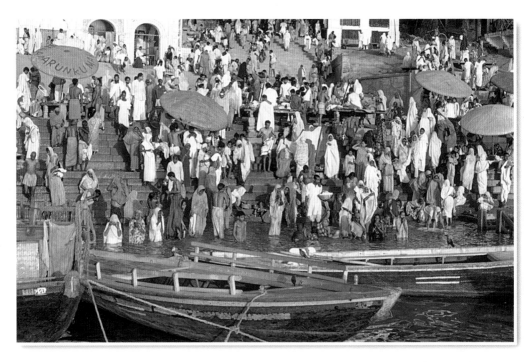

▲ *Hindus believe that bathing in the mighty river Ganges in India can wash away their sins. When a Hindu dies, they scatter the ashes of their cremated body on the waters.*

- **German legend says** that beautiful mermaids called Lorelei lived on rocks in the river Rhine, luring fishermen to their deaths.

- **In Greek mythology**, a Triton is a sea creature like a merman who can control the waves.

- **Norse mythology says** that the goddess of the sea, Ran, owned a huge fishing net she used to catch sailors.

● **Scottish legends tell of kelpies** – watery ghosts of rivers and lakes.

● **Irish legend says** that the hero Finn McCool slew a phantom and a serpent in Loch Ree. In 1960, three Dublin priests fishing on Loch Ree watched a long-necked monster move through the waters for two minutes.

● **Greek myth** says that the Aegean Sea is named after King Aegeus, who drowned himself in the ocean when he was led to believe that his son, Theseus, had been killed.

● **According to Hindu myth**, the goddess Ganga lived in heaven until there was a terrible drought on Earth. Then the god Shiva helped her flow safely down into the world as the sacred river Ganges.

● **A Finnish myth** says that the goddess of the sea and creation, Luonnotar, was once pregnant for 730 years. She finally gave birth to a man, Vainamoinen. He swam ashore to the country that became Finland.

▲ *The Irish hero Finn McCool performed feats of amazing strength and bravery.*

● **A Persian myth** tells of a hero called Keresaspa, who battled for nine days and nights in an ocean with a monster called Gandarewa, who could swallow 12 people at once.

● **The sacred animal** of the Greek sea god Poseidon was the horse. This is perhaps why waves are sometimes described as white horses.

Gauls and Franks

- **The Gauls** were a Celtic people who lived in Western Europe, mainly in France.

- **The Gauls** could be brave warriors, and because the men had long hair and beards, the Romans thought them wild.

- **In 390 BC**, Gauls crossed the Alps, swept down on Rome and sacked the city. They later withdrew, but they occupied northern Italy for almost 200 years.

- **In 278 BC**, Gauls invaded what is now Turkey, settling the area called Galatia.

- **In the 50s BC**, Julius Caesar led a lightning Roman campaign to crush the Gauls. What is now France became Roman Gaul.

- **The Franks** were a German people split into two branches, the Salians and Ripurians.

- **In AD 486**, Clovis, a king of the Salian Franks, invaded Roman Gaul to create a big kingdom covering modern France and Belgium.

- **The first period** of Frankish rule in Gaul is called Merovingian (from AD 486 to 751); the second is called Carolingian (AD 751–987).

◀ *Charles II of France, or Charles the Bald (AD 823–877), fought many wars against his half brothers Louis the German and Lothair. In AD 843 the Treaty of Verdun gave Charles the rule over the part of the empire that formed the basis for France.*

● ●

> ...**FASCINATING FACT**...
> Franks were outnumbered 20 to one by Gallo-Romans
> – but France is named after them.

● **After Clovis's death** in AD 511, the Merovingian kingdom was divided and weakened. About AD 719, some Merovingian kings allowed a man called Charles Martel – *martel* means 'hammer' – to take control in the north with the title 'Mayor of the Palace'. Before long, Martel controlled the whole of Gaul.

▶ *In 52 BC, the Gallic chief Vercingetorix led a last-ditch attempt to drive out the Romans. However, he was beaten, taken to Rome as Caesar's prize and executed.*

Early Africa

- **The world's first known civilizations** appeared in Africa along the Nile valley, in Egypt and further south in Nubia.

- **The first Nubian civilization**, called the A-group culture, appeared about 3200 BC in the north of Nubia, known as Wawat. It was taken over by the Egyptians in 2950 BC.

- **About 2000 BC**, a new Nubian culture emerged in the then-fertile south, called Kush. The Kushites were black Africans.

- **Egypt conquered Kush** in 1500 BC, but the Kushites, led by King Shabaka, conquered Egypt in 715 BC. For 50 years, the Kushites were pharaohs and their capital, Napata, was seen as the centre of the ancient world.

- **In 666 BC**, Assyrians drove the Kushites out of Egypt. However, the Kushites had learned iron-making from the Assyrians.

- **Napata** had iron-ore, but little wood for smelting the ore. So the Kushites moved their capital to Meroe – where they built great palaces, temples, baths and pyramids.

- **From Kush**, iron-making spread west, to Nigeria.

- **From AD 100**, the city of Axum – now in northern Ethiopia – grew rich and powerful on ivory. About AD 350, the Axumite king Aezanas invaded and overthrew Kush.

- **Kings of Axum** (later Ethiopia) were said to be descended from Jewish King Solomon and the Queen of Sheba. The Sheba were an Arab people who had settled in Axum.

- **King Aezanas** was converted to Christianity, but for 1500 years Axum/Ethiopia was Africa's only Christian country.

▲ *Africa was the birthplace of humanity, and rock paintings dating back 30,000 years are found all over the continent.*

Tales from Africa

▲ *Animals feature prominently in African culture. The chameleon, with its highly developed ability to change colour, lives in the trees of African forests.*

- **Numerous tribal groups** have lived in Africa for thousands of years, all with their own different myths and legends, although many shared beliefs.

- **Most African tribes** believe in one supreme creator god (who judges people wisely) and many minor gods.

- **Many myths** say that the creator god grew weary of constant demands from people, so he left the Earth and went to live in heaven.

- **The Yoruba people** of Nigeria believed that in the beginning the universe consisted of the sky, ruled by the chief god Olorun, and a watery marshland, ruled by the goddess Olokun.

- **The Yoruba** believed that a god called Obatala shaped the Earth with the help of magic gifts from other gods.

> ...FASCINATING FACT...
> Different tribal names for the creator god
> include Mulungu, Leza, Amma and Nyambe.

- **The Fon people** of Benin believed that the world was created by twin gods: the moon goddess Mawu and her twin brother Lisa, the Sun.

- **The Dogon people** of Mali believed that the creator god moulded the Sun, Moon, Earth and people out of clay.

- **The Pygmies** believed that the first man and woman were brought forth by a chameleon who released them from a tree in a gush of water.

- **The Yoruba** believed that the chief god, Olorun, breathed life into the first people, who were modelled from mud.

▶ *The Fon people of Benin, where this sculpture comes from, were known from the early 17th century for their skill in battle. Male warriors fought alongside a female army.*

Gassire's Lute

- **An African tribe** called the Soninke have an epic poem called *Gassire's Lute.* It was composed between AD 300 and AD 1100 as part of a group of songs called the *Dausi.*

- **Most other songs** in the Dausi have been forgotten.

- *Gassire's Lute* is a tale about the ancestors of the Soninke, a tribe of warrior horsemen called the Fasa.

- **The Fasa lived** around 500 BC in a fertile area of Africa bordered by the Sahara Desert, Senegal, Sudan and the river Nile.

- **The hero of the legend**, Gassire, is a Fasa prince who longs for his father to die so he can become a famous king.

- **The heroes** of other epic poems usually put their lives at risk trying to help other people. This epic is strikingly different, because the hero puts his own desires in front of everything else.

- **Gassire realizes** that all things die, and that the only way to win lasting fame is to be remembered as a hero in battle songs.

▲ *A musician plays a lute by plucking its strings, similar to playing the guitar.*

- **He has a lute made,** so he can sing of his own adventures. However, the lute will only play once it has been soaked with blood in battle.

- **Gassire leads** his eight sons and followers into war against an enemy tribe. It is only when all but one of Gassire's sons have been killed that his lute finally sings.

- **Gassire grieves** for the dead, but is filled with joy now he has a great battle song to bring him fame.

◀ *The Fasa ancestors of this Soninke woman were like medieval knights. They fought on horseback with spears and swords, not just in battle but also for sport.*

Famous disasters

- **Many ancient civilizations** had legends of great floods.

- **In the Middle East**, a Sumerian named Ziusudra, the Babylonian Gilgamesh and the Jewish Noah all built an ark (boat) to ride out a flood that drowned everyone else.

- **In India**, Manu, the first man and first king, was warned of great flooding by fish and survived by building a boat.

- **In the Americas**, the Aztecs believed four previous worlds had been destroyed by jaguars, hurricanes, thunder and lightning and a huge, 52-year flood.

- **The huge eruption** of the Aegean island volcano of Thera (Santorini), in 1500 BC, effectively destroyed Minoan civilization on Crete – and may have started legends of the lost civilization of Atlantis, drowned by a tidal wave.

- **While the Jews were slaves there**, Egypt was ruined by a flood of blood that had been predicted by the Jew Moses – now thought to have been the Nile River in flood, stained by red algae.

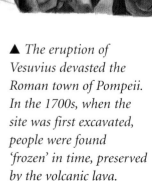

▲ *The eruption of Vesuvius devasted the Roman town of Pompeii. In the 1700s, when the site was first excavated, people were found 'frozen' in time, preserved by the volcanic lava.*

- In **464** BC, 10,000 people were killed by a powerful earthquake that struck the Greek city of Sparta.

- In **436** BC, a famine drove thousands of Romans to jump into the Tiber River to escape the pain of starvation.

- In AD **64**, the Rome of Emperor Nero was destroyed by a great fire. Angry people said that Nero had started it.

- In AD **79**, the Roman city of Pompeii was buried under ash from nearby volcano Vesuvius – and preserved to this day.

▼ *The Greek island of Santorini was blown apart in 1500 BC by a giant volcanic eruption, ending the Minoan civilization.*

Sacrifices for gods

- **The Maya used to play** a ball-game a bit like football. Historians think that at the end of the match, one side was sacrificed to the gods – but they do not know whether it was the winners or the losers!

- **The first wife** of the Hindu god Shiva was Sati. Sati's father tried to disgrace Shiva, and in protest, Sati sacrificed herself by throwing herself onto a sacred fire.

- **The chief Norse god, Odin,** demanded that warriors did not just give themselves up to death fearlessly, but that they actually welcomed death, in his honour.

- **The ancient Hindu fire god**, Agni, had seven tongues to lick up sacrifices of butter burnt on a sacred fire.

- **A Bible story tells** how God asked Abraham to offer him his only son, Isaac, as a sacrifice. God stopped Abraham from doing so just in time, once he had tested his obedience.

- **A sacred fire** to the Roman goddess Vesta was tended by specially chosen girls called the Vestal Virgins. They had to sacrifice ever having a boyfriend or getting married.

▲ *The Maya had a ball-game in which players used their elbows, hips and knees to hit the ball. A similar game is still played in Central America today.*

- **In Native American tribes**, dancers wearing 'false face masks' designed to ward off evil spirits often made offerings of food and 'corn animals' to the good spirits in nature.

- **Thousands of people were sacrificed** at a time to the Aztec sun god Huitzilopochtli, who demanded plentiful offerings of human hearts.

- **The Romans often** offered the deaths of gladiators to honour a particular diety.

- **Druid priests** sometimes made sacrifices to the Celtic gods by hanging up criminals or prisoners of war in big wicker cages and burning them alive.

▲ *In the film* Gladiator *(DreamWorks, 2000) Maximus Meridius competes in a gladiatorial battle to the death. The wealthy backer of a Roman gladiatorial games often dedicated the deaths of the gladiators to his or her favourite god or goddess.*

Gifts from gods

▲ *The French heroine Joan of Arc was made a saint by the Catholic Church 500 years after she had been burned at the stake for witchcraft and lying against God.*

- **In Greek myth**, when Perseus went to kill the monster Gorgon, the gods gave him a helmet of invisibility, a pair of winged sandals and a highly polished bronze shield – with a clue to use it as a mirror.

- **According to Egyptian myth**, the god Osiris taught people the skill of farming and provided them with laws and religious rites.

- **A French story says** that Joan of Arc heard a voice from God instructing her to go into an ancient church and dig behind the altar. She did so and found a great sword, which had been used in holy wars called the Crusades, and which no one knew had been buried there.

- **In Greek myth**, the goddess Athena gave a hero called Bellerophon a golden bridle with which he could catch the magical winged horse, Pegasus.

- **A Japanese myth says** that when the sun goddess, Amaterasu, was hiding in a cave, the other gods enticed her to come out with the gift of the first ever mirror.

- **Inuit myths** tell how it was the raven who brought many gifts to humans.

▲ *Greedy King Midas won the gift of 'the golden touch' – but ended up begging the gods to take it back.*

- **In Greek myth**, the goddess Thetis knew her hero son, Achilles, would die in the Trojan Wars. She tried to protect him with armour made by the gods' blacksmith, Hephaestus, but she failed.

- **A Christian story says** that when Jesus was on his way to die on the cross, a woman called Veronica wiped his bleeding face. The imprint of Jesus's features was left on her handkerchief.

- **A Greek myth says** that King Midas asked the gods for 'the golden touch' – anything he touched was turned into gold. He soon regretted the gift when he tried to eat and drink.

- **The *Ramayana*** tells how the god Indra gave the monkey hero Hanuman the power to choose his own death, as a gift for helping Prince Rama.

209

Who were the Celts?

- **The Celts** are an ancient group of peoples who first appeared in the Danube valley in Germany about 3300 years ago.

- **The first Celts** are known as the Urnfield culture, because they put their cremated dead in urns.

- **From 800 to 400** BC, Celts spread across northern Europe. They took over modern-day France as people called Gauls, England where they were known as Britons, and Ireland where they were called Gaels.

- **The first wave of expansion** is called Halstatt culture. With bronze, Celts developed supreme metal-working skills.

- **Around 500** BC, Celts learned to make iron and came into contact with Greeks and Etruscans. The 'La Tene' culture emerged.

- **In La Tene**, the distinctive Celtic swirls and spiral decoration was used on weapons and ornaments.

◀ *Created in the early* AD *800s, in Iona and Ireland, the Book of Kells is one of the great treasures of Celtic art.*

- **After the Gauls sacked Rome** in 390 BC, it seemed Celts might over-run Europe. But they were split into many tribes, and from 200 BC they were pushed ever further west.

- **Some early Celts used Greek letters** to write in their own language, but our knowledge of them comes mostly from Greek and Roman authors.

- **Celts were fierce warriors** who charged into battle shouting, naked and stained with blue woad dye. But they valued poets more highly than warriors. Their poets' tales of heroes and magic tell us how rich their culture was.

- **Celtic clan society** was highly organized and revolved around the chief of a clan, who made all the laws.

▶ *To face a Celtic warrior was a terrifying experience. Their bodies tattooed with blue dye (woad), they would let out bloodcurdling battle cries as they charged into combat.*

211

Celtic religion

- **Centuries before Christianity**, the Celtic peoples of Great Britain, Ireland and Northern France, were led in worship of their gods by priests called Druids.

- **The name 'Druid'** comes from the Celtic word 'druidh', which is connected with the Greek word for oak, 'drus'. The oak was a sacred symbol and Druids held their ceremonies in oak groves.

- **Celts in different places** called their gods different names and worshipped them in different forms.

▼ *Around 2000 BC, early Celts built a circle of enormous stones on Salisbury Plain in England. Some historians think it may have been used for worshipping the Sun. It is known today as Stonehenge.*

212

▶ *The leafy face of the nature god known today
simply as the Green Man is found carved into
old buildings across Europe.*

- **Many myths tell** of a horned god
  who leads a terrifying wild hunt
  across the sky. Some call
  him Herne.

- **An important race of gods** and
  goddesses, the Tuatha De Danann,
  had a mighty chief called the
  Dagda. He was the lord of magic,
  knowledge, weather and fire.

- **Another great leader** of the Tuatha De
  Danann was the warrior god Nuada. He had a
  magic sword, which conquered all his enemies.

- **The hero Lugh** was master of all skills – including magic. After many mighty
  deeds, he became an immortal.

- **Three important goddesses** are concerned with battle and death: the cruel
  Morrigan, Macha the goddess of Ulster, and Badb who sometimes took the
  form of a raven.

- **A Celtic god** known today as 'the Green Man' was carved into early
  Christian churches across the British Isles and Europe. He represented
  the power of nature, which died and was reborn each year.

- **In England**, traditional Morris dances re-enact Celtic springtime
  celebrations. Morris men leap into the air as a symbol of life triumphing
  over death.

213

The Celts
in Ireland

- **Following the Roman invasion** of Britain in the first century AD, the Celts were a people who lived mainly in Ireland, Scotland, Wales, Cornwall and northern France.

- **Celtic myths were told as stories** by poets called bards and priests called druids. Christian monks later wrote down the tales.

- **In Celtic creation mythology**, Ireland existed at the beginning of time and was the whole world.

- **According to Celtic myth**, the first people to settle in Ireland all died in a flood.

- **The second race of settlers** were male and female gods called the Partholons. They fought off a race of invading monsters called the Formorians, before being wiped out by a plague.

▼ *The Celts made tools, weapons, armour and jewellery from many different metals, decorated skilfully in intricate, flowing patterns. This heavy, twisted neckband is called a torque.*

214

- **Another race of gods** called the Nemedians then settled in Ireland, but were forced out by Formorian attacks.

- **Tribes called the Fir Bolgs** then invaded. These were humans who knew magic.

- **A wise, skilled race** of god-like people called the Tuatha De Danaan arrived and defeated the Fir Bolgs and the Formorians.

- **Finally, a race of humans** called the Children of Mil invaded Ireland. They became the ancestors of the Celts.

- **When the Children of Mil** settled in Ireland, the Tuatha De Danaan used their magic powers to vanish from human sight, but have stayed in Ireland to this day.

▶ *Celtic tribes across Britain and Northern Europe worshipped a fearsome horned god who hunted human souls. One name for him was Cernunnos.*

The first Britons

- **Human-like creatures have inhabited** Britain for over 500,000 years. The oldest known settlement, at Star Carr in Yorkshire, dates back 10,000 years.

- **About 6000 to 7000 years ago**, Neolithic farmers arrived from Europe. They began to clear the island's thick woods to grow crops and build houses in stone.

- **The early farmers** created round monuments of stones and wooden posts called *henges*. The most famous is Stonehenge in Wiltshire.

- **Around 2300 BC**, new people from the Rhine arrived. They are called Beakerfolk, after their beaker-shaped pottery cups. They were Britain's first metal-workers.

- **Legend has it** that the name Britain came from Brutus, one of the sons of Aeneas, who fled from Troy.

- **Around 700 BC**, Celts arrived, often living in hillforts.

- **Iron axes and ploughs** enabled huge areas to be cleared and farmed, and the population rose.

- **When Julius Caesar invaded**, in 55 and 54 BC, the Celtic people of England, known as Britons, were divided into scores of tribes, such as the Catuvellauni and Atrebates.

- **Resistance from tribal leaders** such as Caratacus meant it took the Romans over a century to conquer the Britons.

- **The last revolt** was that of Queen Boudicca, in AD 60.

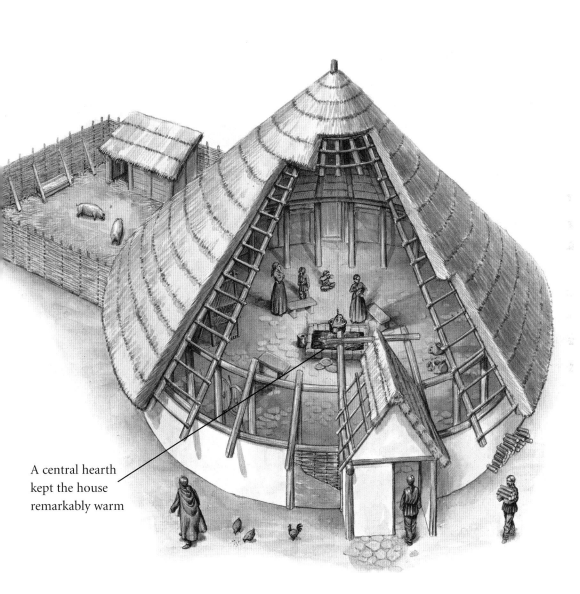

A central hearth
kept the house
remarkably warm

▲ *People of Bronze Age Britain lived in round houses like this,
with thick stone walls and a steeply pitched, thatched roof.*

217

The fall of Rome

- **After the death of Marcus Aurelius**, in AD 180, Rome was plagued by various serious political struggles.

- **The Praetorian Guard** (the emperor's personal soldiers) chose or deposed emperors at will, and there were 60 emperors between AD 235 and 284 alone.

- **The empire fell** into anarchy and was beset by famine, plague and invasion.

▼ *After the emperor Constantine moved his capital there in AD 330, Byzantium (now Istanbul in Turkey) became the main defender of Roman civilization.*

- **Diocletian** (emperor from AD 284) tried to make the empire easier to govern by splitting it in two – East and West. He asked Maximian to rule the west.

- **Diocletian retired** 'to grow cabbages' at his palace in Dalmatia, and soldiers tried to choose a new emperor.

- **Constantine**, commander of the Roman armies in Britain, defeated his rivals to become emperor. It is said that before the main battle, he saw a Christian cross in the sky. After his victory, he became Christian.

- **In AD 330**, Constantine made Byzantium (modern-day Istanbul) his capital and called it Constantinople.

- **After Constantine's death**, the empire fell into chaos again. It became split permanently into East and West.

- **The Western empire** suffered attacks from barbarians. Vandals invaded Spain and North Africa. Goths and Huns such as Attila attacked from the North.

- **In AD 410**, Visigoths led by Alaric invaded Italy and sacked (burned and looted) Rome. In AD 455, Vandals sacked Rome again. In AD 476, the Western empire finally collapsed.

▶ *This coin was minted during the reign of Constantine. The inscription translates as 'Constantine, dutiful and wise ruler'.*

Early Christians

- **The first Christians** were Jews in Palestine, but followers like Paul soon spread the faith to gentiles (non-Jews) and countries beyond Palestine.

- **At first**, Roman rulers tolerated Christians, but after AD 64, they saw Christians as a threat and persecuted them.

- **Persecution** strengthened Christianity by creating martyrs such as St Alban.

- **In AD 313**, Emperor Constantine gave Christians freedom of worship and called the first great ecumenical (general) church council in AD 325.

- **By AD 392**, Christianity was the official religion of the empire.

- **When the Roman Empire** split into East and West, so too did Christianity, with the West focused on Rome and the East on Constantinople.

- **The head of the Western church** was the Pope, and the head of the Eastern church was called the Patriarch. The first Pope was Jesus's apostle St Peter, and there has been an unbroken line of popes ever since. But the power of the popes really began with St Gregory, in AD 590.

- **To separate themselves** from the official religion, some Christians, such as St Benedict, began to live apart as monks in monasteries.

- **After AD 500**, monks spread Christianity over northwestern Europe.

- **Monasteries** became the main havens for learning in the West in the Dark Ages, which followed the fall of Rome.

▶ *Early Christian texts were manuscripts (hand-written) and monks spent years illuminating (decorating) them. The illuminated manuscripts of this time are among the most beautiful books ever made.*

NOMINE DNI INCIPIT LIBER AVGVSTINI EPI DE CIVITATE
MIRIFICE DISPVTATVS CONTRA PAGANOS ET DEOS
RVOS DEMONES

LORIOSISSI
MA CIVITATE DI

SIVE IN HOC TEM PORVM CVRSV

nter impios peregrinatur ex fide uiuens siue in illa stabilitate sedis
quam nunc expectat per pacientiam quoadusq iusticia conuer
iudiciu deinceps adeptura per excellente uictoria ultima & pace
ta hoc opere ad te instituto & mum pmissione debito defendere
rsus eos qui conditori eius deos suos preferut fili kme Marcelline
pi magnu opus & arduu sed ds adiutoi noster est Nam scio quib

prima

Byzantine Empire

- **When Rome collapsed**, in AD 476, Constantinople (modern-day Istanbul, Turkey) became the capital of what historians call the Byzantine Empire. It became the centre of Western civilization for the next thousand years.

- **In the six years after Constantine** made Constantinople his capital, builders, architects and artists created one of the world's most magnificent cities.

- **Constantinople** was at the focus of trade routes between Asia and Europe. Silks, gems and ivories were traded for gold, grain, olives and wine. By charging 10 percent on all goods coming in and out, the city became rich.

- **When the great emperor Justinian I** came to the throne in AD 527, he tried to rebuild the Roman Empire. His general, Belisarius, reconquered Italy, and by AD 565 the Byzantine Empire stretched right around the Mediterranean.

- **Justinian built hundreds** of churches, including the famous Hagia Sophia.

- **Justinian also modernized** Roman law to create the basis of all Western legal systems. This is called the Code of Justinian.

- **The Byzantine Empire** was under constant attack – from Goths, Huns, Persians, Avars, Bulgars, Slavs, Vikings, Arabs, Berbers, Turks, Crusaders and Normans. But it repelled attackers, often with its secret weapon, 'Greek fire', invented in AD 650. This was a mix of quick-lime, petrol and sulphur, which burst into flames when it hit water.

▶ *Justinian I was the greatest Byzantine emperor, although his general's secretary, Procopius, described him as 'a demon incarnate'. He ruled with his beautiful former actress wife, Theodora. Justinian relied on her for support and advice, and it was she who changed laws to improve the lives of women and the poor.*

...FASCINATING FACT...
29 Byzantium's 88 emperors died violent deaths, and the endless
conspiracies at court have given us the word 'Byzantine' for dark intrigues.

- **In 1204**, Constantinople was ransacked by Crusader knights who were
  short of money. Almost every treasure in the city was stolen and it never
  recovered from this devastating blow. The city's population dwindled from
  one million to just 60,000 over the next 200 years.

- **Constantinople was finally conquered** by the Turkish Sultan Mehmet II
  in 1453.

The Hippodrome
was based on the
Circus Maximus
in Rome

60,000 spectators watched
chariot races here

The Hagia Sophia, now a
museum, is the world's oldest
Christian cathedral

▶ *At its height,
Constantinople
was graced by
some of the
ancient world's
most magnificent
buildings. This
picture shows the
tranquil palace
quarter. The rest
of the city was
noisy and crowded.*

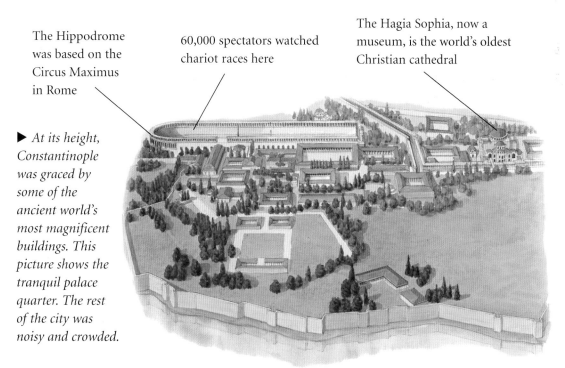

Sui, Tang and Song

- **In AD 581, Yang Chien** seized the throne in the north of China and founded the Sui dynasty.

- **Yang Chien conquered** the south and reunited China for the first time since the fall of the Han in AD 220.

- **Under the second Sui emperor**, Yang Di, China's Grand Canal was rebuilt on a huge scale, linking China's main rivers. Other canals extended the network.

- **Yang Di was betrayed** by one of his 3000 mistresses and was strangled in AD 618. Li Yuan, an ambitious Sui minister, then seized the throne to found the Tang dynasty.

- **Under the Tang**, trade grew, China became rich again and the arts and sciences flourished.

- **By AD 751**, China was the world's largest empire and the capital, Chang'an, was the world's largest city, with over one million inhabitants.

- **Chinese people were the first** to drink tea and sit on chairs.

- **Poets such as Li Po** (AD 701–762) wrote of his love of wild mountains and the fleeting nature of happiness. China's tradition of great landscape painting began and one of the earliest printed books, *The Diamond Sutra*, was made in AD 868.

- **By AD 800**, the Tang dynasty was beginning to break up, Chang'an declined and China descended into turmoil.

- **Order was restored** in AD 960, when the Song family began to rule from the city of Kaifeng. The Song lasted until 1276, when the Mongol Kublai Khan conquered China.

▶ *Gunpowder was invented in the Tang era. The Chinese used it first to make fireworks, and later weapons.*

Barbarians

- **Barbarians** is what the Romans called all the peoples living outside the empire, who they thought of as uncivilized.

- **Barbarian people rarely lived** in large towns. Instead they lived in forts or small farming villages.

- **Many were brave warriors** but many were also skilled craftsmen, poets and farmers.

- **The Romans thought barbarians** wild and crude, but they survived and built a lasting civilization as the peoples of northern and western Europe.

- **To the Romans**, the barbarians seemed ill-disciplined in battle. They rode horses and appeared in vast, wild, terrifying hordes.

- **The Goths** were German peoples who overran the western Roman empire in the 4th and 5th centuries AD. They were divided into Ostrogoths in the east, near the Black Sea, and Visigoths on the Danube. It was the Visigoths who, under their king Alaric, finally broke Rome in AD 476.

- **Italians later used** the term 'gothic' to sneer at what they saw as the ugly cathedrals of northern Europe and the term stuck.

- **The Vandals** were a German tribe who arrived in Europe from the east in the 1st century BC. When driven west by the Huns in c.AD 380, they took over Spain and North Africa.

- **Vandals swept down** through Italy in AD 455 to sack Rome and gave us the current word 'vandal' for destructive troublemakers.

- **The Huns** were nomadic Mongols from eastern Asia who arrived in Europe in about AD 370, driving everyone before them, until they were finally defeated in AD 455. The Huns were bogeymen for the Romans. One Roman said, 'They have a sort of shapeless lump, not a face, and pinholes for eyes' – perhaps because Huns bandaged children's skulls in order to deform them as they grew. The most feared Hun was Attila.

▶ *Alaric was the great Gothic leader who took Rome in AD 410. He looted the city but spared the churches. Alaric planned to settle in Africa, but a storm forced him to stop at Cozenza in southern Italy, where he died.*

Roman Britain

- **The Roman occupation** began in earnest when the armies of Claudius landed at Richborough in Kent in AD 43. All of England and Wales was conquered by AD 78.

- **Scotland remained** beyond Roman control. In AD 122–130, the 118-km-long stone wall that is now called Hadrian's wall was built right across the country to act as a frontier.

- **The Roman army** in Britain was powerful. There were three legions (5000 men each) at York, Chester and Caerleon, plus 40,000 auxiliaries.

- **Roman Britain was ruled** by a Roman governor, but the Romans co-opted local chiefs to help.

- **The Romans built** the first proper towns in Britain – like St Albans, Gloucester and Lincoln – with typical Roman features such as baths and theatres.

- **Demand for food** and leather from the army and the new towns boosted farming. Large estates centred on Roman-style villas grew rich, but even small farmers did well.

- **Most people** were bilingual, speaking both Celtic and Latin, and many adopted Roman lifestyles.

▶ *King Arthur became the greatest hero in British legend, but the real Arthur was probably a British chief who, for a while, turned the tide against the Anglo-Saxons with a victory at Mt Badon around AD 530–550.*

- **When barbarians attacked** the empire on the continent in the AD 300s, leading generals from Italy were sent to reorganize defences. Power fell into the hands of tyrants like the British king Vortigern (AD 425–450).

- **Vortigern invited** Anglo-Saxons from Germany to settle in the east to help him against rebel Britons. But the Anglo-Saxons soon turned against him and invited in others of their kind to join them.

- **Villas and towns** were abandoned and Britons fled west or abroad as the Anglo-Saxons moved in.

▲ *Hadrian's wall may have acted as a defence, keeping 'barbarians' out of Roman territory. It is generally accepted that the emperor Hadrian wanted to mark the northern boundary of his empire. The wall itself took six years to build, and was modified for many years after.*

Muhammad

- **Muhammad** (*c.*AD 570–632) was the Arab prophet whose teachings form the basis of the Islamic religion.

- **Muslims** (followers of Islam) believe Muhammad was the last and greatest prophet of God, who they called Allah.

- **Muhammad was born** in Mecca in Arabia.

- **His father died** before he was born and his mother died when he was a child. He was raised by his grandfather and uncle, tending sheep and camels.

- **At the age of 25**, Muhammad entered the service of a rich widow of 40 called Khadija and later married her. They had two sons and four daughters.

- **When he was 35**, Muhammad was asked to restore a sacred stone that had been damaged in a flood. He had a vision that told him to become a prophet and proclaim the word of God.

- **The people of Mecca** resented Muhammad's preaching, and in AD 622 he emigrated to Medina, in Saudi Arabia.

▼ *Each year, thousands of Muslims from all over the world flock to the Ka'ba shrine at Mecca, in modern Saudi Arabia.*

▲ *The Qu'ran is Islam's holy book of Muhammad's teachings.*

● **In Medina**, he attracted many followers. The Meccans went to war against Medina, but were driven back.

● **In AD 630**, Muhammad re-entered Mecca in triumph, pardoned the people and set up a mosque there.

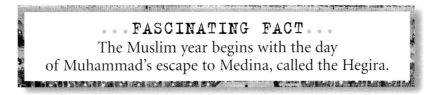

. . .FASCINATING FACT. . .
The Muslim year begins with the day
of Muhammad's escape to Medina, called the Hegira.

What people wore

- **The earliest people** wore animal skins to keep warm.

- **The oldest signs** of woven cloth are marks in clay at Pavlov in Czechoslovakia, which date back 26,000 years.

- **Most of our knowledge** of ancient costumes comes from vases, statues and wall paintings. Colours have often faded, but we know from paintings such as those in the Roman city of Pompeii, preserved under volcanic ash, that ancient clothes were often colourful.

- **The oldest surviving clothes** come from 5000-year-old Egyptian tombs.

- **The deep-blue dye** indigo, from the indigo plant, has been found in Egyptian cloth from 4400 years ago.

- **Tyrian purple** was a purple dye, much-prized in ancient times. It came from Tyre (modern Lebanon) and was made from Purpura and Murex snails.

▲ Egyptians wore clothes made mainly of white linen. At first, men wore a short kilt, but later they wore long, wrap-around skirts. Egyptian women at first wore sheath-like dresses. After 1500 BC, men and women both wore loose robes like these, made from rectangles of cloth.

▲ Greek clothes were very simple – essentially pieces of wool or linen wrapped round to make a tunic, dress or cloak. Young men typically wore a short cloak (chlamys) over a tunic sewn up at the side and fastened at the shoulder. Women wore a dress (chiton) made from a rectangle of cloth. They wore a longer cloak called a himation.

> ...FASCINATING FACT...
> The first people to wear trousers were probably the ancient
> Persians, 4000 years ago. The ankles were tight-fitting.

- **People such as the ancient Egyptians** often wore simple sandals or shoes of papyrus or leather. But the Greek dramatist Aeschylus is said to have invented the platform shoe, with 8-cm heels.

- **Minoan women** of 3500 years ago, unusually for ancient times, wore tight-waisted dresses. Their breasts were left exposed.

- **Ordinary Roman citizens** wore an unbleached white toga. Coloured borders showed a particular status. Public officials at functions had togas with purple borders, called a *toga praetexta*. Early Roman generals wore togas dyed in Tyrian purple. From the time of Augustus, only the emperor wore a purple toga.

▲ *In the north of Europe, Celtic peoples wore warm clothes made mainly of dyed wool and leather. Women wore thick dresses and headscarfs. Men wore long tunics, leggings and a cloak.*

▲ *Roman clothing was quite similar to the Greeks'. Men and women wore tunics, called* stola *(women) or* tunica *(men). Citizens of Rome were allowed to wear a carefully draped cloth called a toga over their tunic.*

233

Monastery life

- **In religions like Christianity and Buddhism**, some devout people step out of ordinary life and live in a monastery, a community devoted to religion.

- **The earliest Christian monastery** was that of the hermit St Anthony of Thebes, who went to live in the Egyptian desert about AD 271, and attracted loyal followers.

- **Basil the Great** (c.AD 329–379) and his sister Macrina the Younger founded monasteries for men and women on their estate in Cappadocia in Turkey.

- **Monasticism spread rapidly** throughout the Byzantine Empire between the 4th and 7th centuries AD.

- **In the West**, monasticism grew more slowly, so St Martin of Tours (AD 316–397) sent out monks to start new communities. They were very successful in Britain and Ireland.

- **Monasteries such as Lindisfarne** and Malmesbury were centres of learning in the Dark Ages.

- **The most famous scholar-monk** was St Bede (c.AD 672–735), known for his history of the English people.

- **The most famous British monastery** was the Scottish Isle of Iona, set up by St Columba in AD 563.

◀ *British and Irish monks laboured to create beautiful illustrated books by hand. This is the* Lindisfarne Gospel.

- **St Benedict** (*c.*AD 480–547) developed a particular way of living for monks at Monte Cassino, Italy. By AD 1000, most monasteries followed Benedictine rules.

- **Monasteries were very vulnerable** to Viking raids. Monks were often killed and many treasures lost, and so the monastic life lost some of its attraction.

▶ *Before the days of mass-printing, monks hand-copied texts because they needed books for their studies.*

The spread of Isla

- **Muslims believe** that their religion began the day a prophet named Muhammad left Mecca in AD 622, but it was after his death in AD 632 that it really began to grow.

- **The spread of Islam** was led by *caliphs* (which means 'successors').

- **Islam expanded** by conquest, and many peoples only became Muslims after they were conquered. But Muslim conquerors were tolerant of other religions.

- **The Muslims regarded** a conquest as a *jihad* (holy war), and this gave them a powerful zeal.

- **The Muslim Arabs conquered** Iraq (AD 637), Syria (AD 640), Egypt (AD 641) and Persia (AD 650).

▼ *Five times a day, devout Muslims face the holy city of Mecca to pray.*

- **By AD 661**, the great Islamic Empire stretched from Tunisia to India. Its capital was at Damascus.

- **The first Muslims** were Arabs, and as Islam spread, so did Arabs, but the empire contained many peoples.

- **Muhammad commanded** men to 'seek knowledge, even as far as China'. Many Muslims became great scholars.

- **The arts and sciences** flourished under Islam to make it one of the most cultured, advanced societies in the world.

▼ *The Dome of the Rock in Jerusalem, built by Abd al-Malik, was one of the first of many beautiful buildings created by Muslims.*

The Fujiwaras

- **The Fujiwaras** were the family who dominated Japan for five centuries from the 7th century AD.

- **In AD 858**, the Fujiwaras' power really began when Fujiwara Yoshifusa married the old emperor. When he died, Yoshifusa became regent to their young son.

- **The Fujiwaras** kept their position by marrying more daughters to emperors, and creating the role of an all-powerful *kampaku* (chancellor).

- **While the emperor** dealt with religious matters, the Fujiwara kampaku or regent ran the country.

- **Fujiwara power** peaked with Michinaga (AD 966–1028).

- **Michinaga's mansions** were more splendid than palaces and filled with banquets, concerts, poetry and picnics.

- **Many women** were novelists and poets, and love affairs were conducted via cleverly poetic letters.

- **The brilliant court life** of Michinaga was captured in the famous novel *The Tale of Genji* by Lady Murasaki.

- **During Michinaga's reign**, warrior families gained the upper hand by quelling rural rebellions, so bringing about the Fujiwaras' downfall.

> ... FASCINATING FACT ...
> Sei Shonagon, a lady at Michinaga's court, wrote a famous *Pillow Book* – a diary about what she saw.

▶ The Tale of Genji *is thought to be the world's oldest full-length novel. It was written about* AD *1000 by Murasaki Shikibu, a lady-in-waiting to the empress of Japan. It tells the story of Prince Genji and his various loves.*

Anglo-Saxons

- **The Angles, Saxons and Jutes** were peoples from Denmark and Germany who invaded Britain and settled there between AD 450 and 600.

- **The Britons resisted** at first, but by AD 650 they were driven back into the west or made slaves.

- **The Angles settled** in East Anglia and the Midlands, the Saxons in Sussex, Essex and Wessex (Dorset and Hampshire).

- **Each tribe** had its own kingdom, yet by AD 700 most people in the south thought of themselves as English.

- **Seven leading kingdoms** formed a 'heptarchy' – Essex, Kent, Sussex, Wessex, East Anglia, Mercia and Northumbria.

- **One king was** *bretwalda* (overlord), but the kingdoms vied for power.

- **When Ethelbert of Kent** was *bretwalda*, in AD 597, St Augustine converted him to Christianity. Christianity spread rapidly throughout England. English monasteries became the universities of Europe. Masons from Gaul and Rome built stone churches.

- **Most Anglo-Saxons** were farmers. Others were warriors, as their famous epic poem of heroism, *Beowulf*, shows.

▲ *In 1939, the burial ship of the overlord Raedwald (died AD 625) was discovered at Sutton Hoo in East Anglia. This helmet is one of the treasures it held.*

240

- **In the AD 700s,** Danish raiders conquered all of England but Wessex. They were pushed back by King Alfred, but attacks resumed in the reign of Ethelred II (AD 978–1016).

- **The last Anglo-Saxon king** was Ethelred II's son, Edward the Confessor (1042–1066).

▶ *The Scandinavian Vikings who made continual raids on Britain were descended from earlier 'barbarian' peoples.*

◀ *Anglo-Saxon villages were made from materials such as wood, thatch and wattle (woven branches).*

Beowulf

- **The epic poem** *Beowulf* was written in the Anglo-Saxon language by an unknown English person around AD 700–750.

- **The legend focuses** on the adventures of a Viking hero, Beowulf. The action takes place in the south of Sweden and Denmark.

- **Christianity was introduced** to England around AD 600. The poem blends traditional elements of Norse myth such as warrior culture and fate with belief in a Christian god.

- **Beowulf risks his own life** to help other people by battling three terrifying monsters: Grendel, Grendel's mother, and a dragon.

- **The monster Grendel** is said to bear 'the mark of Cain'. This is a reference to the Bible story in which Adam's son Cain killed his brother Abel.

- **Beowulf is fatally wounded** when all his chosen warriors desert him through fear – except for his courageous nephew Wiglaf.

- **At the end of the poem**, the dead Beowulf is laid to rest in a huge burial mound. A similarly impressive burial mound, dating around AD 650, was discovered at Sutton Hoo in Suffolk in 1939.

- **The oldest manuscript** of *Beowulf* that exists today was made from an original by monks in about AD 1000. Many other older copies were destroyed when King Henry VIII ordered the monasteries and their libraries to be closed down in the late 1530s.

- **The only remaining copy** is kept in a controlled environment behind glass in the British Museum, London, England.

- **The modern-day film** *The Thirteenth Knight*, starring Antonio Banderas, is based on the Beowulf legend.

▲ *Beowulf has to descend to the depths of a murky lake to fight the monster, Grendel's ferocious mother.*

Bulgars

- **An Asian people** called the Bulgars arrived in Europe – on the Volga River – around AD 370.

- **The Bulgars** were skilled horse-warriors. They were ruled by *khans* (chiefs) and *boyars* (noblemen).

- **They attacked the fringes** of the Byzantine Empire until they were in turn attacked by another Asian people called the Avars.

- **After Kurt became** the Bulgar Khan in AD 605, the Bulgars re-established themselves on the steppes, but when Kurt died, the Bulgars split into five hordes, or groups.

- **Four of the five Bulgar hordes** vanished from history, but the fifth was led by Asparukh Khan, west into the Danube valley. Here they overpowered the Slavs living there to create a Bulgarian Empire.

- **Bulgarian Khans** were called *caesars* or *czars* after helping Byzantine emperor Justinian II in AD 710.

- **The Bulgars were more** often at odds with the Byzantines and were usually defeated. However, after one victory, Krum Khan (AD 803–814) lined Byzantine emperor Nicephorus's skull with silver to make a drinking cup.

- **The Byzantines sent** St Cyril and his brother St Methodius to convert the Bulgar people to Christianity. They succeeded when Czar Boris I was baptized in AD 864.

- **St Cyril invented** the Cyrillic alphabet, still used by Russians and other eastern Europeans today.

- **The Bulgarian empire** peaked under Simeon I (AD 893–927). Its capital, Preslav, imitated Constantinople in splendour.

▶ *In the* AD *800s, the Bulgars were converted to Christianity and adopted the Eastern Orthodox Church of the Byzantines. They began to create icons (religious images) like this.*

245

The caliphs

- **The caliphs** were the rulers of Islam. The word *caliph* means 'successor', and they were all meant to be successors of Muhammad after he died in AD 632.

- **The first caliph** was Muhammad's father-in-law, Abu Bakr. After that came Umar, Uthman and Ali.

- **The first four caliphs** are called the Rashidun ('rightly guided') because they were the only caliphs accepted by everyone.

- **When Ali died**, in AD 661, Islam was torn apart by civil war. Some Muslims, called Shi'ites, saw only Ali's successors, the *imams*, as leaders. Most Muslims followed the Umayyad family, who became caliphs in Damascus.

- **The 14 Umayyad caliphs** expanded the Islamic empire by conquest through North Africa and into Spain. But it proved too much for them to handle.

- **In AD 750**, the last of the Umayyad caliphs – Marwan II – was beaten at the Battle of the Great Zab by the rival Abbasids, who were descended from Muhammad's uncle.

- **The 38 Abbasid caliphs** turned their eyes eastwards and made a new capital at Baghdad, which soon became the richest city in the world.

- **Under the Abbasids**, Islam became famous for its science, learning and art, especially during the time of Harun al-Rashid.

- **One Umayyad escaped** to set up a rival caliphate in Spain (AD 756–1031).

- **Descendants of Muhammad's daughter** Fatimah became caliphs in Egypt, creating the great city of Cairo.

▶ *Under the Abbasid caliphs, Islamic artists made beautiful ceramic tiles and glassware.*

▼ *This mosque in Cairo, Egypt, is dedicated to the caliph Ali, one of the original caliphs who was accepted by all the people.*

247

Alfred the Great

▲ *This enamel and gold jewel was found near Athelney. It is inscribed with the words* Aelfred me ech eh t gewyrcan – *Old English for 'Alfred ordered me to be made'.*

- **Alfred the Great** (AD 849–899) was the greatest of the Anglo-Saxon kings.

- **Alfred became king** of Wessex in AD 871, at a time when the Danes (Vikings) had overrun East Anglia, Northumbria and Mercia.

- **In AD 878**, a series of ferocious Danish attacks drove Alfred to hide on the isle of Athelney – in the Somerset marshes.

- **While on the run**, Alfred is said to have hidden in a pigherd's cottage. He was so tired he fell asleep by the fire, letting some cakes burn. Not realizing he was the king, the pigherd's wife scolded him.

- **From Athelney**, Alfred secretly assembled an army and emerged to score a decisive victory over the Danes at Edington. The Danes agreed to withdraw to East Anglia and their king Guthrum became a Christian.

- **In AD 886**, Alfred recaptured London and forced the Danes to stay within an area called Danelaw.

- **Alfred built forts**, reorganized his army and also created England's first navy to defend the country against invasions.

- **Alfred was a wise** and kindly king who created sound laws, protected the weak from corrupt judges and made laws to help the poor and needy.

- **Alfred was a scholar** who encouraged learning. He decreed that all young men should learn to read English, and made important books available in English.

▶ *Alfred encouraged the building of new ships. He realized that a strong fleet would help his navy defend against invasion.*

...FASCINATING FACT...
Alfred translated many books from Latin into English so that his people could read them.

249

The Berbers

- **The Berbers** were the people who lived in North Africa before various other peoples arrived.

- **'Berber' comes from** *barbara*, Roman for 'barbarians'.

- **Numidian Berbers** allied themselves with Carthage (modern-day Tunisia), the great city created when Phoenician traders from Lebanon settled there 3000 years ago.

- **The Berbers coped with invasions** from Carthaginians, and then Romans, Vandals and Byzantine people, by withdrawing south into the desert, living their lives as bands of marauders.

- **In the 7th century** AD, Islamic Arabs invaded North Africa and many Berbers became Muslims.

- **The Berbers kept their independence** by changing Islam to their own tastes. They based their religion around *marabouts*, holy men who lived very frugally and morally.

- **After** AD **740**, Berbers regained control of North Africa from the Umayyad caliphs.

- **The Berbers built empires** extending into Spain under the Almohads (1121–1269) and Almoravids (1061–1145).

- **Ibn Tumart** was the first Almohad leader, from *c*.1121. He claimed to be the Mahdi, the holy man whose coming was predicted by Muhammad.

- **The Berber empires fell** to the Arabs in the 12th century.

▲ *When their empires fell, the Berbers survived in the harsh conditions of the Sahara Desert.*

The Vikings

- **The Vikings were daring** raiders from Norway, Sweden and Denmark. Between AD 800 and 1100, they swept in on the coasts of northwest Europe in their longships, searching for rich plunder to carry away.

- **People were terrified** by the lightning raids of the Vikings. A prayer of the time went, 'Deliver us, O Lord, from the fury of the Norsemen (Vikings). They ravage our lands. They kill our women and children'.

- **Vikings prided themselves** on their bravery in battle. Most fought on foot with swords, spears and axes. Rich Vikings rode on horseback.

- **Shock troops** called *berserkers* led the attack. *Berserk* is Norse for 'bare shirt' as they wore no armour. Before a battle, they became fighting-mad through drink and drugs and trusted in their god Odin to keep them safe.

- **The word 'Viking'** was only used later. People of the time called them Norsemen. The word Viking probably came from Vik, a pirate centre in Norway. When Norsemen went 'a-viking', they meant fighting as a pirate. Swedish Vikings who settled in eastern Europe may have been called Rus, and so Russia was named after them.

- **Not all Vikings** were pirates. At home, they were farmers, fishermen, merchants and craftworkers. Many went with the raiders and settled in the north of France, northern England and Dublin.

- **The Vikings attacked** mainly Britain and Ireland, but raided as far as Gibraltar and into the Mediterranean.

- **In Eastern Europe**, the Vikings' ships carried them inland up various rivers. They ventured far through Russia and the Ukraine, sometimes marauding as far south as Constantinople, which they called 'Miklagard', the big city.

...FASCINATING FACT...
In November AD 885, Count Odo and 200 knights fought heroically to
defend Paris against Viking hordes, but the city was reduced to ashes.

● **The Norsemen who settled** in northern France were called Normans. The
Norman king, William the Conqueror, who invaded England in 1066, was
descended from their leader, Rollo.

▼ *At home, most Vikings were farmers.*
The women were left in charge when their
husbands went raiding.

▶ *A hammer like this*
one was used at many stages
in a Viking's life – raised over
the newborn, laid in the bride's lap at
weddings, or carved on a grave. The
hammer was the symbol of the great
Viking god, Thor.

253

Viking voyages

- **Great seafarers**, the Vikings made some of the most remarkable voyages of ancient times.

- **The Vikings sailed east** through the Baltic Sea and up the Vistula and Dnieper rivers.

- **The Vikings sailed west** around the British Isles, and south around Spain into the Mediterranean.

- **The most daring Viking voyages** were out across the then-unknown open ocean of the North Atlantic.

- **From AD 900**, the Vikings sailed to, and settled on, remote islands to the far north – including Iceland, the Faroes and Greenland.

▼ *The Vikings' wooden ships, called longships, are masterpieces of boat-building – light and flat-bottomed enough to sail up shallow rivers, yet seaworthy in the open ocean.*

The ships often had a high prow, sometimes carved with a dragon's head

Shields were strapped in rows down each side

When the wind was still, they relied on banks of rowers each side

At sea, ships were driven along by a large, square sail made from strips of woollen cloth stitched together

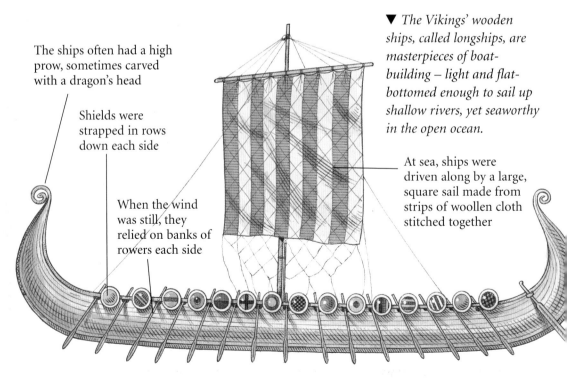

- **About AD 800,** Vikings led by Ohthere reached the remote Siberian islands of Novaya Zemlya in the Arctic.

- **In AD 1000,** Bjarni Herjulffson was blown off course sailing home from Greenland and saw an unknown shore.

- **Leif Eriksson** sailed west to find this shore. Stories called *Sagas* tell how he found a new land. The Vikings called it 'Vinland', as it was abundant in 'wine berries' (probably cranberries).

- **Most experts now think** Vinland is North America, and Leif was the first European to reach it.

- **In 1004,** the Viking Thorfinn took 130 people to settle in Vinland and stayed three years. Remains of Thorfinn's settlement were found in 1963, at L'Anse aux Meadows, on the northern tip of Newfoundland.

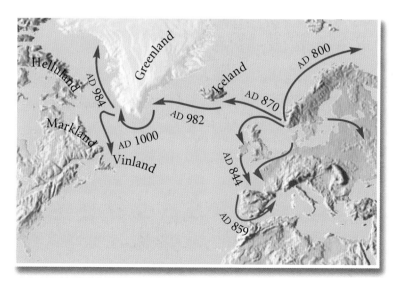

▶ *Viking weapons included a spear, knife and protective shield. Vikings held their weapons sacred.*

◀ *This map shows just some of the remarkable voyages made by the Vikings, and their approximate dates. The names shown are the Viking names.*

255

Viking society

- **Vikings ate beef**, cheese, eggs and milk from their farms, meat from deer, elks and seals caught by hunters and fish such as cod, herring and salmon.

- **The houses Vikings lived** in were one-storey and wooden, with slanted roofs of turf or straw and no windows. At the centre was a hearth for warmth and cooking. The man of the house sat on a chair called the high seat; the rest of the family sat on benches.

- **Viking men wore** trousers and a long-sleeved smock shirt. Women wore long woollen or linen dresses.

- **Viking men were allowed** to have two or three wives, and marriages were arranged by parents.

- **A Viking woman**, unusually for the time, could own her own property and divorce her husband.

- **Skalds** (Viking poets) went into battle to report on them in verse.

- **The Vikings were great storytellers**. They told of their adventures in long stories called *Sagas*.

◀ *Viking god Odin was said to ride on an eight-legged horse called Sleipnir, accompanied by two ravens that brought him news of any battles.*

- **At first**, *Sagas* were only spoken. From 1100 to 1300, they were written down.

- **Vikings were religious** and had several gods. They believed if they died fighting they would go to Valhalla, a special hall in Asgard, the gods' home.

◄ *Viking women looked after the children and the home, but also had rights, which was unusual for women at this time.*

Scandinavian stories

- **Norse mythology** comes from people who lived in Scandinavia in the Bronze Age. These were the ancestors of the Vikings.

- **Myths say that in the beginning** was a huge emptiness called Ginnungagap. A fiery southern land called Muspellheim first came into existence, then a freezing northern land called Niflheim.

- **The fires eventually** began to melt the ice, and the dripping waters formed into the first being: a wicked Frost Giant named Ymir. More Frost Giants were formed from Ymir's sweat.

- **The next being** that grew from the thawed ice was a cow called Audhumla. Audhumla licked an ice block into a male being called Buri.

- **Buri's grandchildren** were the first three Norse gods: Odin, Vili and Ve. They killed Ymir and threw his body into Ginnungagap. His flesh, blood, bones, hair, skull and brains became the earth, seas, mountains, forests, sky and clouds.

- **Dwarves came into existence** before human beings. They grew from maggots in Ymir's flesh.

- **Odin, Vili and Ve** created the first man, Ask, from an ash tree and the first woman, Embla, from an elm. The gods gave humans a world called Midgard.

- **The gods tried** to keep the evil giants away by giving them a separate land, Jotunheim.

- **The gods built** themselves a heavenly homeland called Asgard.

- **A rainbow bridge** links the realm of the gods to the world of humans. The god Heimdall was set as watchman to make sure only gods and goddesses could cross.

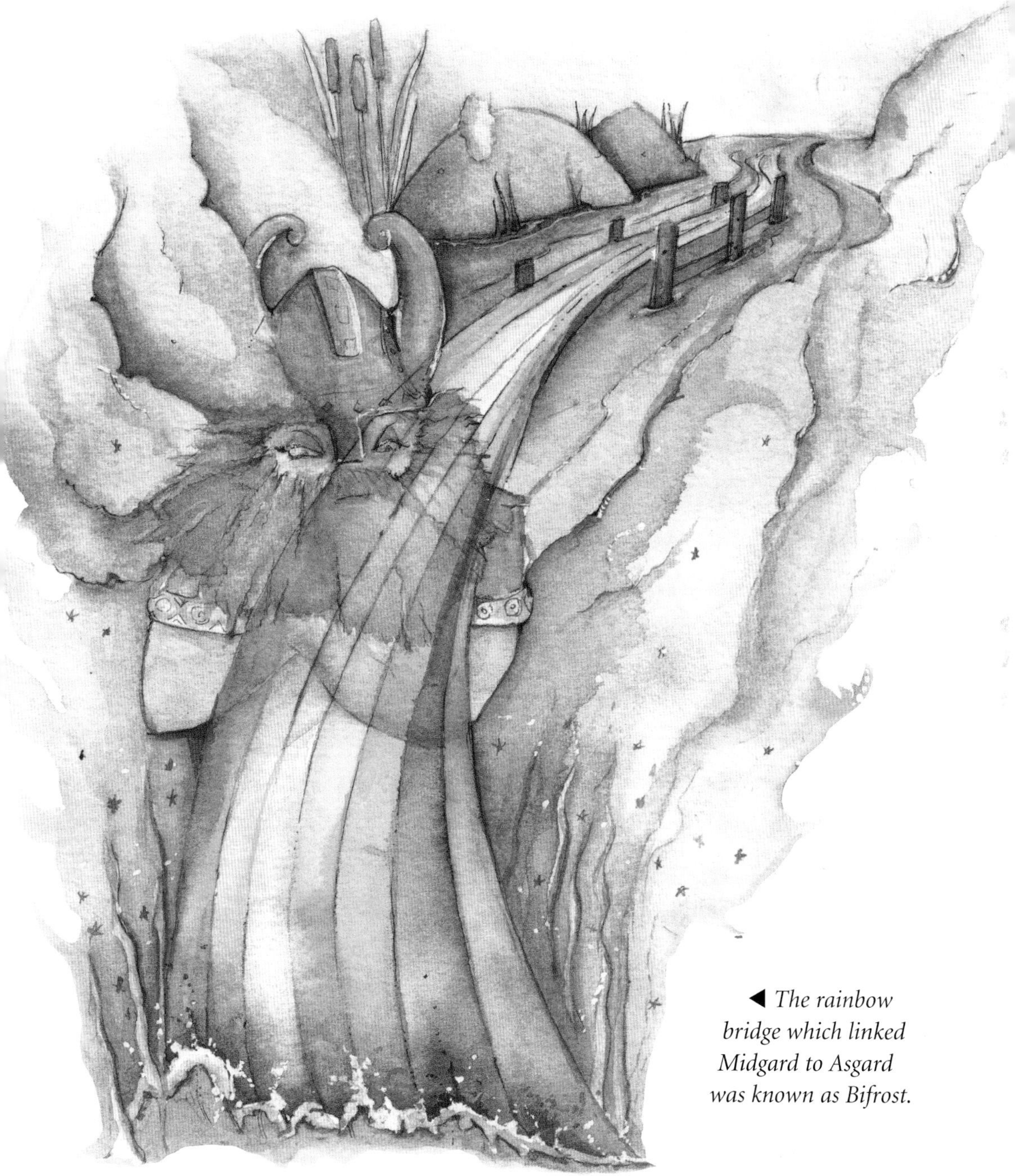

◀ The rainbow
bridge which linked
Midgard to Asgard
was known as Bifrost.

259

Norse warrior gods

- **Ancient Norse peoples told stories** about a race of gods and goddesses called the Aesir. They were brave warriors, just like the Vikings themselves, with similar feelings and fears.

- **Odin, the chief** of the warrior gods, has a high throne called Lidskialf, from which he can see anything happening in the universe.

▶ *Norse stories said that the thunder god, Thor, raced across the heavens in a chariot pulled by two enormous, vicious goats.*

▶ *Norse stories are the mythology of the Vikings – seafaring warriors from Norway, Sweden and Denmark who invaded other parts of Europe.*

- **The Norse gods** do not take much notice of humans. They are more concerned with battling giants and dealing with other magical creatures.

- **Odin occasionally likes** to disguise himself as a traveller and wander undetected through the world of humans.

- **Norse gods and goddesses** are not immortal. They can be killed by cunning magic or simple bravery, just like humans.

- **The most important warrior** goddesses are Odin's wife, Frigg (a mother goddess with fertility powers) and the beautiful Freya (goddess of love).

- **The daughters of Odin** were beautiful spirits called Valkyries. They flew over battlefields and took warriors who had died bravely to live happily in a place in Asgard called Valhalla.

- **Two days of the week** are named after Norse warrior gods. Wednesday means Woden's Day – Woden was another name for Odin, the father of the gods. Thursday means Thor's Day, after the Norse god of thunder.

- **The Aesir once fought** against gods and goddesses called the Vanir (or 'shining ones'). They finally made a peaceful alliance against the giants.

- **The ruler of the Vanir** was the fertility god Njord, ruler of the winds and the sea.

261

Norse world order

- **Two main written sources** tell us what the Norse people believed about the universe. *The Prose Edda* is a collection of myths recorded by an Icelander called Snorri Sturluson (1179–1241). *The Poetic Edda* is a collection of 34 ancient poems recorded in the 17th century.

- **Many Viking carvings** show pictures of what the Norse people believed the universe to be like.

- **The Norse people thought** there were nine worlds arranged on three levels.

- **The uppermost worlds** were Alfheim – home of the light elves, Vanaheim – home of the fertility gods, and Asgard – home of the warrior gods.

- **The middle worlds** were Midgard – home of humans, Nidavellir – home of the dwarves, Jotunheim – home of the giants, and Svartalfheim – home of the dark elves.

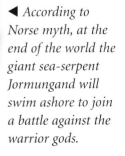

◀ *According to Norse myth, at the end of the world the giant sea-serpent Jormungand will swim ashore to join a battle against the warrior gods.*

● **Norse myth** said that a giant serpent called Jormungand lived in the sea surrounding the middle worlds, circling them.

● **The underworlds** were Muspellheim – a land of fire, and the freezing land of Niflheim, which included Hel – home of the dead.

● **The Norse warrior gods** kept young and strong by eating the Golden Apples of Youth belonging to a goddess called Iduna. Without these, they would face old age and death.

● **Characters from the Norse worlds** such as giants, dwarves and elves also found their way into many European fairy tales.

▲ *Norse kings had court poets who composed gripping poems about heroes and their battles. The poets performed them as entertainment.*

...FASCINATING FACT...
Inspiration for the names in JRR Tolkien's *The Lord of the Rings* trilogy came from characters in the nine Norse worlds.

The first Russians

- **Little is known** of the earliest days of Russia, because it was inhabited mainly by nomadic peoples who left few records – such as the Cimmerians (1200–700 BC) and later the Huns and the Khazars.

- **In the 800s** AD, Russia was on the major trade route from northwestern Europe to the world's richest cities – Constantinople and Baghdad.

- **Slavic peoples** set up trading towns such as Novgorod. They traded in amber, furs, honey, wax and wood.

- **From around** AD **860**, Viking adventurers raided and traded in the region. They were known as the Varangian Rus. The most famous of them was Rurik of Jutland, who took over Novgorod.

- **The city of Kiev** grew up further south, on the Dnieper River.

- **Soon the Varangian 'grand prince'** of Kiev ruled over a vast area historians call Kievan Rus. This covered what is now the Ukraine and eastern Russia.

- **Around** AD **970**, the Slavs took over the city of Kiev – under Prince Svyatoslav and his son, Vladimir.

- **Vladimir** made Kievan Rus the first Russian nation.

- **Legend says** that Vladimir sent people far and wide to study different religions. Nothing impressed them until they reached the Hagia Sophia in Constantinople. They were so stunned 'they knew not whether they were in heaven or on earth'.

- **Kiev quickly adopted** Byzantine Christianity. Within 50 years it had 200 beautiful churches – including its own Hagia Sophia – and Vladimir was Russia's first saint.

▶ *The beautiful cathedral of St Sophia in the city of Kiev resembles the Hagia Sophia in old Constantinople.*

Harun al-Rashid

- **Harun al-Rashid** (AD 766–809) was the most famous of all the caliphs.

- **In Harun's time**, Baghdad became the most glamorous city in the world, famed for its luxury as well as its poetry, music and learning.

- **Harun was famous** far and wide. He sent ambassadors to the Chinese emperor and an elephant to Charlemagne.

- **Zubaydah, Harun's wife**, would only drink from silver and gold cups studded with gems.

- **A great patron of the arts**, Harun gave lavish gifts to poets and musicians. Yet he also enjoyed watching dogs fight – and often had people executed.

- **Stories tell** how Harun would wander in the moonlight with his friend Abu Nuwas, the brilliant poet, as well as Masrur the executioner.

- **Harun has become famous** because he features in the famous collection of 200-odd tales of *The Thousand and One Nights*, or *The Arabian Nights*.

- *The Arabian Nights* includes such famous characters as Aladdin and his genie, Ali Baba and Sinbad the Sailor.

- **The tales begin** with King Shahriyar of Samarkand feeling distraught by his wife's unfaithfulness. He vows to marry a new girl each night and behead her in the morning.

- **The lovely princess Scheherazade** insists on marrying the king, then at night tells him a tale so entertaining that he lets her live another day to finish it. One story leads to another for 1001 nights, by which time the king has fallen completely in love with her.

◄ *The magic and romance of Harun's Baghdad is captured in the tales of* The Arabian Nights.

Holy Roman Empire

- **The Holy Roman Empire** was a mostly German empire, which lasted from AD 800 until 1806.

- **The empire began** when Pope Leo III tried to gain the protection of Charlemagne, the King of the Franks, by reviving the idea of the Roman Empire.

- **Pope Leo III** is said to have taken Charlemagne by surprise in St Peter's church in Rome – on Christmas Day AD 800 – and to have placed the crown of the empire on his head.

- **Charlemagne's Frankish Empire**, including France, Germany and Italy, became the Holy Roman Empire.

- **When Charlemagne died**, in AD 814, the new Holy Roman Empire fell apart.

- **In AD 962**, 150 years later, the German king, Otto I, gained control of Italy as well as Germany and insisted the Pope crown him Holy Roman Emperor.

- **Over the centuries**, the empire was continually beset by conflicts with both powerful Germans and the pope.

- **In 1076**, Pope Gregory VII and Emperor Henry IV were vying for control. Henry's subjects sided with the pope, so Henry had to give way.

- **Gregory forced Henry** to stand barefoot in snow for three days outside his castle in Tuscany to beg for a pardon.

- **The pope's Vatican** and other Italian cities gained almost complete independence from the emperor.

▲ *In 1250, the Holy Roman Empire extended from the North to the Mediterranean Sea. This is highlighted in brown. The Papal states (yellow), separated the Kingdom of the Two Sicilies, which also belonged to the Emperor.*

The Toltecs

- **By AD 900, the city of Teotihuacán** was destroyed and much of Mexico was in the hands of warrior tribes from the north.

- **Legend says** that Teotihuacán was destroyed by one of these warrior tribes called the Toltecs, led by their ruler Mixcóatl. The name Mixcóatl means 'Cloud Serpent'.

- **Under Mixcóatl's son**, Topiltzin, the Toltec were said to have built an empire and a capital at Tollan, now thought to be Tula, 45 km north of Mexico City.

- **Topiltzin** introduced the cult of the god Quetzalcóatl ('Feathered Serpent'), and took the name himself.

- **The Toltecs** were not only great warriors but fine builders and craftsmen. Tollan was full of pyramids, temples and other huge, impressive buildings.

- **Legend says Topiltzin Quetzalcóatl** was driven out of Tollan by jealous rivals – including the priests of the god Tezcatlipoca ('Smoking Mirror').

- **After leaving Tollan**, Quetzalcóatl sailed east into the Gulf of Mexico, vowing to return one day.

- **The Aztecs** were greatly influenced by the Toltecs. The Aztecs got the idea of human sacrifices from the priests of Tezcatlipoca. Some Aztecs believed that, when the Spanish arrived in 1519, it was Quetzalcóatl returning in vengeance.

- **The Toltec empire** broke up in the 12th century and Tollan vanished.

▶ *Toltec temples in Tollan were guarded by stone statues of warriors such as this.*

271

Toltec and Aztec tales

- **In Mexico between AD 900 and 1200,** the Toltecs were a great civilization. The Aztecs were a race of warriors who came to power in 1376. Their first ruler claimed to be a descendant of the chief Toltec god, and they adopted Toltec myths and legends.

- **The Toltecs built** huge pyramid temples, which still stand, covered in pictures telling their myths.

- **We know about Aztec myths** from an ancient Aztec calendar, and a document that explains how Aztec gods fit into the calendar.

- **The Toltecs and Aztecs believed** that both humans and the gods needed to make sacrifices in order to keep the universe alive.

- **In the beginning,** the gods created and destroyed four worlds one after another, because humans did not make enough sacrifices.

- **In order to create a sun** for the fifth world, two gods sacrificed themselves by jumping into a flaming bonfire.

◄ *The name Quetzalcóatl means 'feathered serpent'. His statue is found carved into many ancient sites in Central America.*

- **At first, the fifth world** consisted only of water with a female monster goddess floating in it, eating everything. The mighty gods Quetzalcóatl and Tezcatlipoca ripped the goddess apart and turned her body into the earth and the heavens.

- **The Aztecs believed** that the sun god and the earth monster needed sacrifices of human blood and hearts in order to remain fertile and alive.

- **Human beings were created** by Quetzalcóatl, from the powdered bones of his dead father and his own blood.

- **Quetzalcóatl and Tezcatlipoca** brought musicians and singers from the House of the Sun down to Earth. From then on, every living thing could create its own kind of music.

▲ *These Toltec ruins, known today as El Castillo, date from the 11th century.*

The Maoris

- **No human set foot** on New Zealand before around 2000 years ago.

- **The first settlers** in New Zealand were Polynesians.

- **The early Polynesian settlers** came to New Zealand by canoe, from islands in the Pacific.

- **Around** AD 100, Polynesians called the Maoris came here to settle from the Cook, Marquesas or Society Islands.

- **Maori tradition** tells how the Maoris arrived in waves of migration, beginning about 1150 and ending with the coming of a great fleet from the mythical land of Hawaiki, 200 years later.

- **Hawaiki** is thought to be the Pacific island of Tahiti.

◀ *The Maoris lived mostly near the coast or by rivers and travelled in light, swift canoes.*

- **Archaeologists** have found signs of Maori settlement in New Zealand dating back to AD 800 and earlier.

- **The first Maoris** lived mainly by hunting and fishing.

- **Maoris were skilled** woodworkers, building beautiful wooden houses covered in carvings.

▶ *The beautiful island of Tahiti is a tropical paradise. It is is said to be the mythical land of Hawaiki, from which fleets of Maori settlers sailed.*

Charlemagne

- **In AD 732**, the Frankish (early French) leader Charles Martel halted the great Muslim invasion of Europe – in battle at Tours in central France.

- **Charles Martel's son**, Pepin the Short, made sure of his family's hold on power in the Frankish kingdom. In AD 768, Pepin's son Charlemagne became 'King of the Franks'.

- **Charlemagne** (AD 742–814) was the greatest European ruler for 1000 years after the fall of Rome.

- **Charlemagne's name** means 'Charles the Great'.

- **Taking his armies** on 53 successful campaigns, Charlemagne was a great military leader. He scored victories against the Moors in Spain, and against Saxons and Avars in central Europe.

- **By AD 796**, Charlemagne had created an empire joining France, Germany, northern Italy and northern Spain.

- **He was a Christian**, and in AD 800, the Pope made Charlemagne Holy Roman Emperor.

- **Charlemagne was a great ruler** who set up an effective law system and introduced the idea of juries in trials.

- **Charlemagne knew Latin**, German and Greek, and he encouraged scholarship, helped by the great teacher Alcuin.

- **The palace school** in Charlemagne's capital, Aachen, was the most important school in Europe.

▶ *This beautiful goblet, known as 'Charlemagne's cup', dates back to the time of the Crusaders.*

▼ *After his death, many legends grew up about Charlemagne.*
We know that he must have been a powerful personality.
One eyewitness said: 'He had a broad
and strong body of unusual
height…and strode with
a firm step and held
himself like a man.'

The Magyars

- **The plains by the river Danube** (an area now in Hungary) were settled early in the history of humankind, although little is known of the region before it formed the Roman provinces Dacia and Pannonia. At this time, it was home to Celts and Slavs.

- **Roman Dacia and Pannonia** fell early to the barbarian invaders – Goths, Huns and Avars.

- **In AD 796,** the Avars were crushed by Charlemagne.

- **In AD 892,** another Frankish king called Arnulf asked a people called the Magyars to help him against the Moravians, who now lived on the Danube plain.

- **The Magyars were a people** who lived from 3000 to 800 BC on the steppes near Russia's river Don.

- **In AD 889,** the Magyars had been driven to the edge of their land by a people called the Pechenegs, so they were grateful for Arnulf's call.

- **Led by the legendary Arpad**, the Magyars swept into Hungary and made it their home.

- **In AD 975,** Arpad's great-grandson, Géza, became a Christian and began to form the Magyars into the Hungarian nation.

- **Géza's son, Stephen** (AD 997–1038), carried on his work and became the first king of Hungary.

- **King Stephen**, also called St Stephen, was crowned by the Pope on Christmas Day, AD 1000.

▲ *King Stephen is a famous figure in Hungarian history and his crown became the symbol of the nation.*

Famous villains

- **Ancient history** has many famous villains – but most were called villains by their enemies, so we can never be sure just how bad they were.

- **Many of the best-known villains** are Roman, including the emperors Caligula and Nero and Sejanus, Emperor Tiberius's minister, who is believed to have poisoned Drusus, Tiberius's son.

- **Emperor Claudius's wife** Messalina (AD 22–48) made Claudius execute any man who resisted her advances.

- **Claudius's fourth wife**, his niece Agrippina (AD 15–59), probably poisoned him to make way for her son, Nero.

- **Many stories** are told of the Chinese emperor Shi Huangdi's cruelty, including his killing of 460 scholars.

- **Artaxerxes** (died 338 BC) was the cruel Persian king who ravaged Egypt in 343 BC.

▲ *Emperor Nero is painted as a corrupt villain of ancient Rome, blamed for the Great Fire of Rome in AD 64.*

- **Artaxerxes and all his sons** except Arses were murdered by his minister Bagoas in 338 BC. Bagoas then killed Arses and tried to poison the next king, Darius III. Darius found out and made Bagoas drink the poison himself.

- **Herod the Great** (73–4 BC) of Judea (modern-day Israel) was a strong king, but he is known best for the murder of his beloved wife Mariamne in a jealous rage and the biblical tale of the 'Slaughter of the Innocents'. This tale relates how Herod ordered soldiers to kill all babies in Bethlehem in order to get rid of the infant Jews, who prophets had said would be a threat to him.

- **Pontius Pilate** (AD 36) was the Roman governor of Judea who allowed Jesus to be crucified.

- **Theodora**, wife of Justinian I, was notorious for her secret police.

▶ *The Roman emperor Caligula was malicious and mentally unstable, striking terror wherever he went.*

Early English kings

- **Egbert, king of Wessex** from AD 802 to 839, became in effect the first king of England when he conquered Mercia at Ellandun in AD 829. But his rule lasted just a year before Mercian king Wiglaf claimed it back.

  - **For 100 years**, much of England was lost to the Danes, but Alfred the Great's son Edward and his daughter Aethelflaed gradually drove the Danes out by AD 918.

  - **England's kingship** really began with Athelstan, crowned 'King of all Britain' at Kingston on 4 September, AD 925.

  - **'Ethelred the Unready'** was king of England AD 978–1013 and 1014–1016. *Rede* was old English for advice, and his name meant he was always badly advised.

▲ King Canute.

  - **Ethelred created** so much distrust among his subjects that the Danes easily reconquered England in AD 980.

- **In 1013**, the Dane Sweyn Forkbeard became king of England.

- **When Sweyn died**, Ethelred made a comeback until Sweyn's son, Canute, drove him out. Canute became king in 1016 by marrying Ethelred's widow.

- **Canute ruled well**. A story tells how he rebuked flatterers by showing how even he could not stop the tide coming in.

- **After Canute**, in 1035, came Harold I (1035–1040), followed by Harthacanute (1040–1042). Ethelred's son, Edward the Confessor, then became king – but the Danes did not want a Saxon king.

- **The Danes called on** their Norwegian allies, led first by Magnus then Harold Hardraada, to win back the throne.

The city of Winchester in southern England was Alfred the Great's capital, and in his time it became a great centre of learning. Canute also made it his capital, and his son Hardecanute is buried here, with Alfred.

King Arthur

◀ *Mont Saint-Michel is a rocky islet off the coast of northwest France, where legend says King Arthur once slew a giant.*

- **Legends about** an extraordinary British king called Arthur have been popular for over 800 years, yet historians have never been able to prove whether he was a real figure in history.

- **If a real Arthur did exist**, he is likely to have lived much earlier than the medieval times of the legends.

- **Many authors have written** Arthurian legends over the centuries, including the French medieval poet Chretien de Troyes, the 15th-century writer Sir Thomas Malory, and the Victorian poet Lord Tennyson.

- **Arthur's father** was said to be King Uther Pendragon. The name means 'dragon's head'.

▶ *King Arthur was finally killed by his own son. One legend says that his body was buried at the holy site of Glastonbury in England.*

- **One legend says** that Arthur slew a fearsome giant at Mont-Saint-Michel in France, then conquered the Roman Empire.

- **Many legends focus** on the knights at Arthur's court and the idea of courtly love, in which women are purer beings in God's eyes than men. A lover knight is required to obey the wishes of his lady without question or reward.

- **Arthur's knights** went on many dangerous quests to test their bravery and honour. The most difficult was a search for the Holy Grail – a goblet that caught Jesus's blood as he died on the cross. It was believed to disappear when anyone who had sinned came near it.

- **The Round Table** was first mentioned in legends written by the French medieval poet, Robert Wace, in 1155.

- **Arthur is finally killed** by his enemy Mordred – who is in fact his own son.

- **Some legends say** that King Arthur was taken to a country of blessed souls called Avalon and will return when Britain falls into greatest danger.

The first Scots

- **The first settlers** came to Scotland around 7000 years ago, and the remains of their huts can be seen on Skara Brae in Orkney.

- **People called Picts** arrived here shortly before the times of the Romans, who failed to conquer Scotland.

- **The Picts may have come** from the Black Sea region. They got their name from the tattooed pictures on their bodies.

- *Brochs* are 15-m-high stone towers built for defence around 100 BC by ancestors of the Picts.

- **Celts called Scots** came from Dalriada in Ireland in *c*.470. They soon conquered the west.

- **After St Columba** came to set up Iona monastery in AD 563, Scotland was slowly converted to Christianity.

- **In AD 563**, Scotland was split into four kingdoms: the Scots' Dalriada in the west, the Picts in the north, the Britons' Strathclyde in the southwest, and Bernicia or Lothian of the Angles in the east.

◄ *The Romans gave the Picts their name – picti is Latin for 'painted people', after the Picts' decorative body tattoos.*

- **In AD 685**, the Picts drove out the Angles, and in AD 843, the Dalriada king, Kenneth McAlpin, conquered the Picts to create a country called Alba, the first Scotland.

- **In the AD 900s and 1000s,** many people fought to be king in Scotland. Kenneth III killed Constantine III to become king. Malcolm II killed Kenneth III and Duncan I who followed him was killed by his general, Macbeth. Macbeth was killed by Malcolm III.

- **Malcolm III's wife** was Saint Margaret (1045–1093), brought up in Hungary where her father was in exile.

▶ *Macbeth (died 1057) was the Scottish king who became the basis for Shakespeare's tragedy* Macbeth. *The real Macbeth killed Duncan in battle, not in his bed as in Shakespeare's famous play.*

287

The Norman invasion

- **On 5 January, 1066,** the English king Edward the Confessor died. As he died, he named as his successor Harold Godwinson – the powerful earl of the kingdom of Wessex.

- **Harold's claim** to the English throne was challenged by William, the duke of Normandy in France. William claimed that Edward had already promised him the throne.

▲ *William's troops rapidly seized control of England. This was the last time the country was conquered by a foreign power.*

- **Harold Hardraade**, the king of Norway, also challenged Harold's claim.

- **In autumn 1066**, Hardraade invaded northern England with Harold Godwinson's brother Tostig. His army was routed by Harold's at Stamford Bridge on 25 September.

- **On 28 September**, William's Norman army of 7000 crossed from France and landed at Pevensey in southern England.

- **Harold marched his army** south to meet the Normans, walking over 300 km to London in just five days.

▲ *The Normans commemorated their victory at the Battle of Hastings with a famous tapestry, made in England, now in Bayeux in France.*

- **Harold's tired army** met the Normans at Hastings in Sussex on 14 October, and took a stand by the Hoar Apple Tree on Caldbec Hill.

- **Harold's army was attacked** by William's archers, but axe-wielding English house-carles (infantry) put the Norman cavalry to flight. Harold was then killed – perhaps by an arrow. The English fought on for a while before fleeing.

- **After the battle**, William moved on London, where he was crowned king in Westminster Abbey on 25 December.

- **Within a few years**, the Normans had conquered England.

289

The great khans

- **The Mongols were nomads** who lived in yurts (huts made of felt) in central Asia, as many still do.

- **In 1180**, a 13-year-old Mongol boy called Temujin was made khan (chief) of his tribe. He soon became a great leader, and in 1206 he was hailed as Genghis Khan (Chief of all Men).

- **Genghis Khan** was a brilliant and ruthless soldier. His armies terrified their enemies, and butchered anyone they met.

- **Genghis's horse archers** could kill at 180 m while riding at full gallop. They once rode 440 km in just three days.

- **In just four years** (1210–1214), Genghis Khan conquered northern China, much of India, and Persia. His empire stretched right through Asia, extending from Korea to the Caspian Sea.

▼ *Genghis Khan was a man of incredible physical strength and willpower. He could be tyrannical and cruel, yet philosophers would travel from far away to talk with him about religion.*

290

- **After Genghis Khan died** in 1227, his son Ogedai ravaged Armenia, Hungary and Poland.

- **Genghis Khan's grandson**, Kublai Khan, conquered the rest of China in 1265 and made himself the first of a line of Mongol emperors of China called Yuans. The Yuans lasted until 1368.

  - **Kublai's rule** in China was harsh, but he was greatly admired by the Venetian traveller, Marco Polo.

    - **Kublai Khan created** a grand new capital called Ta-tu ('the Great Capital') – now Beijing.

    - **Kublai Khan adopted** Chinese ways of government and ruled with such efficiency that China became very rich.

◄ *A man of vision, energy, and a certain ruthlessness, Kublai Khan encouraged the arts and sciences, rebuilt Beijing and made Buddhism the state religion – suppressing Taoism in the process. First emperor of the Yuan dynasty, he gave China a strong separate identity and led a glittering court that was famed far and wide.*

The Aztecs

- **In the 1200s**, people called the Aztecs found that the only place to settle in crowded Mexico was on a lake.

- **By 1325**, the Aztecs were powerful and their lake home Tenochtitlán was a splendid city with canals and temples.

- **Aztec farmers** walked or rowed dugout canoes for hours to markets in cities like Tlatelolco to sell farm produce in return for cocoa beans, which they used as money.

- **In Aztec society**, a powerful priest-king plus priests and nobles ruled ordinary folk and slaves with an iron hand.

- **The Aztecs built vast pyramids** topped by temples where priests made bloody human sacrifices on a huge scale.

- **The Aztecs made human sacrifices** to their god Huitzilopochtli. They believed that this gave him the strength to fight off the night and bring the morning.

- **In a special, sacred ball game** teams hit a rubber ball through a small ring in an I-shaped court – using their hips, knees and elbows. This very violent game caused serious injury, even death.

- **One of the ways we know** about the Aztecs is from folding books of picture-writing called codices, written by Aztec scribes. The most famous is the *Codex Mendoza*.

- **By 1521**, the Aztec Empire was finished. Spanish treasure-seekers led by Hernando Cortés defeated Montezuma II, the Aztec emperor, and plundered the Aztecs' land and riches.

▲ *The vast Pyramid of the Sun, built as four huge steps, is part of the ruined Aztec city of Teotihuacán. Archaeologists have found a human skeleton at the corner of each step – buried alive as part of the Aztecs' rituals of human sacrifice.*

...FASCINATING FACT...
Every year Tenochtitlán took in 9000
tonnes of corn, beans and seeds in taxes.

The Magna Carta

- **John I was king of England** from 1199 to 1216. He was one of the most unpopular kings in history.

- **He was nicknamed** 'Lackland' by his father Henry II because, unlike his older brothers Richard and Geoffrey, John did not inherit land to provide him with an income.

- **John was hated** for his cruelty, for the demands he put on his barons for tax and military service and for trying to seize the crown while his popular brother King Richard the Lionheart was Crusading.

- **On 15 June, 1215**, rebellious barons compelled John to meet them at Runnymede on the Thames and agree to their demands by sealing the Magna Carta ('Great Charter').

- **At the time**, ordinary people gained little at the time from the Magna Carta but it is now seen as the world's first bill of rights and the start of fair government in England.

- **The Magna Carta showed** that even the king had to obey the law.

- **The Magna Carta contained** 63 clauses, most relating to feudal customs.

- **Clause 39** gave every free man the right to a fair trial. Clause 40 gave everyone the right to instant justice.

- **Some parts of the Magna Carta** dealt with weights and measures, foreign merchants and catching fish.

- **John got the Pope to annul** the document three days later, but it was reissued in 1225, after John's death.

▼ *The barons compelled King John to put his seal (wax stamp) on the Magna Carta at Runnymede in 1215.*

Saladin

- **Saladin was perhaps the greatest** Muslim (Islamic) leader of the Middle Ages. To his people he was a saintly hero. Even his Christian enemies were awed by his honour and bravery.

- **He is famed as a brilliant soldier**, but Saladin was also deeply religious. He built many schools, mosques and canals.

- **Saladin was a Kurd**, born in Tikrit, now in Iraq, in 1137, but he was brought up in Syria.

- **He became a soldier** at the age of 14. Right from the start he had an intense belief in the idea of *jihad* – the holy war to defend the Islamic religion.

- **Saladin's leadership** brought him to prominence and in 1169 he was effectively made sultan (ruler) of Egypt.

- **By diplomacy and conquest**, he united the different Muslim peoples, which had been torn apart by rivalries for the 88 years since the Crusaders captured Jerusalem in 1099.

- **In 1187**, with Islam united, Saladin was able to turn his attentions to driving the Crusaders out of the Near East.

◄ *Saladin must have been a single-minded and ambitious man, but those who met him said he was the most humble, moral and generous of rulers. Strangely, he died virtually penniless.*

- **On 4 July, 1187**, Saladin routed the Crusaders at Hattin in Palestine. This victory was so devastating to the Crusaders that within three months the Muslims had recaptured almost every bit of land they had lost.

- **Shocked by the fall of Jerusalem**, the Christian countries threw themselves into their last major Crusade, led in part by the great Richard the Lionheart.

- **Such was Saladin's leadership** that the Muslims fought off the Crusaders' onslaught. Eventually, Richard and Saladin drew up a truce that ended the Crusades.

▶ *Here, a knight and his personal page prepare to do battle in the Crusades. These were holy wars fought between 1099 and 1291, in order to recapture Christian holy sites from Muslims.*

Bannockburn

- **In 1286, King Alexander III** of Scotland died. His grand-daughter – Margaret, 'Maid of Norway' – died four years later. Their deaths left no obvious successor to the Scottish throne.

- **The Scottish lords agreed** to the suggestion of English king Edward I that he should decide between the 13 rival claimants, including John de Balliol and Robert Bruce.

- **Edward I marched** into Scotland and imprisoned the leading claimant John de Balliol. Some of Balliol's rivals, such as Robert, supported Edward, and he was soon recognized as king.

- **The Scottish lords** did not react, but a small landowner called William Wallace began a heroic fight. With a band of just 30 men, he attacked Lanark, took the garrison and killed the English sheriff. Commoners flocked to his aid.

- **On 4 May, 1297**, Wallace's small rebel army scored a stunning victory over the English at Stirling. He drove the English from Scotland and marched on into England. But the Scottish lords still gave him no support.

  - **Wallace was captured** by the English in 1305. He was hanged, drawn (disembowelled) and quartered (cut in four pieces). His head was stuck on a pole on London Bridge.

  - **Wallace's heroism** inspired Robert Bruce to lead a rebellion that finally included the Scottish lords.

◀ *The story goes that, while in hiding, Robert Bruce was inspired to go on fighting after seeing a spider struggle up its thread again and again – and eventually succeed.*

- **Letting his enemies think** he was dead, Robert launched a campaign from Ireland in 1306. Within two years he had cleared the English from Scotland again.

- **Robert scored a last decisive victory** over the English under Edward II at Bannockburn on 23–24 June, 1314. With this victory, the Scots regained their independence.

····FASCINATING FACT····
At Bannockburn, just 9000 Scots may
have routed an English army of 25,000.

▶ *Scottish hero Robert Bruce freed the Scots from English control at the Battle of Bannockburn, in 1314.*

African empires

▶ *The splendid ancient city of Great Zimbabwe, now in ruins, flourished in southern Africa and gave its name to modern Zimbabwe. At its height, the city's population was up to 18,000.*

- **From *c.*1230 to *c.*1600**, the interaction of black, Bantu-speaking Africans with Arab Muslims shaped African history.

- **In East Africa**, Bantu people and Arabs mixed to create the culture and language called Swahili.

- **Trade in gold and ivory** created thriving ports down the East African coast – such as Zanzibar and Kilwa.

- **Inland, the city of Great Zimbabwe** (the name means 'house of stone') flourished within its huge granite walls. It is now a ruin, but in the 1400s, gold made this city the heart of the Monomatapa Empire.

- **Further inland**, by the lakes of Uganda, were the extraordinary grass palaces belonging to the Bugandan kings.

- **In West Africa**, trade across the Sahara made kingdoms like Ghana flourish. Two great empires grew up – first Mali (1240–1500) and then Songhai, which peaked in the 1500s.

- **The Mali Empire** centred on the city of Timbuktu.

- **Timbuktu's glory began** in 1324, when King Mansa Musa went on a grand trip to Mecca with camels laden with gold and brought back the best scholars and architects.

- **Timbuktu** means 'mother with a large navel', after an old woman said to have first settled here. But from

▲ *A bust made by the Edo people of Benin, Africa's greatest city during the 1600s.*

1324 to 1591 Timbuktu was a splendid city with what may have been the world's biggest university, catering for up to 25,000 students.

- **The Songhai Empire** in the 1400s stretched right across West Africa from what is now Nigeria to Gambia. It reached its peak under Sunni Ali (1464–1492), who conquered Timbuktu, and his son Askia the Great (1493–1528).

Serfs and lords

- **When the Roman Empire** collapsed, a new way of ordering society, called the feudal system, emerged.

- **In the feudal system**, a king or overlord gave a lord a fief (a grant of land). In return, the lord swore to train and fight for the king as a knight (horse warrior). Land was the security because it could not be moved. Any lord who got a fief was called his king's vassal.

- **In AD 732, Charles Martel**, ruler of the Franks (now France) drove back the invading Muslims at the Battle of Tours. But he was worried he might not beat the brilliant Muslim horsemen if they came back. So he developed one of the first feudal systems.

- **There were different levels** in the feudal system. The count of Champagne had 2017 vassal knights, but he himself was vassal to ten overlords, including the king of France.

- **Only noblemen** could join the feudal system, but it soon took over most land in Europe, as kings tied their subjects by grants of land.

- **There was a saying**: 'No land without a lord; and no lord without a land'.

- **With so much land in fiefs**, most peasants were serfs, legally bound to their lords by the 'manorial' system, which centred on a lord's manor or castle.

▶ *Most people in medieval Europe were poor serfs tied to their lord. They lived in basic huts clustered round the lord's manor house and scraped a meagre living.*

- **In return for** working their lord's land, serfs were given small plots of land to live off.

- **Serfs could not** be evicted, but had few rights. They could not leave the village, marry or sell their possessions without their lord's permission.

- **The feudal and manorial systems** reached their peak in the 1100s but then began to decline.

▲ *In return for basic food and housing, serfs worked their lords' lands and had virtually no personal freedom. In the Middle Ages, most people in Europe worked on the land. Almost everything they owned, from food and clothing to land and animals belonged to the local lord.*

Crusades

- **In the 11th century**, western Christian countries were threatened by the Muslim Seljuk Turks. In 1095, they were just outside Constantinople, capital of the Byzantine Empire and the centre of Christianity in the east. The emperor Alexander Comnenus appealed to the Pope, Urban II, for help.

- **Urban II held a meeting** of church leaders at Clermont in France. He called for warriors to drive back the Turks and reclaim the Holy Land. This became a holy pilgrimage or Crusade. 'Crusade' comes from the Latin *crux*, meaning 'cross'.

- **Before the armies** could set out, 50,000 peasants began marching from western Europe on their own 'People's Crusade' to free the Holy Land. They had been stirred by tales of Turkish atrocities, spread by a preacher called Peter the Hermit. Many peasants died or got lost on the way; the rest were killed by Turks.

- **In 1096**, armies of French and Norman knights set out on the First Crusade. At Constantinople, they joined up with the Byzantines. Despite quarrelling on the way, they captured Jerusalem in 1099 and then set about massacring Jews and Turks.

◄ *When the Crusader knights set out to fight for control of Jerusalem, in the Holy Land, they went with different motives. Some were courageous men with a deep sense of honour and a holy purpose. Others were adventurers, out for personal gain or glory. This Crusader wears the famous uniform of the Knights Templars.*

- **After capturing Jerusalem**, the Crusaders divided the Holy Land into four parts, together known as Outremer (say: *oot-rer-mare*), which meant 'land beyond the seas'. The Crusaders ruled Outremer for 200 years and built great castles like Krak des Chevaliers in Syria.

- **Two bands of soldier-monks** formed to protect pilgrims journeying to the Holy Land – the Knights Hospitallers of St John and the Knights Templars. The Hospitallers wore black with a white cross. The Templars wore a red cross on white, which became the symbol of all Crusaders.

- **By 1144**, Crusader control in Outremer weakened, and the Turks advanced. King Louis VII of France and King Conrad of Germany launched a Second Crusade. But by 1187, Saladin had retaken most of Outremer.

- **In 1190**, the three most powerful men in Europe – Richard I of England, Philip II of France and Frederick Barbarossa (Holy Roman Emperor) – set off on the Third Crusade. Barbarossa died on the way and Philip II gave up. Only Richard went on, and secured a truce with Saladin.

- **In 1212**, thousands of poor people set off on what is known as the Children's Crusade to take back Jerusalem, led by French farm boy Stephen of Cloyes. Sadly, most were lured on to ships in Marseilles and sold into slavery or prostitution.

> ...FASCINATING FACT...
> The most famous Crusader in England was King
> Richard I, known as the Lionheart for his bravery.

305

Marco Polo

- **Marco Polo** was a famous Italian traveller. Born *c*.1254 in Venice, he spent many years in the court of Kublai Khan, emperor of China.

- **In the 1200s**, most of Europe knew China only as the romantic land of 'Cathay'. But Marco's father Niccolo and uncle Maffeo were well-travelled merchants who had already been there.

- **In 1271**, Niccolo and Maffeo invited 17-year-old Marco to come with them to Cathay again.

- **The Polos took** four years to reach China, travelling on foot and horse along the 'Silk Road' – a route north of the Himalayan mountains. The Silk Road was the way merchants brought silk from China to Europe.

- **Kublai Khan welcomed** the Polos. Marco had a gift for languages and became one of the Khan's diplomats.

◀ *While in China, Marco Polo is said to have served as governor of Yangzhou.*

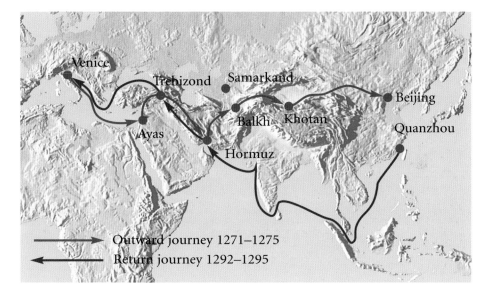

▲ *Marco Polo was one of the few Europeans to journey all the way to China and back in the Middle Ages.*

● **After 17 years**, the Polos decided to return, but the Khan would only let them go if they took a princess who was to be wed to the Khan's grand-nephew in Persia.

● **The Polos arrived back** in Venice in 1295, laden with jewels, silks and spices.

● **Marco Polo later wrote** an account of his time in China while a prisoner of war in Genoa, dictating it to a man called Rustichello.

● **Marco's tales** were so fantastic that some called the book *Il milione* ('The million lies'). Some experts now think that he reported the truth as he saw it. Others think he just recycled other travellers' tales.

● **Christopher Columbus** was just one of many people who were inspired by Marco Polo's accounts.

307

The Black Death

- **The Black Death** was the terrible epidemic that ravaged Europe between 1347 and 1351.

- **The Black Death** was perhaps the worst disaster ever to have struck humanity.

- **Worldwide,** it is estimated that the Black Death killed around 75 million people.

▲ *The Plague brought death so close to people that they began to think of it as a real person.*

- **The Black Death** killed 25 million people in Europe.

- **The disease probably started** in China. It was transmitted to Europeans when a Kipchak (Mongol) raiding party catapulted infected corpses into a Genoese trading centre in the Crimea.

- **The plague reached Genoa** in 1347 and spread west and north, reaching London and Paris in 1348.

- **The plague was carried** first by rat fleas that could also live on humans. It then changed to pneumonic plague, which was spread through coughs and sneezes.

- **After the Black Death,** fields were littered with bodies. Houses, villages and towns stood silent and empty.

- **Afterwards** there was such a shortage of labour that wages soared and many serfs gained their freedom.

▲ *Plague returned several times over the centuries, including London's Great Plague of 1665. Houses struck by this highly infectious scourge were marked with a cross.*

...FASCINATING FACT...
The Black Death killed more than one in
every four Europeans in just four years.

309

The Hundred Years War

- **The Hundred Years War** was a long war between France and England, lasting from 1337 to 1453.

- **The war was caused** by disputes over Guyenne (English land in southwest France), English claims to the French throne, French support for the Scots and French efforts to block the English wool trade in Belgium.

- **In 1337**, French king Philip VI tried to take over Guyenne. English king Edward III, whose mother was sister to three French kings, retaliated by claiming the French throne.

  - **In 1340**, Edward won a great naval battle off Sluis, Belgium.

  - **In 1346**, Edward III's archers – outnumbered three to one – routed the greatest French knights at Crécy with their 2-m-long yew bows, and so hastened the end of knighthood.

  - **In 1347**, Edward III took the French port of Calais.

  - **In 1356**, Edward III's son, the Black Prince, won a great victory over the French at Poitiers.

  - **In 1415** was the last great English victory was Henry V's at Agincourt – 6000 English beat a French army of 30,000.

  - **The English** won most battles, but the French won the war because they had three times the resources.

◄ The greatest knight of the war was Edward the Black Prince (1330–1376), hero of the Battles of Crécy, Poitiers and Navarette.

▲ *In the Battle of Agincourt (1415), the French failed to learn lessons from previous defeats and Henry V won a glorious victory.*

...FASCINATING FACT...
The tide turned for the French in 1429, when
Joan of Arc led them to victory at Orléans.

The Hanseatic League

- **By the 1400s**, the feudal system of knights fighting part-time in exchange for land was outmoded. Kings now relied on full-time armies.

- **Kings turned** to newly rich merchants to pay for their armies, so merchants gained power. The Italians invented banks to give loans.

- **From the 1300s**, many serfs gained freedom and became prosperous 'yeoman' farmers. They needed merchants to sell their produce.

- **After the Crusades**, silks, spices and riches from the east were traded in the Mediterranean region for cloth, hides and iron. In northern Europe, the wool trade thrived.

- **In the 1300s and 1400s**, trading towns grew up across western Europe – Antwerp, Flanders, Bruges, Bristol, Norwich, York, Florence, Venice, Milan and many others.

- **Trading towns** grew powerful. In England, many became boroughs with charters giving them some self-rule.

- **Merchants** and traders set up guilds (like trade unions) to defend their rights.

- **In 1241**, the German ports of Hamburg and Lübeck set up a *hanse* (guild) to protect merchants against pirates. The *hanse* grew into a very powerful Hanseatic League that monopolized trade around the Baltic Sea.

- **The Hanseatic League** set up special areas in cities across north Europe and controlled most trading routes. The League also put financial pressure on kings and lords to keep them at peace, and not to disrupt trade.

- **Hanseatic merchants** brought raw materials, spices and silks from eastern Europe and traded them for cloth, linen, silverware and woollen clothes from the west.

► *Riches from the Hanseatic traders helped Hamburg build a great cathedral in the Middle Ages.*

The Great Schism

- **In the Middle Ages,** kings and lords battled with the Church over who had the right to run people's lives.

- **The Church** was all-powerful but riddled with corruption. Men like John Wycliffe (1320–1384) began to argue that it had too much power. He was supported by English kings.

- **Between 1214 and 1294,** scholars called 'scholastics', such as Roger Bacon, tried to use reason to understand Christian ideas.

- **The French scholar Peter Abelard** argued that we should ask questions. 'By doubting, we come to inquiry, and by inquiry we come to truth.'

- **Churchmen** like Bernard of Clairvaux opposed scholastics: 'the faith of the righteous believes; it does not dispute.'

- **In 1302,** Pope Boniface VIII issued a decree called the *Unum sanctum*, stating that everyone was subject to him.

- **French king Philip IV** said Boniface was trying to claim authority over the French king and French people.

- **In 1309,** Pope Clement V moved from Rome to Avignon in France. This became home for a series of French Popes, until Pope Gregory XI went back to Rome in 1377.

- **When Gregory XI died** in 1378, there was a Great Schism (split) in the Church. Some claimed Italian Urban VI as Pope. Others supported Robert from Switzerland. Urban stayed in Rome and Robert went back to Avignon. In 1409, some church leaders declared a third Pope.

- **In 1417,** the Great Schism was ended when a council of all Church leaders elected Martin V as Pope in Rome. But the dispute had weakened the Church's authority fatally.

▲ The impressive Palace of the Popes in Avignon, southern France, was built between 1314 and 1370. It was the home of the French Popes for 100 years during the time of the Great Schism.

315

The Ottoman wars

- **In 1281, a new power** began to emerge in Turkey from a tiny state called Sögüt, which was led by a ruler called Osman.

- **Over 200 years** a huge Muslim empire was built up, called the Ottoman Empire after Osman's descendants. It stretched from the Euphrates River on the borders of Persia to the Danube in Hungary.

- **In 1453**, Christian Constantinople fell to the Ottoman Turks and became their capital.

- **For centuries**, the Christian countries of Europe were threatened by Turkish expansion.

▲ *The Barbarossa brothers, Aruj and Khir, were Turkish pirates who helped to bring Tunisia and Algeria into the Ottoman Empire.*

- **Ottoman power peaked** in the 1520s under Suleiman, known as Qanuni ('law-giver') by Turks and 'the Magnificent' by Europeans because of his splendid court.

- **Suleiman** took all Hungary and attacked Vienna in 1529.

- **In 1522**, Suleiman took the island of Rhodes from his sworn enemies, the Knights of St John, who moved to Malta and built the fort of Valetta.

- **In the 1520s,** the Turkish pirate Khayr or Barbarossa (Spanish for Redbeard) took most of North Africa and became an Ottoman admiral. Algeria and the Barbary coast (North Africa) became a feared base for pirates for 300 years.

- **In 1565**, Suleiman attacked the Knights of St John in Valetta, but they survived.

- **When the Turks attacked** Cyprus in 1571, Venetian, Spanish and Papal fleets combined to crush them at the crucial battle of Lepanto in Greece. Turkish power declined after this.

▶ *Lepanto was the last great battle between fleets of galleys – warships powered by huge banks of oarsmen.*

317

The Wars of the Roses

- **The Wars of the Roses** were a series of civil wars in England in the 1400s as two branches of the Plantagenet family fought for the English throne.

- **On one side** was the house of York, with a white rose as its emblem. On the other was the house of Lancaster, with a red rose as its emblem.

- **The wars began** when Lancastrian king Henry VI became insane in 1453. With the country in chaos, Warwick the 'kingmaker' set up Richard, duke of York as Protector in Henry's place.

- **In 1455, Henry VI** seemed to recover and war broke out between Lancastrians and Yorkists.

- **Richard was killed** at the Battle of Wakefield in 1460, but Henry VI became insane again.

- **A crushing Yorkist victory** at Towton, near York, in 1461, put Richard's son on the throne as Edward IV.

- **Edward IV made enemies** of his brothers Clarence and Warwick, who invaded England from France in 1470 with Henry VI's queen Margaret of Anjou and drove Edward out.

◀ *The white – and red – roses were emblems of the rival houses of York and Lancaster. When Henry VII married Elizabeth of York, he combined the two to make the Tudor rose.*

- **Henry VI was brought** back for seven months before Edward's Yorkists defeated the Lancastrians at Barnet and Tewkesbury. Henry VI was murdered.

- **When Edward IV died** in 1483, his son Edward V was still a boy. When young, Edward and his brother vanished – probably murdered in the Tower of London – and their uncle Richard III seized the throne.

- **Richard III** made enemies among the Yorkists, who sided with Lancastrian Henry Tudor. Richard III was killed at Bosworth Field on 22 August 1485. Henry Tudor became Henry VII and married Elizabeth of York to end the wars.

▲ *Richard was a harsh man, but not the evil monster portrayed in Shakespeare's play,* Richard III.

319

Monasteries

- **Monasteries played an important role** in medieval life in Europe, reaching a peak in the 1200s.

- **The most famous monastery** was Cluny in France, but there were thousands of others in France and England.

- **Most had a church** called an abbey, some of which are among the greatest medieval buildings.

- **Monasteries were the places** where the poor went for welfare and they were also the only hospitals.

- **They were also** places for scholars to study. They were the only libraries. Most great works of medieval art, literature and scholarship came from monasteries.

▲ *Like most English monasteries, the great 12th-century Cistercian monastery at Tintern in Wales was destroyed by Henry VIII.*

- **Monasteries were great landowners** with immense power and wealth. In England, monasteries owned a third of the land and a quarter of the country's wealth. They were also Europe's biggest single employers.

- **Many monsteries oppressed** the poor by taking over land and taking a heavy toll in tithes (church taxes).

- **Many became notorious** for the indulgence of their monks in fine food and high living.

- **New orders of monks** attempted every now and then to go back to a simpler life, like the Cistercians from Citeaux in France and the Premonstratensians from Laon in France.

▲ *Franciscan friars. The Franciscan order was founded by St Francis of Assisi in the early 1200s.*

- **Cistercians** founded monasteries in barren places like Fountains in Yorkshire. But even they grew rich and lazy.

China

- **After almost a century of chaos**, the Song dynasty (family) of emperors came to power in China in AD 960. The Songs ruled until the early 1200s, when the Mongol Khans invaded and their time is perhaps the golden age of Chinese civilization.

- **The Song rulers** renounced the warlike policies that had kept China in strife, and brought peace by paying tribute money to the barbarian peoples in the north. They had a huge army, but this was partly to give jobs to hundreds of thousands of poor Chinese.

- **The Song slowly got rid** of soldiers from the government and replaced them with civil servants.

  - **In earlier times**, only aristocrats tended to hold key posts in government, but under the Song, anyone could enter for the civil service exams. Competition to do well in the exams was intense, and the main yearly exams became major events in the calendar.

◀ *When the Mongol Khans seized China from the Song, they made a new capital in the north at Beijing. At its centre lies a walled area containing the emperor's palaces. It is called the Forbidden City because only the emperor and his servants could enter it.*

- **The civil service exams** stressed not practical skills but the study of literature and the classic works of the thinker Confucius. So the Song civil service was full of learned, cultured men, known in the west as mandarins. Ou Yang-hsiu was a typical mandarin – statesman, historian, poet, philosopher, wine and music connoisseur and brilliant player of the chess-like game *wei-ch'i*.

- **Under the Song**, the Chinese population soared, trade prospered and all kinds of advances were made in science and technology – from the invention of gunpowder and the sailors' compass to paper and printing. Technologically, China was about 500 years ahead of Europe.

- **The Song period** is also known for its exquisite landscape paintings and fine porcelain, which is why good porcelain is called 'China'.

- **In 1126**, barbarian invasions forced the Song to move their capital from Kaifeng in the north to Hangzhou (modern Shanghai) in the south.

- **By 1275**, Hangzhou was the world's largest city, with a population of a million. Its warm climate encouraged a lively, leisurely lifestyle. The city was full of luxury shops, bars, restaurants, tea-houses and clubs where girls sang. Often, people went out to stroll in the gardens by the West Lake or lazed over long meals on the lake's scores of floating restaurants, pushed along by poles like Venetian gondolas. Marco Polo later complained that the people here were 'anything but warriors; all their delight was in women, nothing but women.'

> ...**FASCINATING FACT**...
> The Song inventions, gunpowder and printing, had a huge influence on Europe when they arrived there centuries later.

323

Joan of Arc

- **St Joan of Arc** (*c.*1412–1431) was the peasant girl who led France from defeat in the Hundred Years War and was burned at the stake for her beliefs.

- **Joan was called** Jeanne d'Arc in France. She called herself Jeanne la Pucelle (Joan the Maid).

- **She was brought up** in the village of Domrémy, near Nancy, northeastern France, as a shepherd girl.

- **By the age of 13**, Joan was having visions and believed that God had chosen her to help the French king Charles VII to beat the English.

- **Joan tried** to see the king but was laughed at until she was finally admitted to the king's court, in 1429.

▲ *Known traditionally as the Maid of Orléans, Joan was made a saint in 1920.*

- **To test Joan**, the king stood in disguise amongst his courtiers but Joan recognized him instantly. She also told him what he asked for in his secret prayers.

- **Joan was given** armour and an army to rescue the town of Orléans from the English and succeeded in just ten days.

- **Joan then led** Charles VII through enemy territory to be crowned at Rheims cathedral.

- **In May 1430**, Joan was captured by the English and accused of witchcraft.

- **Joan insisted** that her visions came from God, so a tribunal of French clergymen condemned her as a heretic. She was burned at the stake in Rouen on 30 May 1431.

▼ *It was said that a short-haired, armour-clad Joan, flying her own flag, pushed back the English at Orléans, in 1429. She then took the Dauphin to Rheims, to be crowned Charles VII.*

Knights

- **Knights were the elite** fighting men of the Middle Ages, highly trained for combat both on horseback and on foot.

- **Knights always wore** armour. At first, the armour was simply shirts of mail, made from linked rings of iron. By the 1400s, most knights wore full suits of plate armour.

- **Knights rode into battle** on a horse called a destrier, or warhorse, and usually had an easy-going horse called a palfry just for travelling, plus a packhorse called a sumpter.

- **Chivalry** was the knights' strict code of honour. It comes from *chevalier*, the French for 'horseman'.

▶ *Medieval knights were always ready to fight to defend their own honour and that of their lord.*

- **The ideal knight** was meant to be bold but good and gentle – fighting only to defend his lord, his lady and the Church. But in reality many were just brutal fighting men.

- **Training to be a knight** was a long and costly process, so most were from wealthy families.

- **A young boy** began his training to be a knight at seven years of age as a page to a lord, then he became a knight's squire (apprentice) at 14.

- **A squire's task** was to look after his master's armour, dress him for battle and serve his food.

- **A squire who passed** all the tests was dubbed a 'knight' at about 21 years old.

- **Knights took part** in mock battles called tournaments, often involving 'jousts', where two knights would charge at each other with lances.

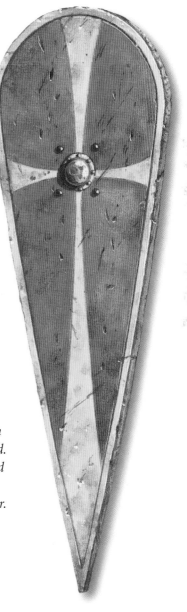

▶ *This is a typical design of an 11th-century shield. As knights wore more and more plate armour, their shields were made smaller.*

327

The Renaissance

▼ *This portrayal of God's creation of man comes from the great Renaissance artist Michelangelo's famous paintings on the ceiling of the Sistine Chapel, in Rome.*

- **The Renaissance** was the great revolution in arts and ideas in Italy between the 1300s and the 1500s.

- **Renaissance is French** for 'rebirth' because it was partly about a revival of interest in the works of the classical world of Greece and Rome.

- **The Renaissance began** when many people started to doubt that the Church had all the answers.

- **Scholars gradually developed** the idea of 'humanism' – the idea that man is the focus of things, not God.

- **A spur to the Renaissance** was the fall of Constantinople in 1453. This sent Greek scholars fleeing to Italy, where they set up academies in cities like Florence and Padua.

- **Artists** in the Renaissance, inspired by classical examples, began to try and put people at the centre of their work – and to portray people and nature realistically rather than as religious symbols.

- **In the 1400s** brilliant artists like Donatello created startlingly realistic paintings and sculptures.

- **The three greatest artists** of the Renaissance were Michelangelo, Raphael and Leonardo da Vinci.

- **The Renaissance saw** some of the world's greatest artistic and architectural masterpieces being created in Italian cities such as Florence and Padua.

- **During the late 1400s**, Renaissance ideas spread to northern Europe.

▶ *Many Renaissance painters ran studios where a team of artists worked on a 'production line' principle, so that the painter himself was not wholly responsible for the work.*

329

The Mogul Empire

- **The Moguls**, or Mughals, were a family who ruled most of northern India from 1526 to 1748.

- **The Moguls were descended** from the Mongol Ghengis Khan via Tamerlane – the great conqueror of the 1300s.

- **The first Mogul emperor** was Babur (1483–1530), who invaded India on swift horses that completely outran the Indians' slower elephants.

- **Babur was a brave** and brilliant leader, as well as a famous poet and diarist.

- **He created gardens** wherever he went and held garden parties there when they were finished.

- **After Babur** came a string of remarkable emperors: Humayun, Akbar, Jahangir, Shah Jahan and Aurangzeb.

- **Akbar** (1556–1605) was the greatest of the Mogul emperors – conquering most of India and setting up a highly efficient system of government.

- **Jahangir** (1569–1627) was a great patron of the arts – but suffered from an addiction to drugs and alcohol. He was also attacked for being under the thumb of his Persian wife, Nur Jahan.

- **The Mogul Empire** reached its peak under Shah Jahan (1592–1666), when many magnificent, luxurious buildings were built – most notably the Taj Mahal.

- **Aurangzeb** (1618–1707) was the last great Mogul ruler. He inspired rebellion by raising taxes and insisting on a strict Muslim code.

▶ *Babur, or Zahir-ud-din Muhammad Babur in full, became the first Mogul emperor, occupying Agra and Delhi in 1526.*

▲ *The breathtaking Taj Mahal, at Agra in northern India, is perhaps the finest example of Mogul architecture. It was built by Mogul emperor Shah Jahan as a tomb for, and love-letter to, his favourite wife – Mumtaz Mahal.*

Voyages of exploration

- **In the late 1300s,** the Mongol Empire in Asia collapsed and Ottoman Turks grew powerful in the Near East. Roads to China and the east were cut off.

- **Italian merchant cities** like Genoa and Venice needed another route. So bold sailors set out from Portugal and Spain to find a way to the east by sea.

▼ *Nearly all European explorers sailed in caravels. These ships were rarely more than 20–30 m long and weighed under 150 tonnes. But they could cope with rough seas and head into the wind, so could sail in most directions. They were also fast – vital when crossing vast oceans.*

Big square sails on the fore and main masts filled like parachutes for high-speed sailing

A raised section at the bow, called the forecastle, gave extra storm protection and extra accommodation

The caravel's strong deck was a platform for guns and made it very storm-proof

The caravel had a deep, narrow hull and a strong, straight keel for speed and stability

A lookout in the crow's nest often saw new land first

A triangular lateen sail on the mizzen (rear) mast helped the ship sail into the wind and manoeuvre along coasts

A small poop (raised deck) held the captain's cabin

- **At first**, they tried to go round Africa, and voyages ventured down Africa's unknown west coast.

- **Many early voyages** were encouraged by Portugal's Prince Henry (1394–1460), who set up a school of navigation at Sagres.

- **In 1488**, Bartholomeu Dias sailed round Africa's southern tip and into the Indian Ocean.

- **In 1497**, Vasco da Gama sailed round Africa to Calicut in India, and returned laden with spices and jewels.

- **Perhaps the greatest voyage** by a European was in 1492, when Genoese sailor Christopher Columbus set out across the open Atlantic. He hoped to reach China by travelling westwards around the world. Instead, he found the whole 'New World' – North and South America.

- **Columbus** only landed on Caribbean islands at first. Even when he reached South America on his last voyage, he thought he was in Asia. The first to realize it was an unknown continent was the Florentine explorer Amerigo Vespucci, who landed there in 1499. A map made in 1507 named North and South America after him.

- **In 1519–1522**, Magellan's ship *Victoria* sailed across the Atlantic, round the southern tip of South America, across the Pacific and back round Africa to Spain. Although this Portuguese explorer was killed in the Philippines, his crew and ship went on to complete the first round-the-world voyage.

> ....FASCINATING FACT....
> Venetian John Cabot set out from Bristol, England in 1497 –
> and 'discovered' North America when he landed in Labrador.

The Medicis

- **The Medici family** of Florence in Italy were one of the richest and most powerful families in Europe between 1400 and 1700.

- **The Medicis' fortunes** began with the bank founded by Giovanni Medici in 1397. The bank was a success and the Medicis became staggeringly rich.

- **Giovanni's son**, Cosimo, built up the bank and there were soon branches in major cities in Europe.

- **By 1434**, Cosimo was so rich and powerful that he became ruler of Florence. Except for brief periods, the Medicis then ruled Florence for 300 years.

- **The Medicis were famed** for paying huge sums of money to commission works of art.

▲ *Lorenzo de' Medici was a tough ruler who put down opposition brutally. But he was also a scholar and a fine poet.*

- **The artist Michelangelo** worked for the Medici family from 1515 until 1534 and created the fabulous Medici Chapel for them.

- **The most famous Medici** was Lorenzo (1449–1492), known as the Magnificent. Under him, Florence became Europe's most splendid city, full of great works of art.

▲ *During the 1400s, art and architecture in Florence flourished under the Medicis' patronage. The city's magnificent domed cathedral was the work of Renaissance architect, Brunelleschi.*

- **Lorenzo** may have been called the Magnificent, but he managed to bankrupt the Medici bank.

- **Three Medicis became Pope** – Leo X (1513–1521), Clement VII (1523–1534) and then Leo XI (1605).

- **Two Medicis became queens** of France. One of these was Catherine de' Medici (1519–1589), queen of Henry II.

The Incas

- **The Incas** were South American people who created a remarkable empire in the Americas in the 1400s.

- **They began as a tribe** in highland Peru, but in 1438 Pachacuti Inca Yupanqui became their Sapa Inca (king) and they built a huge empire in an amazingly short time.

- **Pachacuti** and his son built a huge empire in just 50 years stretching 4000 km through what is now Peru and Chile.

- **Inca soldiers** were highly disciplined and deadly with slings, bronze axes and spears.

- **Inca engineers** swiftly built 30,000 km of paved roads across the empire, spanning deep ravines with dizzying suspension bridges.

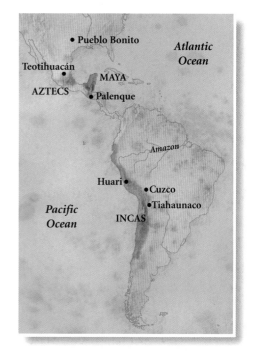

▲ The darker brown area shows the extent of the Inca empire at the height of its power.

- **The Incas kept** in close touch with local officials by relays of runners 2.5 km apart. A message could travel 250 km in under a day.

- **Inca builders** cut and fitted huge stones with astonishing precision to create massive buildings.

- **The royal palace** had a garden full of life-like corn stalks, animals and birds made of solid gold.

336

▼ *The remains of Inca buildings at Pisac, in modern-day Peru. The Incas built impressive palaces, temples, fortresses and warehouses, and covered some buildings in sheets of beaten gold.*

...FASCINATING FACT...
The Inca capital was called Cuzco, which means 'navel', as it was the centre of their world.

Christopher
Columbus

▶ *The beautiful shores of the Bahamas were*
probably those first spotted by Columbus on
his voyage westward.

- **Christopher Columbus**
  (1451–1506) was the Genoese
  sailor who crossed the Atlantic
  and 'discovered' North and
  South America for Europe.

- **Columbus was not** the first
  European to cross the Atlantic.
  The Vikings, for instance, settled in
  Newfoundland in 1004. But it is
  Columbus's discovery that lasted.

- **Other sailors** were trying to find their way to
  China and the east by sailing south round Africa. Columbus, realizing the
  Earth is round, wanted to strike out west across the open Atlantic Ocean
  and reach China that way.

- **After years spent trying** to get backing, Columbus finally got support from
  Queen Isabella of Spain.

- **Columbus set sail** off southwestern Spain on 3 August, 1492, in three
  caravels – the *Santa Maria*, the *Niña* and the *Pinta*.

- **They sailed west** into the unknown for three weeks, by which time the
  sailors were ready to mutiny with fear.

- **On 12 October**, a look-out spotted the Bahamas. Columbus thought he was in the Indies (hence the 'West Indies'). He called the native people Indians.

- **Columbus left 40 men** on a large island that he called Hispaniola and went back to Spain a hero.

- **In 1493 and 1498**, he set off on two more trips with large fleets, as Viceroy of the Indies. He set up a colony on Hispaniola, but it was a disaster. Spaniards complained of his harsh rule and many Indians died from cruelty and disease. Columbus went back to Spain in chains.

- **Columbus was pardoned**, and began a fourth voyage in 1502. He died in Spain in 1506, still thinking his journeys had taken him along the east coast of Asia.

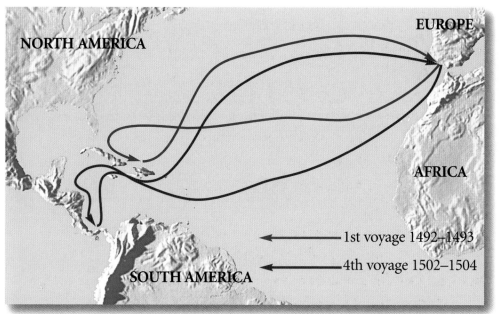

▲ *Columbus made four voyages across the Atlantic, and they are all given great significance today. He died in 1506, still refusing to believe the New World existed.*

The Reformation

- **In the early 1500s,** many people were starting to question the teachings of the Catholic Church. They were angered by the power of the church leaders and the life of idleness that many of the monks appeared to lead.

- **Many critics were angered** by the amounts of money the Church made by selling 'indulgences' – a pardon for sin bought with cash.

- **Martin Luther** (1483–1546) was a poor miner's son from Saxony in Germany. As a monk at Wittenberg University, he earned a reputation for his great biblical knowledge.

- **Luther attacked** the sale of 'indulgences' (pardons for sin) by Pope Leo X, who was selling them by the score to raise money to build St Peter's church in Rome.

- **In 1517,** Luther nailed a list of 95 grievances on the door of Wittenberg Castle's chapel, hoping to start a debate.

◀ *St Peter's Basilica, Rome – the world's largest Christian church. Begun in 1506, this expensive undertaking was partly funded by pardons 'sold' by the Pope.*

- **The Pope issued** a bull (demand) that Luther go back on his views or face expulsion from the Church. Luther burned the bull – and the Church expelled him in 1521.

- **The development of printing** in Europe in the 1400s meant that pamphlets explaining Luther's views could be read by thousands, and support grew rapidly.

- **Luther set up** his own church, whose members soon came to be called Protestants – because of their protests.

- **Other more extreme rebels** joined the cause, such as John Calvin (1509–1564) and Ulrich Zwingli (1484–1531), and the movement gathered pace across northwest Europe.

- **Soon the Protestant movement** was so strong and widespread that the split with the Catholic Church seemed permanent. This is called the Reformation.

▶ *Martin Luther was the monk whose radical views sparked off the great Reformation, which divided Christians in Europe into Catholics and Protestants.*

The conquistadors

- **The conquistadors** ('conquerors') were Spaniards who landed in the 'New World' shortly after Columbus. They came to conquer the peoples there.

- **The most famous conquistadors** were Hernán Cortés (1485–1547) and Francisco Pizarro (*c.*1478–1541).

- **Cortés landed** in Mexico with just 500 men in 1519. The Indian girl Malintzin became his interpreter and lover.

- **Joining with Indians** rebelling against the Aztecs, he marched to Tenochtitlán, the Aztec capital (modern-day Mexico City).

▼ *The Aztec people of Central America created a great, advanced civilization – until Cortés's conquistadors finally crushed it, in 1521.*

- **Perhaps thinking** that Cortés was the god Quetzalcoatl, the Aztec leader Moctezuma let Cortés take him prisoner and become ruler in his place.

- **When Cortés** left Tenochtitlán six months later, the Aztecs rebelled. Cortés returned and destroyed the city.

- **Pizarro set off** to find the Incas in 1524.

- **Pizarro reached** Peru when the Incas were hardly over a civil war between the Inca Atahualpa and his brother.

- **The Incas**, terrified of Pizarro's horses and guns, were easily slaughtered. Pizarro took Cuzco in 1533.

▶ *The typical conquistador was essentially an adventurer and bounty-hunter, ill-suited to the job of ruling. Once the conquistadors had defeated local peoples, Spanish administrators moved in to govern the region.*

> ...**FASCINATING FACT**...
> When Spaniards got off their horses, the Incas
> thought they were beasts splitting in two.

Shoguns and samurai

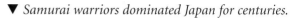

▼ *Samurai warriors dominated Japan for centuries.*

- **In the 12th century**, the civilized Japanese Fujiwara rulers were replaced by powerful warrior clans from country areas – notably the Taira and Minamoto.

- **In 1185**, the Minamoto Yoritomo crushed the Taira clan and made himself ruler of Japan as sei-i-dai-shogun, which means 'barbarian conquering great general'.

- **Warrior shoguns** ruled Japan until the mid-1800s.

- **Japan became dominated** by samurai. The samurai warriors lived to fight and trained in fighting skills to a fanatical degree.

- **A samurai's prized possession** was his massive two-handed sword, which was sharpened and honed to such an extent that a skilled samurai could slice a man in half with a single stroke.

- **Samurai** *means* 'one who serves'.

- **The warrior culture** drove many to seek refuge in nature and men started to live for long periods in remote huts.

- **A kind of Buddhism** called Zen appealed to many Japanese. It showed how meditation could make them see beyond the material world.

- **In the 1300s, samurai** began to take a more Zen approach to their skills.

- **In the 1300s, these Zen Buddhists** began to develop their own forms of elegant entertainment, like flower-arranging and tea-drinking.

▲ *Today it is fashionable all around the world to incorporate Zen principles in the home and garden. The simple lines of this Zen garden promote calm feelings of peaceful meditation.*

Henry VIII

- **Henry VIII** (1491–1547) was the Tudor king of England who separated the Church in England from Rome, and who married six wives, beheading two of them.

  - **Henry's wives:** Catherine of Aragon (1509–1533, divorced); Anne Boleyn (1533–1536, beheaded); Jane Seymour (1536–1538, died); Anne of Cleves (1540, annulled); Catherine Howard (1540–1542, beheaded); and Catherine Parr (1543–1547).

  - **When Henry VIII** became king at 18, in 1509, he was handsome and athletic, spoke several languages, played the lute well and was keen on new 'humanist' ideas. As he grew old, he became grossly fat, riddled with sickness and inclined to terrible outbreaks of anger.

- **Henry was served** by clever ministers like Wolsey and Cromwell. Many were executed when things went wrong.

◀ *We have an astonishingly clear picture of what Henry and his court looked like from the brilliant portraits of Hans Holbein. This picture is based on Holbein's striking painting of Henry from 1537.*

▶ *Catherine Parr – the only one of Henry VIII's six wives to survive him.*

- **Catherine of Aragon** bore Henry a daughter, Mary, but not the needed son. The Pope refused a divorce, so Henry broke with Rome to become head of the English Church.

- **Split from Rome**, the Church of England moved towards Protestantism and the monasteries were destroyed.

- **Anne Boleyn** gave Henry a daughter, Elizabeth, but not the son he wanted, and her strong views made her enemies. She was beheaded on a charge of treason.

- **Jane Seymour** gave Henry a son, Edward, but died in childbirth in 1538.

- **Henry found Anne of Cleves** so ugly, he cancelled the marriage after five months.

- **Young Catherine Howard** was beheaded when she was found to have a lover. Only Henry's last wife, twice-widowed Catherine Parr, survived him when he died in 1547.

Catholics vs Protestants

- **In the 1500s**, the Roman Catholic Church was determined to fight against the Protestant Reformation and other threats. Their fight is called the Counter-Reformation.

- **In 1534**, St Ignatius Loyola founded the Society of Jesus (Jesuits) to lead the Counter-Reformation.

- **Investigative bodies** called Inquisitions were set up to seek out and punish heretics – anyone who held views that did not agree with the Catholic Church's.

- **From 1483**, the Spanish Inquisition became a byword for terror, swooping on suspected heretics – Protestants and Jews alike – torturing them and burning them at the stake.

▲ *Thomas More (1478–1535) was executed when he refused to acknowledge Henry VIII as head of the English Church.*

- **The battle between** Catholics and Protestants created many victims and many martyrs in the late 1500s.

- **In the St Bartholomew's Day massacre** in 1571, up to 70,000 French Protestants, called Huguenots, were killed on the orders of the Catholic queen Catherine de' Medici.

◀ *The Spanish Inquisition was notorious for public burnings of anyone they considered to be dangerously anti-Catholic. Their activities continued until the 1800s.*

- **English Protestants** were burned in Catholic Queen Mary's reign, earning her the name 'Bloody Mary'.

- **English Catholics** such as Edmund Campion (1540–1581) were hanged, drawn and quartered in Protestant Queen Elizabeth I's reign.

- **In Germany**, a terrible Thirty Years' War was started in 1618 as rivalries between Catholics and Protestants flared up.

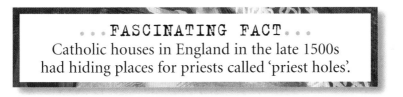

...FASCINATING FACT...
Catholic houses in England in the late 1500s
had hiding places for priests called 'priest holes'.

349

The Spanish Empire

- **Within half a century** of Columbus's arrival in America in 1492, Spanish conquistadors had conquered Latin America – from California to Argentina.

- **By the Treaty of Tordesillas** (1494) Portugal allowed Spain to take any territory more than 370 leagues (about 2000 km) west of the Cape Verde islands – all of Latin America but Brazil.

- **Thousands of Spaniards** came to colonize Latin America in the 1500s, creating cities such as Cartagena in Colombia and Guayaqil in Ecuador.

Hull and decking of winter-cut oak, cedar or cypress hardwood

Three masts with square sails – or, as here, with a triangular lateen on the mizzen (rear) mast

Banks of 20 or so cannons for 'broadsides' – firing together down one side

◀ *Once a year, two Spanish treasure fleets would leave from Havana in Cuba guarded by the galleons of the Armada de la Guardia. Galleons were the biggest warships, 35 m long and weighing around 500 tonnes.*

- **Spanish rulers tried** to deal with local people with the *encomienda*, whereby Native Americans were assigned to Spaniards who were supposed to look after them in return for taxes and labour. Many Spaniards were cruel to these people, and Spaniards now talk of how cruelly they abused the Native Americans. In 100 years, the number of Native Americans dropped from 50 million to 4 million, through cruelty, poverty and diseases brought by Spaniards.

- **Many Spanish Dominican friars** condemned the *encomienda* – especially Bartolomé de Las Casas – and fought unsuccessfully for better conditions for Native Americans.

- **Indians mined silver**, gold and gems in huge amounts in South America. The Muzo and Chivor mines in Colombia were famous for their emeralds.

- **Every year**, in the calm months between March and October, ships laden with treasure left the Americas bound for Spain.

- **Besides American treasure**, Spanish ships carried spices from the East Indies and silks from China. These were shipped across the Pacific from the Philippines to Mexico, then carried overland to be shipped from the Caribbean to Europe.

- **By the 1540s**, the Spanish ships were suffering pirate attacks, so the ships crossed the Atlantic every year in two great *flotas* (fleets) protected by an armada of galleons (warships).

...FASCINATING FACT...
The Spanish brought new foods such as tomatoes, potatoes and chocolate back to Europe from their American empire.

Elizabeth I

- **Elizabeth I** (1533–1603) was one of England's greatest rulers. The time of her reign is called the Elizabethan Age or England's Golden Age. Under her strong and intelligent rule, England became an enterprising, artistically rich and peaceful nation.

- **Elizabeth was daughter** of Henry VIII and his wife Anne Boleyn, who was beheaded when Elizabeth was three.

- **She was a brilliant** scholar, fluent in many languages by the time she was 12.

- **When Henry VIII died**, Elizabeth's nine-year-old half-brother became King Edward VI, but he died in 1553. He was succeeded by her older sister 'Bloody' Mary.

◀ *Elizabeth loved the theatre. Here, Shakespeare himself (at the front of the acting group) performs in a play in front of the queen.*

▶ *William Shakespeare was one of several important English writers whose work flourished during Elizabeth I's reign.*

- **Mary** was staunchly Catholic. For a while Elizabeth was locked up, suspected of involvement in a Protestant plot.

- **In 1558**, when Mary died, Elizabeth became queen.

- **At once Elizabeth** strengthened the Protestant Church of England by the Act of Supremacy in 1559.

- **Elizabeth was expected** to marry, and she encouraged foreign suitors when it helped diplomacy. But she remained single, earning her the nickname 'The Virgin Queen'.

- **Elizabeth sent troops** to help Protestants in Holland against their Spanish rulers, and secretly urged Francis Drake to raid Spanish treasure ships. In 1588 Spain sent an Armada to invade England. Elizabeth proved an inspiring leader and the Armada was repulsed.

- **Elizabeth's reign** is famed for the poetry and plays of men like Spenser, Marlowe and Shakespeare.

The colonization of America

▲ 'Pilgrims' on their way to church. Pilgrims were devout Puritans who had been persecuted for their beliefs in England and so set up a colony in America in the 1600s.

- **In the 1580s,** English people tried unsuccessfully to set up colonies in North America.
- **The first successful English colony** was set up at Jamestown, Virginia, on 24 May, 1607, with 104 colonists.

- **Many of the Jamestown colony** died in 'the starving time' of the winter of 1609.

- **In 1610**, fighting broke out with the local Indians as the desperate colonists took the Indians' food supply.

- **Colonist leader John Smith** was captured by the Indians, but the chief's daughter, Pocahontas, saved his life.

- **In 1612**, colonist John Rolfe introduced tobacco from the West Indies. It became the basis of Virginia's economy.

- **Pocahontas** was held hostage by the colonists in 1613. While captive she met, fell in love with and wed John Rolfe.

- **In December 1620**, 102 'Pilgrims' arrived from Plymouth, England, in the *Mayflower* and set up a new colony near Cape Cod. They survived thanks to help from Wampanoag Indians.

- **In November 1621**, the Pilgrims invited the Wampanoags to celebrate their first harvest. This first Thanksgiving Day is now celebrated every year in the USA.

▶ *Daughter of a Native American chief, Pocahontas wed prominent colonist John Rolfe.*

FASCINATING FACT
Pocahontas died of influenza while in London, raising money for the colonists.

Dutch independence

- **In 1500**, there were 17 provinces making up what is now Belgium, the Netherlands and Luxembourg. The most important was Holland.

- **The provinces** came under Spanish rule in 1516, when their ruler Charles became the king of Spain.

- **In the 1500s**, Holland's capital Amsterdam became the leading commercial centre of Europe. With the growth of trade, Protestant ideas started taking hold.

- **Charles's son Philip II** and his deputy the duke of Alba tried to crush the Protestants by executing their leaders.

- **As Alba became** more ruthless, opposition spread.

- **In 1566**, William, prince of Orange, led the Dutch in revolt. Although the Dutch controlled the sea, they gradually gave way before the Spanish army.

- **In 1574**, the Dutch opened dikes holding back the sea to sail over the flood to Leiden and rescue the besieged.

- **Protestants retreated** to the northern provinces, and in 1581 declared themselves the independent Dutch Republic. The fighting ceased.

- **The 1600s proved** a Golden Age for the Dutch Republic.

- **The Dutch merchant fleet** became the biggest in Europe. Dutch banks and businesses thrived and Dutch scientists like Leeuwenhoek and Huygens made great discoveries.

▶ *In the 1400–1600s, Dutch artists like Steen, Vermeer and Rembrandt created vibrant, technically brilliant paintings, often of everyday scenes. This is by Van Eyck, who was said to have invented oil painting in the 1430s.*

Toyotomi Hideyosh

- **Toyotomi Hideyoshi** (1536–1598) was the great Japanese shogun who unified Japan.

- **Hideyoshi was the son** of poor, hard-working peasants.

- **As a boy**, Hideyoshi believed that if he became a shogun, he'd make sure peasants wouldn't have to work so hard.

- **As a man**, Hideyoshi became a soldier for shogun Oda Nobunaga, who was trying to unify Japan through force.

- **Legend says** that one day Hideyoshi warmed Nobunaga's shoes for a winter walk. Nobunaga made him a general.

▲ *Hideyoshi helped to perfect the Japanese art of making and taking tea.*

- **Hideyoshi proved himself** a brilliant general, and when Nobunaga was murdered, Hideyoshi carried on his work in unifying Japan – but by good rule as well as by arms.

- **By 1591**, Hideyoshi had unified Japan, but he kept warriors and peasants firmly separated as classes.

- **To establish** a mystique for his court, Hideyoshi had the Zen master Sen No Rikkyu perfect the tea ceremony.

- **Later, Hideyoshi became** paranoid. Suspecting his chief adviser Hidetsugu of plotting, he had Hidetsugu's family killed – including the beautiful Princess Komahime.

- **Komahime's father**, Yoshiaki, sided decisively with Hideyoshi's enemy, the hero Tokugawa Ieyasu, in the great battle that led to Hideyoshi's downfall.

▲ *Hideyoshi did much to develop international trade, and in 1597 became the first person to ban the Christian religion on political grounds.*

Russia

- **In 1237**, Tatar hordes, the descendants of Genghis Khan, swept into Russia, burning cities and slaughtering people. The Tatars stayed for 200 years.

- **Some Russians thrived** under the Tatars and a trading post called Moscow grew into a powerful city at the centre of a province called Muscovy. In 1318, Prince Yuri of Moscow married the Tatar Khan's sister. A later prince called Ivan began collecting taxes for the Tatars.

- **Moscow grew strong** as the Tatars grew weak. In 1453, Ivan III ('the Great'), Grand Prince of Muscovy, was strong enough to drive out the Tatars.

- **Russians were Christians** of the Eastern Church, ruled from Constantinople. Constantinople had become the second focus of Christianity when Rome fell to barbarians in the AD 400s. When Constantinople fell to the Turks in 1453, Ivan III called for Moscow to be the Third Rome. He wed a Byzantine princess, and his grandson Ivan IV took the title tsar after the Roman caesars.

- **Ivan's ambitions** left him in need of money and food, so he forced thousands of peasants into serfdom – at a time when peasants in western Europe were gaining their freedom. Those who would not submit fled to the southern steppes, where they became known as Cossacks.

▶ *Ivan rebuilt Moscow's Kremlin as a vast, walled complex of palaces and churches. It has remained the centre of Russian government ever since.*

- **Ivan IV** (1544–1584), the first tsar, drove the Tatars out of Russia, conquering Kazan, Astrakhan and much of Siberia – creating the first Russian Empire.

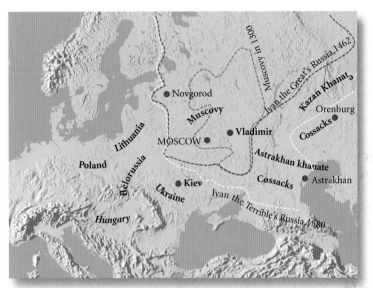

▲ *Under Ivan the Great and his grandson Ivan the Terrible, Russia grew to be a great empire.*

- **Ivan IV was called** 'the Terrible' because of his brutality. He formed the Oprichniki – a police force to control people – and had hundreds of boyars (aristocrats) murdered. He even beat his son Ivan to death in a fit of rage.

- **Ivan IV was an effective ruler**, who encouraged scholars and brought Moscow its first printing presses.

- **Fyodor**, Ivan IV's second son, was a simpleton, and his wife's brother Boris Godunov seized the throne in 1598.

- **When Godunov died** in 1606, Moscow fell into a period of chaos that is called the 'Time of Troubles'. A monk named Gregory Otrepiev claimed to be Dmitry, another of Ivan IV's sons who was thought to have died. He invaded Moscow with a Polish army and rebellious Cossacks, and Russia was torn apart a by civil war.

Mary Queen of Scots

- **Mary Queen of Scots** (1542–1587) was the Catholic queen of Scotland held captive in England by Elizabeth I for 19 years, then beheaded.

- **Mary became queen** when she was a baby but was brought up at the French court, where she enjoyed hunting and learned six languages.

- **Mary married** the French king Henry II's son Francis at 15 and was briefly queen of France, but Francis died in 1560.

- **In 1561**, Mary returned to Scotland to rule there. By this time, Scotland had become Protestant, while Mary was a Catholic.

- **In 1565**, Mary fell in love with her cousin Henry Stuart, Earl of Darnley. She married him and they had a child, but Darnley was only interested in power.

- **Led by Darnley**, Protestant nobles stabbed Mary's Catholic secretary David Rizzio to death before her.

- **The Earl of Bothwell** was in love with Mary and murdered Darnley. They married three months later. The Scots were so outraged by the marriage that Mary had to flee to England.

◀ *Mary with her cousin and second husband, the highly ambitious Earl of Darnley – an ill-starred marriage that ended in deception and double murder.*

- **After Elizabeth**, Mary was next in line to the English throne. Many Catholics felt she was first in line, since they did not recognize Henry VIII's marriage to Anne Boleyn.

- **Mary posed a danger** to Elizabeth, so she was kept in captivity in English houses, where she became the focus for plots against Elizabeth.

- **Elizabeth's spy-master** Walsingham trapped Mary into going along with a plot by Babington. Mary was found guilty of treason and beheaded at Fotheringay in 1587.

▶ *Mary, about to meet her death at the executioner's block. Her presence in England had made her a dangerous focus for Catholic plots against Elizabeth I.*

363

Native Americans

- **When the first European colonists** arrived in North America, there were one and a half million Native Americans living there.

- **There were hundreds of tribes** in North America, each with its own language.

- **There were six kinds** of tribal area: the Southwest, Great Plains, Far West Plateau, Northwest, Eastern Woodland and Northern.

- **Southwest Native Americans** like the Pueblo Indians lived by growing corn, beans and squash.

- **Plains tribes** like the Blackfoot, Comanche and Cheyenne hunted buffalo on foot.

- **With Woodland tribes** like the Delaware, the men hunted deer and fished while the women grew crops.

- **Plateau and Northwest Native Americans** like the Nez Percé and the Kwakiutl lived by fishing and gathering berries. They are famous for their baskets.

- **Northern tribes** like the Cree lived mainly by hunting caribou.

- **Until Europeans arrived**, Native Americans got around mainly on foot or by canoe. The Europeans introduced horses in the 1700s – and Indians quickly became skilled riders.

◄ *Native North Americans typically wore 'buckskin' clothes – made from the tanned hides of deer. Eagle feathers provided decoration and held a special meaning.*

▲ *Native Indians who lived on the Plains were often on the move, looking for buffalo to hunt. As they went from camp to camp they made tepees, large tents built with poles and covered by buffalo skins.*

...FASCINATING FACT...
Woodland tribes lived in wigwams,
domes of sticks covered in hide and moss.

The Manchus

- **In the 1600s**, the Ming emperors of China were unpopular after three centuries in power. Rebellions became all too common.

- **In 1644**, the last Ming emperor hanged himself as the bandit Li Zichen and his men overran Beijing.

- **Guarding the Great Wall** were Manchu troops, from Manchuria in the north. A desperate Ming general invited them to help get rid of Li Zicheng.

- **The Manchus marched** into Beijing and proclaimed their own child-emperor as the 'Son of Heaven' and set up the Qing dynasty of emperors.

- **Resistance to the Manchu emperors** went on in the south for 30 years, but was eventually suppressed.

- **At first, the Qing forced** Chinese men to put their hair in pigtails to show they were inferior to Manchus.

- **Manchus and Chinese** were also made to live separately and were not allowed to marry each other.

▲ *Under the Qing, China remained as it had been for 3000 years, while much of the world was changing dramatically.*

- **In time, the Qing adopted** Chinese ways, and even Manchu civil servants had to learn the classic works of Confucius, just like the Chinese.

- **Under the Qing**, China reached its greatest extent.

- **In the 1800s**, the power of the Qing was weakened by rebellions, Muslim uprisings and growing European influence.

▲ *Manchu troops guarded China's ancient Great Wall against bandits, but the Manchus eventually seized power for themselves.*

Roundheads and Cavaliers

- **The English Civil War** (1642–1649) was the struggle between 'Cavalier' supporters of King Charles I and 'Roundheads', who supported Parliament.

- **A key issue** was how much power the king should have. Charles wanted to be free to set taxes and his own brand of religion. Parliament demanded a say.

- **On the royalist side** were those who wanted the English Church more Catholic; on the other were Puritans.

- **Puritans** were extreme Protestants. They believed that churches (and people) should be stripped of the wasteful luxury they saw in the Catholic Church and the aristocrats at the court of Charles's French, Catholic wife.

- **'Cavalier'** is from the French *chevalier* (horseman). It was meant as a term of abuse. Many Cavaliers were rich landowners.

- **Puritans thought** that long hair was indulgent, and the Roundheads got their name from their short-cropped hair. Many Roundheads were rich merchants and townspeople.

▶ *A Cavalier soldier. The term Cavalier was coined because many of Charles' supporters were seen as frivolous courtiers who loved fighting for its own sake.*

- **Many revolutionary groups** emerged among poorer people, such as the 'Diggers' and 'Levellers'.

- **The war turned against** the royalists when the parliamentarians formed the disciplined New Model Army.

- **Charles I** was beheaded in 1649.

- **Oliver Cromwell** (1599–1658) became Roundhead leader and signed Charles I's death warrant. In 1653, he made himself Lord Protector – England's dictator.

▶ *Many Cavaliers had long hair and wore colourful and elaborate clothes, after the style of the French court. Some, like Lovelace, were poets.*

The Sun King

- **Louis XIV** (1638–1715) was king of France for 72 years, a longer reign than any other European king in history.

- **Louis became king** in 1643, when he was five, and the first minister Cardinal Mazarin effectively ruled France.

- **In 1648**, heavy taxes and other grievances inspired a rebellion – the Fronde – against the hated Mazarin.

- **During the Fronde**, Louis was forced into hiding, and vowed never to let the same happen again.

- **Louis said** '*L'état c'est moi*' ('I am the State') and believed it was his God-given right to command his people totally.

- **When Mazarin died**, in 1661, Louis decided to run the country himself, and devoted huge energy to administering every detail of the nation's business.

- **Louis made France** the most efficiently run country in Europe. It hummed with new industries, roads and canals.

- **He used the finest** artists to turn the French court into a glittering spectacle to distract nobles from rebellion. His palace was filled with banquets, plays and art.

- **Louis got the nickname** 'The Sun King' from his favourite dance role, that of Apollo the Sun God. He adopted the Sun as his personal emblem.

◄ *Louis used the image of the Sun in his emblem, as he loved to play the part of Apollo the Sun God in dances and masques.*

▲ *Court life at the magnificent palace and gardens of Versailles, just outside Paris, formed the stunning centrepiece of the Sun King's reign.*

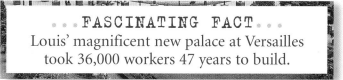

. . .FASCINATING FACT. . .
Louis' magnificent new palace at Versailles
took 36,000 workers 47 years to build.

Gustavus Adolphus

- **Gustavus Adolphus** (1594–1632) was Sweden's greatest king and military leader.

- **He was a brilliant** speaker and inspiring general who always led his men into battle from the front.

- **Gustavus had** a perfect ally in his chancellor Axel Oxenstierna (say: erks n sherna). Gustavus ran the foreign wars while Oxenstierna ran Sweden.

- **When Gustavus came** to the throne at the age of 17, Sweden was involved in three wars: with Denmark (1611–1613), Russia (1611–1617) and Poland.

- **Gustavus quickly made** peace with Denmark and Russia.

- **In skirmishes with the Poles**, Gustavus began to develop the first modern army – a large, highly mobile force combining foot soldiers and horsemen.

- **Gustavus was a devout** Protestant. When he saw the Protestants of Germany facing defeat in the Thirty Years' War against the Catholic Austrian emperor Ferdinand II, he decided to intervene.

- **In July 1630**, Gustavus's armies landed in Germany.

- **In 1631**, Gustavus won a great victory over Ferdinand's army at Breitenfeld near Leipzig.

- **On 6 November, 1632**, the Swedes scored a crucial victory over Bohemian general Wallenstein, but Gustavus himself was killed leading a charge.

▶ *Gustavus's great flagship, the* Vasa, *sank on its maiden voyage in 1628, but it has been recovered almost intact and can now be seen in Stockholm.*

Pirates

◄ *The famous 'Jolly Roger' flag, flown from pirate ships.*

- **Barbary corsairs** were pirates from North Africa who raided ships in the Mediterranean between 1520 and 1830. Many corsairs were Muslims and regarded Christian merchant ships as fair game.

- **The most famous corsairs** were the Barbarossa brothers and Occhiali.

- **Sea dogs** were pirates like Sir Francis Drake, secretly encouraged by Queen Elizabeth I to raid the ships of her Spanish enemies in the Caribbean.

- **'Letters of marque'** from the monarch gave English raiders official blessing, so they were called privateers.

- **When King James I** withdrew letters of marque in 1603, privateers were replaced by lawless 'buccaneers' like Henry Morgan, who terrorized the Caribbean from bases on Jamaica like Port Royal.

- **Buccaneer** comes from the French *boucan* (barbeque) as many were poor hunters who grilled the meat of cows and pigs that they scavenged.

- **Piracy reached its height** between 1690 and 1790, preying on traders plying between Europe and its new colonies around the world.

- **In the Indian Ocean** were pirates like William Kidd from Madagascar. In the Bahamas, there was 'Calico Jack' Rackham and female pirates Anne Bonny and Mary Read.

- **The most notorious pirate** of this time was 'Blackbeard' (Edward Teach), who leaped into action with lighted firecrackers tied to his big, black beard.

- **Piracy diminished** after 1720, when the British navy clamped down worldwide.

▼ *Female pirates Anne Bonny and Mary Read plied the high seas when piracy was at its height.*

The Restoration

- **For 11 years** after the execution of Charles I in 1649, England was without a king. It was ruled instead by the Commonwealth, run by the Puritans.

- **At first**, the Commonwealth consisted of Parliament and its Council of State, but its failure to make progress spurred general Oliver Cromwell to make himself Lord Protector and rule through army officers.

- **Cromwell's Protectorate** proved unpopular. When he died in 1658, the army removed his son Richard Cromwell as successor and called for Charles I's exiled son Charles II to be recalled as king.

- **The Restoration** of Charles II as king was in May 1660.

- **Charles II proved** on the whole to be a skilful ruler, tactfully easing tensions between rival religious groups.

- **Charles II was known as** the Merry Monarch, because his love of partying, theatre, horse-racing and women was such a relief after years of grim Puritan rule.

▶ *The sedan chair was a popular way for the rich to get about in the years after the Restoration.*

- **Of Charles II's** many mistresses, the most famous was Nell Gwyn, an orange-seller who worked in the theatre.

- **The Restoration** saw the Puritan ban on Christmas and the theatre lifted. Plays like Congreve's *Way of the World* made Restoration theatre lively and outrageous.

- **Charles II took** a keen interest in science, encouraging great scientists like Isaac Newton, Edmund Halley and Robert Hooke to form the Royal Society.

▲ *Exiled after his father's death, Charles first attempted to bring back the monarchy in 1651 but was defeated. After nine more years in exile, he was finally invited to return as king.*

. . . **FASCINATING FACT** . . .
When London burned down, in 1666, Charles II personally organized the fire-fighting.

377

Slavery

- **Slaves were used** a great deal in the ancient world, as warring people put their captives to work. The pyramids of Egypt were probably built mostly by slaves. One in three people in ancient Athens was likely to have been a slave.

- **Slavery diminished** in Europe when the Roman Empire collapsed, although in the Middle Ages, Russian and African slaves were used on sugar plantations in the Mediterranean.

- **Slavery grew hugely** when Europeans established colonies in the Americas from the 1500s onwards.

- **At first**, the settlers used Native Americans as slaves, but as numbers dwindled, they took slaves from Africa to work on new sugar plantations. British and French sugar planters in the West Indies used African slaves too.

▼ *Europeans established huge, highly profitable sugar plantations in the Caribbean, worked by African slaves who were treated appallingly.*

- **From 1500 to 1800**, Europeans shipped 10–12 million black slaves from Africa to the Americas. Of these 40 percent went to Brazil, 30 percent to Cuba, Jamaica and Haiti, and 5 percent to the USA.

- **The slave trade** involved shipping several hundred thousand Africans across the Atlantic from the 'Slave Coast' of West Africa to the West Indies and the USA, or from Angola to Brazil. Once the slave ships had unloaded their slaves, they would return to Europe with a cargo of sugar, then sail for Africa with cotton goods and guns to exchange for slaves.

- **Slavery was rife** in the American south in the 1700s, where owners of large plantations needed cheap labour to grow first tobacco and then cotton.

- **In the West Indies and Brazil**, there were more blacks than whites, and slaves often revolted. The greatest revolution was on French Haiti, where the slave Toussaint l'Ouverture (1743–1803) led 500,000 slaves to take over the country in 1791. For a while Haiti was black-governed – but Napoleon's troops reasserted control in 1802.

- **In the 1790s**, some Europeans began to speak out against slavery. Denmark banned the Atlantic slave trade in 1792. William Wilberforce got Britain to ban the trade in 1807. The USA banned the import of slaves in 1808. When Latin-American countries became independent in the early 1800s, they freed slaves. Britain abolished slavery in its empire in 1833, but the USA had to go through a civil war first.

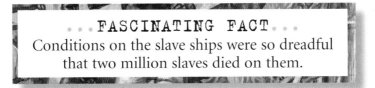

...FASCINATING FACT...
Conditions on the slave ships were so dreadful
that two million slaves died on them.

The Glorious Revolution

- **The Glorious Revolution** of 1688 was when the English Parliament replaced James II with William III and Mary, as king and queen.

- **James II became king** when his brother Charles II died in 1685.

- **James II upset people** by giving Catholics key jobs in the army, the Church and the universities.

- **He jailed** any bishops who refused to support his Declaration of Indulgence in favour of Catholics.

- **In 1688**, James II and his Catholic wife Mary had a son. It seemed England was set to become Catholic.

- **Leading Protestants** decided to invite the Dutch prince William of Orange to help. William was married to James II's Protestant daughter Mary.

◀ *Mary sided with her Protestant husband, William, against her Catholic father James II.*

- **William** landed with his army at Brixham in Devon on November 5, 1688. James's army refused to obey its Catholic generals and so he was forced to flee to France.

- **Parliament** decided James's escape meant he had abdicated, and offered the throne to William and Mary.

- **James tried** a comeback, landing in Ireland with French troops. Defeat came at the Battle of the Boyne (July 1689).

▶ *William III, or William of Orange (1650–1702), suffered much political opposition and countless assassination plots in the latter years of his reign.*

...FASCINATING FACT...
Ulster Protestants are called Orangemen because they once helped William of Orange at the Boyne.

381

The Age of Reason

- **The Age of Reason** is the time in the 1700s when many people began to believe that all-important questions about the world could be answered by reason.

- **The Age of Reason** is also called the Enlightenment.

- **The idea that human reason** has the answers was revolutionary. It meant that even the lowliest peasant was just as likely to be right as the highest lord. So why should a lord rule over a peasant?

- **In earlier times**, kings had ruled by 'divine right' – and their power over other people was God's will. The Age of Reason questioned this right.

- **As the 1700s progressed**, the ideas of the Age of Reason turned into real revolutions in France and America.

▶ *The French philosopher Diderot (1713–1784) spent much of his life compiling and writing the* Encyclopedia, *a work of reference that greatly reflected his views on philosophy and science.*

► Thomas Jefferson, *painted by John Trumbull. Jefferson (1743–1826) was America's third president. He caught the spirit of the age when he drafted the USA's Declaration of Independence.*

- **The hero of the Age** was Isaac Newton. His discovery of the Laws of Motion proposed that every single event in the Universe could be worked out mathematically.

- **American revolutionary leader Jefferson** had a portrait of Newton before him as he wrote the Constitution.

- **In France**, the great ideas were worked out by philosophers like Rousseau and Voltaire. People discussed the ideas earnestly at fashionable 'salons' (supper parties).

- **In Britain**, thinkers like Hume showed how important it was to work things out for yourself – not just be told.

- **To sum up all human knowledge**, the first great encyclopedia was created – by Diderot in France.

Peter the Great

- **Peter the Great** (1672–1725) was the greatest of all the Russian tsars (emperors). He built the city of St Petersburg and turned Russia from an inward-looking country to a major European power.

- **Standing at** well over 2 m tall, Peter towered above everyone else.

- **Peter had** incredible willpower and a burning interest in new ideas. But he was very impatient and often went into rages. When his son Alexei plotted against him, Peter had him put to death.

- **At the age of ten** Peter became tsar. His step-sister Sophia ruled for him until 1689, when her enemies drove her out and Peter took charge.

- **In 1697–1698** Peter travelled to Holland and England disguised as a ship's carpenter in order to learn about western European technology and culture.

  - **When Peter returned** from Europe, he brought with him many western European craftsmen and teachers.

  - **Peter insisted** on Russian men shaving off their old-fashioned, Russian-style beards.

  - **Peter was very keen** on boats. He built the first Russian navy – on the Volga River. His wars later ensured that Russia had, for the first time, a sea port on the Baltic.

  - **He led the Russian armies** to crucial victories in battle – notably against the Swedes at Poltava in 1709.

  - **Peter created** the first Russian Academy of Sciences, started Russia's first newspaper, and founded many schools, technical institutions and art galleries.

◀ Peter the Great brought sweeping changes to Russia and carried many of them out with great brutality.

▶ *The Cathedral of St Peter and St Paul, in St Petersburg – the grand city built by Peter the Great.*

British India

- **Shortly after Vasco da Gama** reached India, in 1498, the Portuguese set up a trading base in Goa.

- **In 1600**, Elizabeth I of England gave a charter to the East India Co. to trade in India. It set up posts at Surat, Madras, Bombay and Calcutta.

- **The French set up** a base at Pondicherry, in 1668.

- **In the 1700s**, rebellions weakened the Mogul empire. The French and British vied to gain control.

- **In 1757**, 3000 British soldiers, led by the East India Co.'s Robert Clive, defeated an army of over 50,000 French and Indian troops at the battle of Plassey.

- **After Clive's victory**, the British gradually gained control over much of India through a combination of bribes, bullying and making well-placed allies.

- **In 1803**, the British captured the Mogul capital of Delhi – so completing their power base.

- **British rule** was resented by many Indians. Hindus felt that the British were undermining their religion.

- **In 1857**, Indian soldiers revolted and other Indians joined them, but the 'mutiny' was crushed after 14 months.

- **In 1858**, the British decided to rule India directly. Their rule was known as the Raj (which means 'rule'). In 1876, Queen Victoria of Britain was named empress of India.

▶ *Robert Clive's victory over Indian and French troops at the Battle of Plassey gave Britain control over much of India – control that would last for 200 years.*

American independence

· ·

- **In 1763**, Britain finally defeated the French in North America, adding Canada to its 13 colonies – but wanted the colonists to help pay for the cost. The colonists resented paying taxes to a government 5000 km away.

- **To avoid costly wars** with Native Americans, George III issued a Proclamation in 1763 reserving lands west of the Appalachians for native peoples, and sent troops to keep settlers out, arousing colonists' resentment.

- **In 1764–1765**, British prime minister George Grenville brought in three new taxes – the Sugar Tax on molasses, which affected rum producers in the colonies; the Quartering Tax, which obliged the colonists to supply British soldiers with living quarters; and the Stamp Tax on newspapers, playing cards and legal documents.

- **Colonists tolerated** sugar and quartering taxes, but the Stamp Tax provoked riots. Delegates from nine colonies met in New York to demand a say in how they were taxed, demanding 'No taxation without representation.'

- **As protests escalated**, Grenville was forced to withdraw all taxes but one, the tax on tea. Then, in 1773, a crowd of colonists disguised as Mohawk Indians marched on to the merchant ship *Dartmouth* in Boston harbour and threw its cargo of tea into the sea. After this 'Boston Tea Party', the British closed Boston and moved troops in.

- **A Congress of delegates** from all the colonies except Georgia met to demand independence, and appointed George Washington to lead an army to fight their cause.

- **In April 1775**, British troops seized military stores at Lexington and Concord near Boston and the war began.

● **At first**, the British were successful, but the problems of fighting 5000 km from home told in the long run. In 1781, Washington defeated the British at Yorktown, Virginia and they surrendered.

● **In 1776**, the colonists drew up a Declaration of Independence, written by Thomas Jefferson. The British recognized independence in 1783, and in 1787 the colonists drew up a Constitution stating how their Union should be run. In 1789, George Washington was elected as the first president of the United States of America.

◀ *The original 13 colonies of North America stretched from Massachusetts in the north, 2500 km south to Georgia. These 13 colonies became the first 13 states of the United States of America. The dates on the map show when they were founded. The green lines show today's states – these, of course, did not exist in 1775.*

Hudson Bay Company

Maine (part of Massachusetts)

New Hampshire 1680

New York 1664

Massachusetts 1629

Rhode Island 1635

Connecticut 1664

Indian Reserve

Pennsylvania 1681

New Jersey 1664

Delaware 1702

Maryland 1632

1763 Proclamation Line

Virginia 1607

N. Carolina 1670

S. Carolina 1670

Georgia 1732

West Florida

East Florida

...FASCINATING FACT...

The Declaration of Independence began with the words: 'We hold these truths to be self-evident, that all men are created equal, that they are endowed by their Creator with certain inalienable rights, and that among these are Life, Liberty and the pursuit of Happiness.'

The French Revolution

- **In 1789**, French people were divided among three 'Estates' – the nobles, clergy and middle class – plus the peasants. Nobles owned all the land, but were exempt from paying taxes, and the tax burden fell on the peasants.

- **In the same year**, France was bankrupt after many wars, and King Louis XVI was forced to summon Parliament, called the Estates General, for the first time in 175 years.

- **The three Estates** had met separately in the past, but now insisted on meeting in a National Assembly to debate how to limit the power of the king. The Assembly was dominated by the Third Estate, the middle class.

- **On 14 July, 1789**, the poor people of Paris, tired of debates, stormed the prison fortress of the Bastille.

▲ *The guillotine had a blade that dropped to cut victims' heads off instantly.*

- **Fired by the fall of the Bastille**, peasants rose all over the country and refused to pay taxes. Parisian women marched to Versailles and dragged the king back to Paris.

- **The National Assembly** became more radical, ending serfdom and attacking the nobles and the Church. Many nobles fled the country in panic.

- **The Assembly speakers** who had the power to move the Paris mobs, like Georges Danton, came to the fore. The Assembly renamed itself the National Convention and set up the Committee of Public Safety to govern France by terror.

- **Many nobles were sent** to the guillotine and in 1793 Louis XVI and his queen, Marie Antoinette, were themselves guillotined.

- **This Reign of Terror** was presided over by Robespierre, who saw more and more of his rivals to the guillotine, including Danton. But in the end even Robespierre himself was guillotined, in July 1794.

- **With Robespierre gone**, conservatives regained control. Emphasis shifted to defending the revolution against foreign kings and to Napoleon's conquests.

▶ *When the French Revolution brought down the old ruling classes, crowds of ordinary people took to the streets to celebrate.*

Agricultural Revolution

- **The Agricultural Revolution** refers to dramatic changes in farming in Britain in the 1700s and later in the USA.

- **Before the 1700s**, farmland was mostly wide open fields, cultivated in narrow strips by peasants growing food for themselves, using traditional methods.

- **The Agricultural Revolution** created large farms, growing food for profit in enclosed fields, using specialist techniques.

- **The most dramatic effect** was enclosure, in which peasants were evicted from open fields as they were parcelled up into small fields for rearing livestock.

- **Crop-growing** was improved by techniques such as the four-field rotation system.

- **The four-field system** devised by 'Turnip' Townshend and Thomas Coke meant growing turnips, clover, barley and wheat in successive years so land was used all the time.

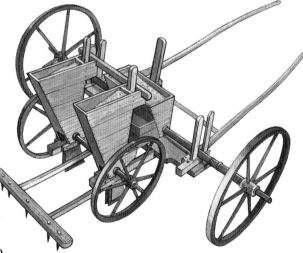

- **Livestock farmers** found how to breed cattle, horses and sheep larger and fatter, like Bakewell's Leicester sheep.

▲ *The first-ever seed drill was invented by Englishman Jethro Tull in 1701.*

- **New machines** were invented. Jethro Tull's drill, for example, made holes and planted seeds in them.

- **In 1793**, Eli Whitney invented a gin machine to separate cotton fibre from the seeds – so making large-scale cotton production profitable.

- **In 1834**, American Cyrus McCormick made the first mechanical harvester.

▲ *Separating the seeds from the fibres of cotton plants by hand is a very slow process. Once American farmer's son Eli Whitney invented the 'gin', mass-production became possible.*

393

Industrial Revolution

- **The Industrial Revolution** refers to the dramatic growth in factories that began in the 1700s.

- **Before the Industrial Revolution**, most ordinary people were farmers who lived in small villages. Afterwards, most were factory hands and foremen living in huge cities.

- **The Revolution began** in Britain in the late 1700s, and in France, the USA and Germany in the early 1800s.

- **The Farming Revolution** created a pool of cheap labour, while the growth of European colonies created vast markets for things like clothing.

- **It was with the invention** of machines for making cloth, like the spinning jenny that the Revolution began.

- **The turning point** was the change from hand-turned machines like the spinning jenny, to machines driven by big water wheels – like Richard Arkwright's 'water powered spinning frame' of 1766.

  - **In 1771**, Arkwright installed water frames at Crompton Mill, Derby, and created the world's first big factory.

◀ *In 1764, Lancashire weaver James Hargreaves created the 'spinning jenny' to help cottage weavers spin wool or cotton fibres into yarn (thread) on lots of spindles, turned by a single handle.*

- **In the 1780s**, James Watt developed a steam engine to drive machines – and steam engines quickly replaced water as the main source of power in factories.

- **In 1713**, Abraham Darby found how to use coke, rather than wood charcoal, to make huge amounts of iron.

- **In 1784**, Henry Cort found how to remove impurities from cast iron to make wrought iron – and iron became the key material of the Industrial Revolution.

▶ *Arkwright's water frame, powered by a water wheel, used four pairs of rotating rollers to stretch fibres before they were spun.*

◀ *During the second half of the 1700s, the Scottish engineer James Watt refined the designs of existing steam engines to produce a model that used heat efficiently and was powerful enough to drive heavy machinery.*

The Jacobites

- **After James II was deposed** as king of England and Scotland in 1688, many Scots still believed he and his Stuart descendants were rightful kings.

- **Supporters of the Stuarts** were called Jacobites after *Jacobus*, Latin for James.

- **James II's son**, James, was called the Old Pretender, because he pretended to (claimed) the English throne.

- **English Queen Anne** died childless in 1714, and the Scottish and English Jacobites rose in revolt in 1715. This revolution is called 'The Fifteen'.

- **The Old Pretender** arrived in Scotland only after The Fifteen and its leaders had been crushed.

- **The Scots hero** of the Fifteen was Rob Roy MacGregor (1671–1734), an outlaw who stole cattle from English-inclined Duke of Montrose, then joined the rebellion. His tale is told in Walter Scott's novel *Rob Roy* (1817).

- **The Old Pretender's son Charles** was Bonnie Prince Charlie, the Young Pretender.

- **In 1745**, Bonnie Prince Charlie led the Jacobites in a rebellion – called 'the Forty-Five' – against George II.

◀ *Rob Roy MacGregor – Scottish outlaw, hero of the Jacobite rebellion of 1715 and the subject of Walter Scott's dramatic 1817 novel,* Rob Roy.

- **The Jacobites defeated** the English at Prestonpans, then invaded England, advancing as far as Derby before they lost their nerve and retreated.

- **In the sleet**, on bleak Culloden moor near Inverness on 16 April, 1746, the Jacobites were routed by the English and lowland Scots under the Duke of Cumberland. Cumberland came to be called Butcher, because of the way he ruthlessly hunted down and killed survivors.

▼ *When Jacobites led by Bonnie Prince Charlie rose up in the 1740s, they were brutally crushed, at the bleak and bloody Battle of Culloden Moor, by England's Duke of Cumberland.*

Napoleon

- **Napoleon Bonaparte** (1769–1821) was the greatest general of modern times, creating a French empire that covered most of Europe.

- **Napoleon was quite short** at just 157 cm tall and was nicknamed le Petit Caporal ('the tiny corporal'). He was an inspiring leader, with a genius for planning and an incredibly strong will.

- **Napoleon was born** on the island of Corsica. At the age of nine he went to army school, and at fourteen he joined the French army.

- **The Revolution** gave Napoleon the chance to shine and by 1794, at just 25, he was a brigadier general.

▼ *The Battle of Waterloo, in 1815, was a hard-won conquest that finally ended Napoleon's bids for power. Leading the victors was British general Wellington, aided by the last-minute arrival of Prussian troops and by some serious French errors.*

▶ *Napoleon, with his right hand hidden, characteristically, inside his jacket.*

- **In 1796**, days after marrying Josephine de Beauharnais, Napoleon was sent with a small troop simply to hold up the invading Austrians. Instead, he drove them back as far as Vienna and conquered much of Austria.

- **By 1804**, Napoleon's conquests had made him a hero in France, and he elected himself as Emperor Napoleon I.

- **By 1812**, Napoleon had defeated all the major countries in Europe but Britain and decided to invade Russia.

- **Napoleon's invasion** of Russia ended in such disaster that it broke his power in Europe. Soon afterwards, he was defeated at Leipzig, Paris was occupied by his enemies and he was sent into exile on the isle of Elba.

- **Napoleon escaped** from Elba in March 1815 to raise another army, but this was defeated by Wellington's armies at Waterloo, Belgium, in June.

- **After Waterloo**, Napoleon was sent to the island of St Helena in the mid-Atlantic, where he died, aged 51.

399

Ireland

- **When the Irish high king**, Turlough O'Connor, overthrew Dermot, the king of Leinster, *c.*1160, Dermot asked Henry II, the Norman king of England, for help.

- **When Dermot died**, the Norman baron Strongbow made himself king of Leinster. Henry II invaded and Normans slowly gained control of all Ireland.

- **Norman English power** in Ireland weakened as many people adopted Irish ways. By the 1400s, they controlled only a small area round Dublin called the Pale.

- **The phrase 'beyond the Pale'** originally meant the dark and wild Ireland that lay outside the Pale.

- **To regain control**, the English began the 'plantation of Ireland' – giving English settlers land there.

- **In the late 1500s**, the English queen Elizabeth I tried to set up Protestantism in Ireland by force.

◄ *Shane O'Neill, who led Irish revolts against Elizabeth I's attempts to force Ireland to accept Protestantism.*

- **The Irish in Ulster** revolted, led first by Shane O'Neill and later his nephew Hugh O'Neill, but Elizabeth crushed the rebellion in 1603.

- **Oliver Cromwell** stamped out another Irish revolt in 1649.

- **After the defeat of James II** at the Battle of the Boyne in 1690, Irish Catholics lost more land to English and Irish Protestants. By 1704, they owned just 15 percent of Ireland.

- **In 1798**, Wolfe Tone led another Irish revolt – aided by a small French army – but the revolution was soon crushed.

▼ *In July, 1690, William III of England fought the former King James II for the English crown at the Battle of the Boyne in Ireland.*

Industrial unrest

- **Wages in the new factories** of the Industrial Revolution were low and working conditions were very poor.

- **Luddites** were English factory workers who, in 1811–1812, smashed new machines that put people out of work.

- **High taxes** on imported corn meant that the poor were first to suffer in times of bad harvest, such as 1816–1819.

- **The 'Peterloo' massacre** of 16 August, 1819, was caused by a cavalry charge into a crowd gathered to hear radical leader Henry Hunt in Manchester's St Peter's field.

- **Welsh-born Robert Owen** (1771–1858) was the first great factory reformer and socialist.

▲ *Welshman Robert Owen did much to promote better conditions for workers.*

- **Owen set up** 'ideal' communities at New Lanark in Scotland and New Harmony in Indiana, USA, where people might work together in good conditions.

- **Trade unions were banned** by British 'Combination' Acts. But these were partly removed in 1824.

- **Owen's** Grand National Consolidated Trades Union of 1833 – the first national union – was instantly repressed by the government.

- **The Tolpuddle Martyrs** were six Dorset farmworkers transported to Australia in 1834 for trying to form a trade union.

▲ *Sheffield, northern England, in 1879 – one of Europe's major centres during the Industrial Revolution, famed for its steel production. Cities such as this became hotbeds of unrest among badly treated workers.*

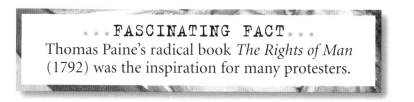

. . .FASCINATING FACT. . .
Thomas Paine's radical book *The Rights of Man* (1792) was the inspiration for many protesters.

Austria and Prussia

◀ *As well as being a ruthless military leader, Frederick the Great played and composed flute music and exchanged long letters with the philosopher Voltaire.*

- **In 1711**, Austria, Hungary, Germany and parts of Italy were part of the Holy Roman Empire. The emperor was Charles VI, the Archduke of Austria.

- **Charles VI** had no sons, but wanted his young daughter Maria Theresa to rule after him.

- **When Charles VI died**, in 1740, three non-Austrians claimed they should be emperor. Maria Theresa rallied her Austrian people to defend her claim.

- **The War of the Austrian Succession** began with Britain, Hungary and the Netherlands backing Maria Theresa. Prussia, France, Bavaria, Saxony, Sardinia and Spain opposed her.

- **In 1742**, Maria Theresa was defeated and Charles of Bavaria became emperor. Charles, however, died in 1745. Maria Theresa's husband Francis I became emperor, though Maria was actually in charge.

- **The rise of Prussia** is linked to the rise of their ruling family the Hohenzollerns, and aristocratic landlords called junkers.

- **In 1417**, Frederick Hohenzollern became elector of Brandenburg. This meant he was one of the chosen few who could elect the Holy Roman Emperor.

- **By 1701**, Brandenburg expanded to become Prussia. Frederick I became its first king and built up its army.

- **Frederick I's son**, Frederick II or Frederick the Great (1712–1786), was Prussia's greatest ruler. Frederick II was ambitious and manoeuvred Austria, France and Russia into wars that he used to gain land.

- **Austria and Prussia** lost much of their power after they were beaten by Napoleon's armies.

▶ *Maria Theresa's fight to become Holy Roman Emperor was crushed and Charles of Bavaria took the title. However, she rose to power once again as the wife of Charles's successor, Francis I.*

Napoleonic wars

- **The Napoleonic wars** were the long and bitter wars (1796–1815) between the France of Napoleon and other European countries, including Britain.

- **The wars began** with Napoleon's victories over the Austrians in Italy in 1796.

- **Napoleon wanted to destroy** British trade with the Middle East, and so attacked Egypt in 1798, defeating Egypt's rulers the Mamelukes. Napoleon's fleet was destroyed on the Nile by the British under Lord Nelson, but Napoleon then beat the Turks at Abuqir.

- **The French Revolution** had introduced a conscript system, which meant that every Frenchman had to serve in the army – Napoleon's army was 750,000 in 1799. Two million more had joined up by 1815.

- **In 1805**, Britain, Russia and Austria allied against Napoleon. Napoleon crushed the Austrians and Russians at Austerlitz. When Prussia joined Russia, Napoleon routed the Prussians at Jena and Auerstadt and the Russians at Friedland. But in 1805 Nelson's ships had destroyed the French and Spanish fleets at Trafalgar. Nelson died at Trafalgar, but his victory ended Napoleon's chances of invading Britain.

▼ *Napoleon's retreat from Moscow in 1812 was one of the worst military disasters. The winter trek was so cold and food so scarce, only 30,000 of the army of 695,000 that set out made it back to France. However, the biggest cause of death was the spread of the disease typhus.*

- **A key element** in the French success was the 'column'. Instead of advancing in a thin line, men marched almost up to the enemy in columns, then spread out.

- **Napoleon tried** to destroy Britain with the 'Continental System', which banned any country from trading with it.

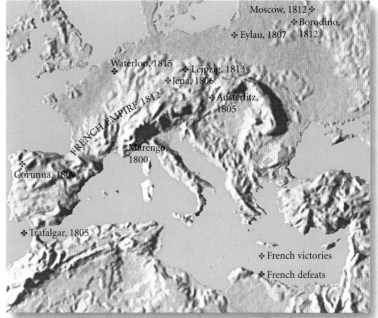

▲ *This map shows some of the major battles of the Napoleonic Wars.*

- **In 1812,** Napoleon captured Moscow, but the Russians burned everything as they fell back – leaving the French without food.

- **After the 1812 disaster**, Napoleon's enemies moved in swiftly. Defeated at Leipzig, Napoleon abdicated. His brief comeback in 1815 ended in defeat at Waterloo.

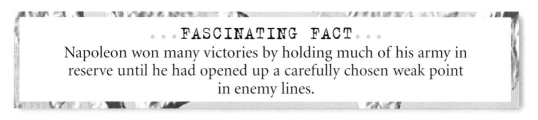

. . . **FASCINATING FACT** . . .
Napoleon won many victories by holding much of his army in reserve until he had opened up a carefully chosen weak point in enemy lines.

The year of revolutions

▲ *When rioters raged through Vienna, the feared Prince Metternich and many of his hated secret police were forced to flee.*

- **The year 1848** saw revolutions break out right across Europe – in France, Germany, Italy, Austria and Hungary.

- **The revolutions** were not linked directly, but the revolutionaries had many of the same grievances.

- **Most revolutionaries** were also angry at repressive governments in which too few people had a say.

▶ *Karl Marx (1818–1883), founder of international communism. The ground-breaking* Communist Manifesto *that he wrote with Engels appeared during the year of revolution – 1848.*

- **Many revolutionaries were angry** too at the poverty suffered by ordinary people in the new industrial cities.

- **Many places**, such as Hungary, Germany and Italy, were under the power of a foreign government, and revolutionaries were often nationalists who wanted freedom from foreign oppression for their country.

- **In Paris**, revolutionaries shouting 'bread or death' stormed government buildings, threw out the king and set up a republic.

- **In Vienna**, the powerful Prince Metternich and emperor were forced to flee as people created their own parliament and freed serfs.

- **In Hungary**, revolutionary leader Louis Kossuth established a short-lived Hungarian republic.

- **In London**, the last and biggest Chartist rally took place. The Chartists had a charter demanding votes for all men and other political reforms. The rally dispersed peacefully.

- **All but the Paris revolution** were quickly dealt with by armies – but the desire for change grew stronger over the century. The *Communist Manifesto*, written by Karl Marx and Friedrich Engels, was to become the basis of the great revolutions in Russia and China.

Latin American revolts

- **By 1800**, Latin Americans were ready to revolt against the centuries of rule by Spain and Portugal.

- **When the Napoleonic Wars** turned Spain and Portugal into a battleground, Latin American revolutionaries seized their chance.

- **Mexicans** led by priests Hidalgo and Morelos revolted in 1810. The Spanish quelled the revolt and executed Hidalgo and Morelos. In 1821, however, Mexico gained independence.

▼ *South Americans under Bolívar fought hard against the Spanish in modern-day Colombia and Peru.*

Simón Bolívar (1783–1830) was South America's greatest revolutionary hero, but as president of Gran Colombia he proved unpopular.

● **In 1810**, José de San Martin led Argentina to independence. In 1816, San Martin made an epic march across the Andes to bring Chile freedom, too – with the help of Bernardo O'Higgins.

● **In the north**, Venezuelans Francisco de Miranda, Simón Bolívar and Antonio de Sucre led a long fight against the Spanish in New Granada (now Colombia) and Peru. In 1819, after a victory at Boyaca in Colombia, Bolívar proclaimed the Republic of Gran Colombia (now Venezuela, Colombia, Ecuador and Panama).

● **In 1824**, Sucre won a crucial victory at Ayacucho in Peru, freeing all of north South America from Spanish rule.

● **The Republic of Bolivia** was named after Bolívar, who wrote its constitution. Sucre became its first president.

● **Brazil gained its freedom** from Portugal without a fight when its ruler Prince John fled. His son became emperor.

● **Miranda died** in a Spanish jail after Bolívar handed him over. Sucre was assassinated in 1830. Bolívar died in 1830, shortly after a failed assassination attempt.

> ... FASCINATING FACT ...
> In 1824, San Martin left for Europe, saddened by disputes after independence and his wife's death.

411

Italian independence

▲ *The glittering city of Venice became part of a united Italy in 1866.*

- **After the Napoleonic Wars**, Italy was split into various kingdoms – some, like Naples, under French Bourbon kings, some under Austrian rule and papal states under the pope.

- **The Carbonari** (meaning 'charcoal burners') were a secret society working for Italian freedom.

- **In 1820**, the Carbonari got the Bourbon king of Naples to agree to a constitution, but the Austrians intervened to abolish it.

- **In 1831**, Giuseppe Mazzini founded 'Young Italy' to unite Italy. The drive to unite the country became known as the *Risorgimento* ('rising again').

- **In 1848**, revolutions broke out across Italy, but were put down.

- **In 1857**, Count Cavour, prime minister of Piedmont, asked France for help with evicting the Austrians.

- **In 1859**, France and Piedmont beat the Austrians at Magenta and Solferino. After political wrangling, northern Italy was joined to Piedmont under King Victor Emmanuel II.

- **The Battle of Magenta** was so bloody that a new purple-red colour was named after it.

- **In 1860**, the great hero Garibaldi led a rebellion and conquered all of southern Italy. Only Cavour's intervention stopped Garibaldi from taking Rome.

- **In 1861**, most of Italy was united under Victor Emmanuel. Venice was added in 1866 and Rome as capital in 1870.

▶ *Garibaldi was the hero who landed in Italy with just his thousand famous 'Red Shirts'. He went on to conquer all of southern Italy.*

The Irish famine

- **The Irish potato famine** (1845–1849) was one of the worst human disasters of the 1800s, when over a million people in Ireland died of starvation.

  - **In the 1800s**, most Irish were poor farmers, working tiny plots of land rented from Anglo-Irish landlords.

  - **Potatoes were introduced** from America in the 1700s. They were such a successful crop that the Irish population grew to 8.4 million by 1844, but most were very poor.

  - **Half the Irish population** depended entirely on potatoes for food because English laws kept the price of bread too high for the poor Irish to buy.

  - **In 1845**, much of the potato crop was ruined by blight, a disease caused by the fungus Phytophthora.

  - **When the blight** ruined even more of the 1846–1849 potato crops, millions of poor Irish farmers began to starve.

◀ Potatoes became the staple food of the Irish poor because laws established by the English made bread too expensive.

- **By August 1847**, three million were fed entirely on rations from soup kitchens set up by landlords and the British.

- **Many poor tenant farmers** were thrown off their land because they had no crop to sell in order to pay the rent.

- **Throughout the famine**, Irish farms exported grain, meat and vegetables too costly for the Irish to buy.

- **One and a half million** desperate Irish people packed up and left for America, leaving the country half-empty.

▼ *The potato famine devastated Ireland.*

The British Empire

- **At its height**, in 1920, the British Empire covered a quarter of the world and ruled a quarter of the world's population.

- **The British** ruled more peoples than any other nation.

- **The British Empire** began to build up in the 1600s, as British merchants started to extend their trading links throughout the world. The British won out over Dutch, Portuguese, French and Belgian rivals through the success of their navy and also their reasonably efficient colonial government.

- **The 13 American colonies** broke away in 1776, but Canada and many West Indian islands remained British.

- **Britain gained control** of India through the East India Company, between 1757 and 1858. In 1877, Queen Victoria was proclaimed Empress of India – the first time the word empire had been used in relation to the British possessions.

- **Many of the British possessions** had similar climates to Britain's – parts of Canada, South Africa, Australia and New Zealand – and British settlers moved to these places in huge numbers in the 1900s, pushing out the native inhabitants. These colonies were given more and more freedom to govern themselves and came to be called 'dominions'.

- **The Empire reached its peak** after World War I, when German and Turkish possessions were added.

- **After World War II**, more countries demanded independence. India and Pakistan became independent in 1947, Ceylon in 1948. By 1980, most African, West Indian and Pacific Island colonies were independent.

◄ *The British Empire was controlled by the British navy and army. The army worked in every continent, from India to Egypt, and Australia to Canada.*

- **Most colonies** remained within the Commonwealth after independence. There are 54 Commonwealth nations, linked essentially by agreed principles, but they all accept the British queen as head of the Commonwealth.

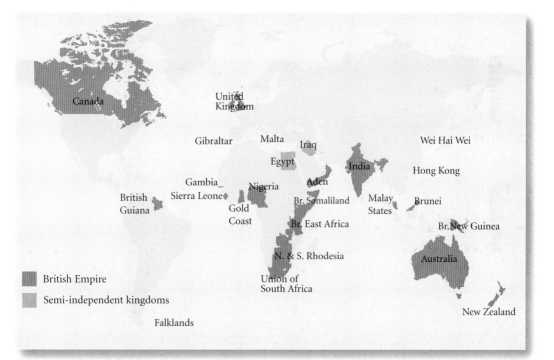

▲ *This map shows the British Empire in the 1930s, when it was beginning to shrink. Egypt was given some independence in 1922, when Sultan Ahmed became King Fuad I. Iraq gained a similar independence when amir Ahd Allah Faisal became King Faisal I.*

. . . **FASCINATING FACT** . . . .
In 1920, 600 million people around the world were ruled from London.

The American Civil War

◀ *The Union flag had stars for all the 13 original states (top). The Confederates had their own version of the flag, also with 13 stars.*

● **The American Civil War** (1861–1865) was fought between northern states (the Union) and southern states (the Confederacy). It split friends and families and resulted in the deaths of over 600,000 Americans.

● **The main cause** of the war was slavery. In 1850, slavery was banned in the 18 northern states, but there were four million slaves in the 15 southern states, where they worked on huge plantations.

● **The conflicts developed** over whether new states, added as settlers pushed westward, should be 'slave' or 'free' states.

● **In 1854**, slavers gained legal victories with the Kansas-Nebraska Act, which let new states decide for themselves.

● **In 1860**, the Abolitionist (anti-slavery) Republican, Abraham Lincoln, was elected as president.

● **The southern states** immediately broke away from the Union in protest, to form their own Confederacy.

- **As the war began**, the Confederates had the upper hand, fighting a mainly defensive campaign.
- **The turning point** came in July 1863, when an invading southern army, commanded by Robert E Lee, was badly defeated at Gettysburg in Pennsylvania.
- **The extra industrial resources** of the north slowly began to tell and General Grant attacked the south from the north, while Sherman advanced ruthlessly from the west.
- **Lee surrendered** to Grant in Appomattox Court House, Virginia, on 9 April, 1865. Slavery was abolished, but a few days later Lincoln was assassinated.

▼ *The American Civil War has been described as the very first 'modern war'. It was basically a fight between two different philosophies of life – the forward-thinking, industrial, anti-slavery north versus the old-fashioned pro-slavery south, with its greater military resources.*

Australia

- **In 1788,** the British sent a fleet of 11 ships, carrying convicts, to start a prison colony in Australia.

- **The fleet landed** at Botany Bay, but the first governor, Arthur Phillip, settled in a new site that eventually became the city of Sydney.

- **Over the next 80 years** 160,000 convicts were sent to Australia, but by 1810 British settlers were arriving voluntarily.

- **After 1850,** settlers set up vast sheep farms in the interior. Many Aborigines were killed as they fought for their land.

- **In 1851,** gold was discovered in New South Wales and Victoria, and many thousands of people came to Australia to seek their fortune, tripling the population to 1.1 million in just nine years.

- **After the gold rushes,** ex-miners campaigned to 'unlock the lands' – that is, free up land from squatters and landowners for small farmers.

- **In the 1880s and 1890s,** Australians began to become aware of their own national identity – partly as Australian cricketers became heroes – and demand self-government.

- **In 1901,** Australia became the independent Commonwealth of Australia, with its own parliament at Melbourne.

- **In 1927,** the Australian government moved to a new capital in Canberra.

- **In 2000,** Australians voted to keep the British queen as head of state, rather than become a republic.

▶ *Famous Yorkshire-born navigator James Cook (1728–1779) sailed around the Pacific, charting New Zealand, Australia and several island groups. Here he is seen on the Cook Islands (some way east of Australia, in Polynesia), which bear his name.*

The scramble for Africa

- **From 1500 to 1800**, Europeans were familiar only with the coast of Africa, from which slaves were taken.

- **After 1800**, many Europeans wanted to explore the interior of Africa, in order to spread Christianity.

- **Some Europeans** wanted to develop trade in products like minerals and palm oil to help combat the slave trade.

- **Many European explorers**, such as David Livingstone and Richard Burton, went to Africa to find out more about its 'dark' (unknown) interior.

- **The wealth brought** to Britain by its colonies, such as India and North America, spurred the European powers to look for more lands to colonize.

▶ *Scottish missionary David Livingstone (1813–1873) undertook several expeditions to Africa. Having gone missing while seeking the source of the Nile, he was famously 'found' by H M Stanley, in 1871.*

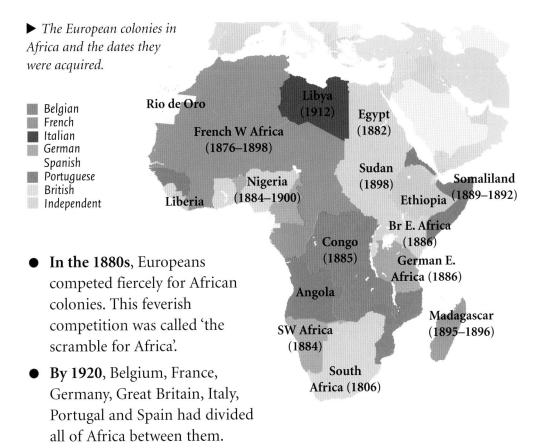

▶ *The European colonies in Africa and the dates they were acquired.*

Belgian
French
Italian
German
Spanish
Portuguese
British
Independent

Rio de Oro

Libya (1912)

Egypt (1882)

French W Africa (1876–1898)

Sudan (1898)

Somaliland (1889–1892)

Nigeria (1884–1900)

Liberia

Ethiopia

Br E. Africa (1886)

Congo (1885)

German E. Africa (1886)

Angola

Madagascar (1895–1896)

SW Africa (1884)

South Africa (1806)

- **In the 1880s**, Europeans competed fiercely for African colonies. This feverish competition was called 'the scramble for Africa'.

- **By 1920**, Belgium, France, Germany, Great Britain, Italy, Portugal and Spain had divided all of Africa between them.

- **In some parts of Africa**, colonial rule was established peacefully by agreement with the Africans.

- **In Nigeria and Ghana**, the Africans fought hard against British rule, and in Tanzania and Namibia, they fought against German rule.

- **Ethiopia and Liberia** were the only countries in Africa to hold on to their independence.

423

The Oregon trail

- **After the USA became independent**, in 1783, waves of settlers began to move west

- **The first settlers** were fur traders. These were followed by cattle ranchers, then other farmers.

- **When cattle ranchers moved** to the Great Plains, they grazed huge herds on the open range and drove them to newly built rail depots for shipment east.

- **The cattle ranchers of the Great Plains** employed cowboys to herd the cattle, and these cowboys became the symbol of the American west.

- **As the settlers pushed west** they came into conflict with Native Americans who already lived there.

- **The settlers made** many treaties with local peoples but broke almost all of them, and Native Americans were gradually driven from their lands or simply slaughtered.

- **In each decade**, new settlers struggled further west, facing great hardship in the hope of finding a new life.

- **Settlers often set out** with all their possessions in a covered wagon, often travelling with other wagons in a convoy for safety.

- **The Oregon trail** was the longest of the routes to the west, winding over 3000 km from Independence, Missouri to the Pacific northwest.

- **The first group of 900 wagons** set out on the Oregon trail in the Great Migration of 1843.

▶ *Would-be settlers packed everything they owned in a covered wagon and joined a train of wagons heading west. They travelled in convoy for safety, as they were passing through, and staking claim to, land that had been inhabited by Native Americans for centuries.*

The Crimean War

▲ Around a third of the cavalrymen of the Light
Brigade died making their heroic but useless charge.

- **The Crimean War** was fought in the Crimea – to the north of the Black Sea – between 1854 and 1856.

  - **On one side** was Russia. On the other were Turkey, Britain, France, and Piedmont/Sardinia, while Austria gave political support.

    - **The main cause** of the war was British, French and Turkish worries about Russian expansion in the Black Sea.

      - **The war began** when Russia destroyed the Turkish fleet.

        - **Armies on both sides** were badly organized. Many British soldiers died of cholera before they even reached the Crimea and wounded soldiers suffered badly from cold and disease.

        - **During the Battle of Balaklava**, on 25 October, 1854, a stupid mistake sent a gallant British cavalry charge straight on to the Russian guns. The heroic 'Charge of the Light Brigade' was made famous in a poem by Tennyson.

          - **Conditions in the battle hospitals** were reported in the first-ever war photographs and in the telegraphed news reports of W H Russell.

          - **Nurses** like Florence Nightingale and Jamaican Mary Seacole went to the Crimea to help the wounded.

          - **Lessons learned** in the Crimea helped to lay the foundations of modern nursing.

          - **The war finally ended** in 1856 with the Treaty of Paris, with few gains on either side.

Germany

- **In 1815**, Germany was divided among 38 different states of the German Confederation.

- **The most powerful** of the German states were Prussia and Austria, who sparred for dominance.

- **In 1862**, Otto von Bismarck (1815–1898) became chancellor of Prussia. He was known as 'the Iron Chancellor 'and it was through his determination and skilful diplomacy that Germany was united.

- **In 1864**, Denmark tried to annex the duchies of Schleswig and Holstein whose duke was the Danish king. The Austrians and Prussians sent an army to drive the Danes out.

- **Austria and Prussia** could not agree on what to do with Schleswig-Holstein.

- **Bismarck proposed** a new North German Confederation, excluding Austria.

- **Austria objected** to Bismarck's plan, but was defeated by Prussia in a very swift war in 1866.

- **To complete Prussian control** over Germany, Bismarck provoked a war against France, which had been the main opponent to German unity. He used the trick of the Ems telegram – a version of a telegram reporting a conversation between the Prussian king and the French ambassador, skilfully edited to imply an insult to France.

- **France declared war** on Prussia, but was swiftly beaten by the Prussians, who marched into Paris in January 1871.

- **After the defeat of France**, all the German states agreed to become part of a united Germany under Prussian leadership. On 18 January, 1871, Wilhelm I was crowned kaiser (emperor).

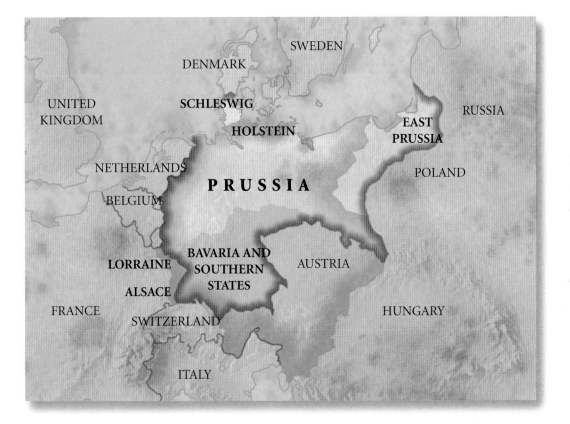

 German Confederation

North German Confederation 1867

German Second Empire 1871

▲ *The North German Confederation was a union of states formed in 1867. Prussia dominated the confederation. Within this union, members were able to keep their own governments, but foreign and military policies were decided by a federal government.*

The rise
of America

◀ *The president and executive in the White House prepare laws and puts them into effect – and also conducts foreign affairs – but only Congress can make laws legal.*

- **In the late 1800s,** the USA changed from a nation of farming pioneers and plantation owners to the world's biggest industrial powerhouse. American inventors and industrialists made products that changed the world – the typewriter (1867), the telephone (1876), the phonograph (1877) and electric light (1879). Then, in the early 1900s, Henry Ford pioneered the mass production of cars and made them affordable for millions of people.

- **The writer Mark Twain** called the era of industrialization 'the Gilded Age', to describe the culture of the newly rich. Without any traditions of their own to draw on, they developed a showy culture aping that of European aristocrats – going to operas and building enormous European-style mansions filled with antiques, works by European painters and rare books.

- **The less rich** enjoyed different kinds of show – circuses, vaudevilles and sport. By 1900, baseball was the national pastime. After 1920, motion pictures drew millions.

- **In the late 1800s,** people started to realize that American progress was leaving many behind, and reformers called Progressives began to demand change. In 1184, farmers and labourers formed the Populist party.

- **In 1903,** Theodore Roosevelt was elected as president and promised Americans a 'square deal'. He tried to curb the power of monopolies like Standard Oil and supported striking miners.

- **Until 1898,** the USA played little part in world affairs. Bismarck said, 'A special Providence takes care of fools, drunkards and the USA'. But in 1898, the US battleship *Maine* was blown up off Cuba. Americans blamed the Spanish and in the war that followed, the USA easily defeated Spain.

- **From 1898 onwards,** the USA became increasingly involved in world affairs, stepping in later in World War I and World War II to play a decisive role. By the late 1900s, the USA saw itself as the world's policeman.

- **By the 1920s,** America was booming. The 1920s were known as the 'Roaring Twenties', because the pace of change was so exciting, and cars and loud jazz music made the new America so noisy and vibrant.

- **The confidence of the 1920s** spurred speculation on money markets, and in 1929 New York's Wall Street stock market crashed. US economic power was now so great that the crash plunged the world into the Great Depression of the 1930s, which saw businesses fold and millions unemployed.

- **The USA has taken a lead** in a 'war on terror' after terrorists destroyed New York's Twin Towers and part of the Pentagon building in Washington by flying planes into them on 11 September, 2001.

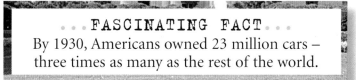

... FASCINATING FACT ...
By 1930, Americans owned 23 million cars –
three times as many as the rest of the world.

Victorian England

- **In 1837**, 18-year-old Victoria became the queen of England and reigned for 63 years until 1901 – the longest reign in British history.

- **Victoria's reign** is called the Victorian Age.

- **In the Victorian Age**, Britain became the world's largest industrial and trading power, and the British Empire reached its peak.

- **British factories and towns** mushroomed and railways were built throughout the country.

- **In 1851**, the Great Exhibition opened in a huge building of glass and iron, later called the Crystal Palace, to show British skills to the world.

- **In 1861**, Victoria's husband, Prince Albert, died. She went into mourning and wore black for the rest of her life.

▲ *Under Victoria, Britain came to wield control over the largest empire the world had ever seen, and made astonishing artistic, scientific and manufacturing advances.*

▶ *Benjamin Disraeli, twice prime minister in Victorian England (1868 and 1874–1880), and one of Victoria's favourite statesmen. Under Disraeli, the British Empire gained even more status when Victoria became Empress of India.*

- **The rapid expansion** of Victorian cities created vast slum areas where living conditions were appalling.

- **Social reformers** and writers such as Charles Dickens highlighted the problems of the slums. Slowly, Parliament passed laws to improve conditions for working people and to provide education for all.

- **The two great prime ministers** of the Victorian Age were the flamboyant Benjamin Disraeli (1804–1881) and the dour William Gladstone (1809–1898).

- **Victorian middle-class life** cultivated cosy moral values, but there was also a seamy side, with widespread prostitution and crime.

The Balkans

▶ *Within just four days after the assassination of Archduke Franz Ferdinand, World War I had started.*

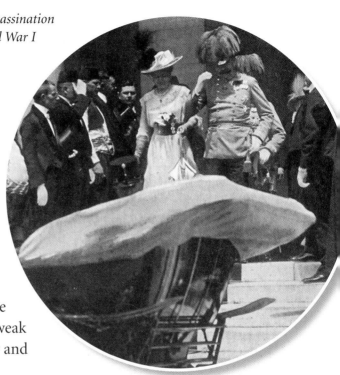

- **The Balkans** are the countries of southeastern Europe. The word *balkan* is Turkish for 'mountain'.

- **In 1800**, people of many nationalities lived in the Balkans – Slovenes, Croats, Serbs, Bulgars, Greeks and Turks.

- **All the Balkan peoples** were ruled over by two old and weak empires – Austria-Hungary and Ottoman Turkey.

- **Throughout the 1800s**, many nationalities in the Balkans worked for independence.

- **European powers** like Russia and Germany encouraged independence movements for their own purposes.

- **Between 1829 and 1908**, Greece, Montenegro, Serbia, Romania and Bulgaria gained some independence, but many of their people were still living within the old empires.

- **Austria refused** Slovenia and Croatia independence and held on to Bosnia-Herzegovina, which Serbia claimed.

- **In 1912**, various Balkan countries conspired to drive the Turks out of Europe in the First Balkan War, but rivalry between them led to a Second Balkan War in 1913, which let the Turks back in and left the Balkans highly unstable.

- **In June 1914**, Archduke Franz Ferdinand was assassinated in Sarajevo by Gavrilo Princip, a Serbian activist from Bosnia-Herzegovina.

- **Austria believed** Serbs were behind the assassination and declared war. Russia defended the Serbs as they had pledged by secret treaty. Soon all of Europe was engaged in World War I.

▲ *Tanks first appeared in World War I. They were effective against gunfire, but often broke down.*

The Opium Wars

▲ *Millions of Chinese became addicted to opium in the early 1800s.*

- **From 1759 to 1842**, Chinese emperors let European merchants trade only in the port of Guangzhou, and buy tea and silk only from the cohong (guild) of Chinese firms.

- **To pay for Chinese goods**, the East India Company used opium, the drug made from poppies. Huge quantities of opium grown in India were sold to Chinese drug dealers.

- **All the silver** used to pay for opium upset the Chinese economy and opium-smuggling got out of hand.

▶ *Opium is obtained from a certain type of poppy. It is made by drying an extract from seed capsules that have not yet ripened.*

- **In March 1839**, Chinese commissioner Lin Tse-hsü seized 20,000 crates of opium from British merchants.

- **Many ordinary Chinese** backed the British, because the British provided them with opium and because the emperor's restrictive rule had brought poverty and hunger.

- **In 1840**, 16 British warships went to Guangzhou, starting the First Opium War. The Chinese were easily beaten.

- **Under the Treaty of Nanjing**, drawn up in 1842, the Chinese gave Britain Hong Kong, abolished the cohong system and opened up trade to specially favoured nations.

- **In 1856**, Chinese police seized the *Arrow*, a ship flying a British flag, thus starting the Second Opium War.

- **British and French armies** invaded China and, after some wrangling, occupied Beijing in 1860.

- **At the Beijing Convention**, China opened more ports to western trade and allowed Europeans to travel inland.

437

Abraham Lincoln

- **Abraham Lincoln** (1809–1865) was America's 16th, and possibly greatest, president. He led the Union through the Civil War and the freeing of slaves.

- **He was born** in a single-room log cabin in Kentucky, to a poor family.

- **He never went to school** but a relative said, "I never seen Abe after twelve 'at he didn't have a book in his hand or his pocket" – often the Bible.

- **He became a lawyer**, known for shrewd common sense and honesty. His defence of Rock Island Bridge (on the Mississippi River) against shipping interests made him famous.

- **Once elected to Congress**, he went on to win political fame as an opponent of slavery through debates over the Kansas-Nebraska Act, in the 1850s.

- **In 1860**, just before the start of the Civil War, between north and south, he was elected president – on the votes of the northern states alone.

▲ *Lincoln was a tall, lanky man. His razor-sharp mind, calm manner and resolutely moral attitudes made him a hero to many Americans.*

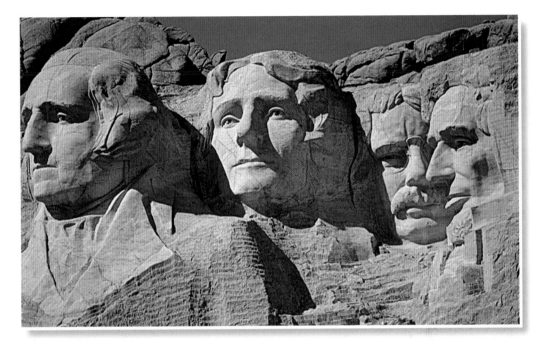

▲ *From left: presidents Washington, Jefferson, Roosevelt, Lincoln, carved into Mt. Rushmore.*

- **On 1 January, 1863**, Lincoln announced his Emancipation Proclamation, which freed all slaves.

- **In 1863**, after the terrible battle of Gettysburg, Lincoln made a famous speech called the Gettysburg Address, which summed up the spirit of democracy. In it he vowed that 'government of the people, by the people, for the people, shall not perish from the Earth.'

- **When the war ended**, in 1865, he made plans for peaceful reconciliation.

- **He was shot dead** at Ford's Theatre, Washington, by John Wilkes Booth, a fanatical southerner.

439

The Second Empire

- **In the 1840s,** the poverty of workers in French towns inspired men like Proudhon and Fourier to devise socialist ideas for solving various social problems.

- **Political meetings** were banned, so agitators held banquets to press their demands for liberal reforms.

◄ Radical politicians came to the fore in the Empire.

- **On 22 February, 1848,** the government banned a huge banquet in Paris, provoking such protest and rioting that King Louis-Philippe was forced to abdicate.

- **After much wrangling,** a new popular assembly set up the Second Republic and Louis-Napoleon Bonaparte was elected president in a vote by all French men.

- **Louis-Napoleon** (1808–1873) was the son of Napoleon's brother and his step-daughter Hortense. In his youth, he had been active in the Italian Carbonari.

▶ *Louis-Napoleon, nephew of Napoleon I and ruler of the Second Empire.*

- **The Assembly proved** conservative and, in 1852, Louis-Napoleon curbed their powers and had himself made Emperor Napoleon III by popular vote. His rule is called the Second Empire.

- **Napoleon III gave state aid** to industry, banks and railroads. Industry boomed and France grew rich. French engineers became world-famous.

- **Napoleon III's Spanish wife**, Eugenie, set the Empire Style for beautiful, lavish fashions and decoration that was mimicked across Europe.

- **Gradually, Napoleon's rule** provoked more and more hostility among radicals, and France's defeat by Germany in 1871 led to his downfall.

...FASCINATING FACT...
The famous boulevards of Paris, with their grand houses, were created on Napoleon III's orders.

The Russian Revolution

▲ *The Tsar's grand Winter Palace at St Petersburg, seized by revolutionaries in 1917.*

- **In 1861,** Tsar Alexander II freed Russian serfs, but they stayed poor. In towns, factory workers were just as poor.

- **Unrest among factory workers** and peasants grew and by 1901 there were two revolutionary parties: Socialist Revolutionary (SRP) and Socialist Democrat (SDP).

- **In 1903,** the SDP split into Bolsheviks (extremist majority), led by Lenin, and Mensheviks (moderate minority).

▶ *Tsar Nicholas II and family, who were fatally shot by Bolsheviks in the aftermath of the Revolution.*

- **In 1905**, after Russia's disastrous war against Japan, workers and peasants rose in revolt and workers from arms factories set up the first soviets (workers' councils).

- **Tsar Nicholas II** was forced to set up a Duma (parliament) but soon began to ignore it.

- **In March 1917**, terrible losses among Russian soldiers in World War I, plus hardship at home, provoked a revolution.

- **The first 1917 revolution** is called the February Revolution, because this was the month in the old Russian calendar.

- **Tsar Nicholas abdicated**. Later, the Bolsheviks shot him and all of his family at Ykaterinburg.

- **The SRP**, led by Kerensky, had the upper hand at first, but more soviets were set up and Bolseheviks gained support.

- **On 7 November** (25 October on the old calendar), the Bolsheviks seized the Winter Palace in St Petersburg. Lenin headed a new government, based in Moscow, and ended the war, while soviets took control of major cities.

World War I

- **World War I** (1914–1918), the Great War, was the worst the world had seen (World War II would prove to be even worse), killing ten million troops.

- **The war was caused** by the rivalry between European powers in the early 1900s. The assassination of Franz Ferdinand in Sarajevo in the Balkans, on 28 June, 1914, made Austria start a war with Serbia. Russia came to Serbia's defence. Germany declared war on Russia and her ally France on 3 August.

- **The Germans** had a secret plan (the 'Schlieffen plan') for invading France. Instead of tackling the French head-on, as expected, they swept round to the north through neutral Belgium. This outrage drew Britain into the war.

- **As the Germans moved into France**, they came up against the British and French (the Allies). The opposing armies dug trenches – and stayed facing each other in much the same place for four years. The trenches, known as the Western front, stretched from the English Channel to Switzerland.

- **The war soon developed** an Eastern front, where the Central Powers (Austria and Germany) faced the Russians. The deaths of millions of Russians provoked the 1917 Revolution, which took Russia out of the war.

- **In the Alps**, the Central Powers were opposed by Italy. At Gallipoli in Turkey, British and Anzac (Australia and New Zealand) troops fought the Turks.

- **The Allies** relied on supplies from North America, so the Germans used submarines to attack ships. The sinking of the *Lusitania* in May 1915, with 128 Americans out of 1198 casualties, brought the USA into the war.

- **In 1918**, there were 3.5 million Germans on the Western front and in March they broke through towards Paris.

- **In July 1918**, British tanks broke the German line at Amiens.

- **An Allied naval blockade** meant many people were starving in Germany. As more US troops arrived, the Germans were pushed back. At 11 o'clock on 11 November, 1918, the Germans signed an armistice (peace).

◀ *Trenches were dug to protect troops from enemy gunfire, but became hell-holes, filled with water, rats and disease. Soldiers had to eat, sleep and stand guard ankle-deep in mud. Every now and then, they were ordered to 'go over the top' – climb out of their trenches and advance towards enemy lines. Out of the trench, they were exposed to enemy fire, and quickly mown down. Millions of soldiers on both sides died. On 1 July, 1916, 60,000 British soldiers were killed in just a few hours in the Battle of the Somme. The four-month Somme offensive killed 600,000 Germans, 400,000 British and 200,000 French – and advanced the Allies 7 km. The horror of war was conveyed in letters and poems by soldiers such as Siegfried Sassoon and Wilfred Owen.*

445

The Ottoman Empire

- **In 1774**, the Turkish Ottoman Empire was defeated by the Russians after a six-year war, and was forced to allow Russian ships to pass through the Straits from the Black Sea to the Mediterranean.

- **During the 1800s**, the Ottoman Empire grew weaker and weaker and was called 'the Sick Man of Europe' by foreign statesmen.

- **In 1829**, the Greeks fought a successful war of independence against the Turks. Other Balkan states followed suit.

- **During the 1800s**, the Turks fought four wars against Russia and lost three. Russia gained Bessarabia (now Moldova and Ukraine) and control of the Black Sea.

- **Trying to stop** the empire's decline, Sultan Abdul-Hamid II crushed opposition violently in the 1890s.

- **The Young Turks** were students and army officers who, in 1908, revolted against Abdul-Hamid and then ruled through his brother Muhammad V.

◀ *A sumptuously dressed Ottoman pasha, or high-ranking official (centre), with his noblemen.*

- **The Turks joined** World War I on the German side to regain territory lost to the Russians and in the Balkans.

- **After World War I** ended, the Allies invaded Turkey and broke up the empire, leaving just modern Turkey.

- **The nationalist hero** Mustafa Kemal became first president of the Turkish republic, on 29 October, 1923.

- **Kemal became known** as Attaturk (father of the Turks). He created modern Turkey by reforming education, law and languages.

▶ *This mosque is a fine example of architecture from the early Ottoman period.*

447

The rise of the Nazis

- **Even before World War I** ended, Germans had risen in revolt against their kaiser (emperor), Wilhelm II.

- **Wilhelm II was driven** out, and in 1919 Germany became a republic with a president elected by the people.

- **The republic was called** the Weimar Republic because that was where the constitution had been drafted.

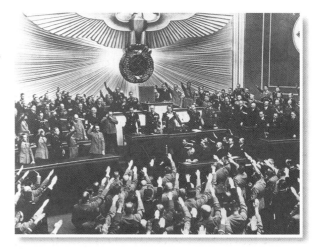

▲ *To boost their support, the Nazis held huge meetings called rallies at which their symbol, the swastika, was prominently displayed.*

- **Under the peace terms** for World War I, Germany was forced to pay huge amounts of money for war damage.

- **The cost of the war** ruined the German economy, and rapidly rising prices made people poor overnight.

- **In 1923**, the National Socialist German Workers Party, or Nazis, led by Adolf Hitler, tried to stage a rebellion in Munich. The rebellion failed, but support for the Nazis grew.

- **The Great Depression** threw six million people out of work, and in 1933 enough people voted for the Nazis to make them the strongest party. Hitler became chancellor and set about destroying the opposition.

- **The Nazis** asserted German superiority over other races, including Jews and Slavs. They removed Jews from all government jobs and took away their rights.

- **On 9 November, 1938**, Nazis broke windows and burned down synagogues and Jewish businesses. This night became known as *Kristallnacht* ('Night of the Broken Glass').

- **The Nazis prepared** for war to give Germans *Lebensraum* ('living space'). In 1936, they marched into the Rhineland. In 1938, they took Austria, followed in 1939 by Czechoslovakia and then Poland.

▲ *The dramatic collapse of the German economy caused by World War I and the Great Depression made the country's currency virtually worthless. Here, a girl is playing with large bundles of Mark notes, using them as building blocks.*

449

Lenin and Stalin

- **Lenin** (1870–1924) was the leader of the Communist revolution in Russia.

- **Lenin's real name** was Vladimir Ilyieh Ulyanov. He took the name Lenin from the River Lena in Siberia when he became a revolutionary.

- **Like Karl Marx** (1818–1883), Lenin believed the world's workers would revolt and take over industry. Unlike Marx, he thought a small band of professionals like the Bolsheviks would need to lead the way.

- **After the 1905 revolution**, Lenin lived in exile, but he returned to Russia when the tsar fell, in 1917.

- **After the October revolution**, Lenin ruled the country as head of the Bolsheviks (now the Communists). The Communists won the civil war that followed and in 1922 changed the Russian Empire into a new nation, called the Union of Soviet Socialist Republics (USSR).

- **Joseph Stalin** (1879–1953) became dictator of the USSR after Lenin died in 1924, and remained so until he himself died, in 1953.

- **Stalin was from** Georgia and his real name was Joseph Vissarionovich Dzhugashvili.

▲ *Lenin and Stalin in rare agreement.*

- **Stalin used terror** to wipe out opposition and ensure the revolution survived. Russians lived in fear of the secret police NKVD (later the KGB), led by Beria, and millions went to their deaths in the Gulags (prison camps).

- **Millions of Russian peasants** starved in the 1930s as Stalin forced government control of farms.

- **Stalin's industrial programme** transformed the USSR into one of the world's great industrial and military powers.

▼ *Lenin's tomb, in Red Square, Moscow. Over the years, countless thousands have queued up to see the embalmed body inside.*

Hitler

- **Adolf Hitler** (1889–1945) was the dictator who turned Germany into a war machine that started World War II and murdered six million Jews in the Holocaust.

- **Hitler was born** in Braunau-Am-Inn, Austria. A failed artist, he painted postcards before joining the German army in World War I.

- **Hitler was so angry** at the terms ending World War I that he joined the National Socialist (Nazi) party, becoming its leader.

- **In 1923**, Hitler was put in prison after a failed Nazi coup, and there he wrote *Mein Kampf* ('My Struggle').

- *Mein Kampf* says Germany's problems were caused by Jews and communists and that it needed a strong *führer* (leader).

◄ *Hitler was a mesmerizing speaker, with the power to get the whole audience at rallies shouting his praise.*

- **As the Depression hit Germany** in the early 1930s, Hitler's ideas gained support. In the 1933 elections, the Nazis got 37 percent of the vote and President Hindenburg asked Hitler to become chancellor (chief minister).

- **The Nazis** established the Gestapo (secret police) and used them to wipe out all opposition. When Hindenburg died in 1934, Hitler made himself *führer*.

- **Hitler built up** Germany's army, rigidly organized all workers and sent millions of Jews to concentration camps.

- **In 1938**, Hitler invaded Austria, then in 1939 Czechoslovkia and Poland too, and so began World War II.

- **Finally, as Germany faced defeat** in 1945, he married his mistress Eva Braun on April 29 in their bomb shelter in Berlin. They shot themselves the next day.

◀ *The worst of the Nazi concentration camps, such as Auschwitz, in Poland, became brutal death-centres. Millions of Jews were killed in these camps, many of them sent to horrific 'gas chambers', where they were poisoned with toxic gas.*

The Spanish Civil War

- **In the 1920s**, a weak economy and political unrest led General de Rivera to run Spain as dictator, alongside King Alfonso XIII.

- **In 1930**, the army drove Rivera out. In 1931, a popular vote for a republic persuaded Alfonso to leave Spain.

- **Spain was split**. On the Left were socialists, communists and ordinary people who supported the republic. On the right were wealthy landowners, army officers, the Catholic Church, and the fascist Falange party, who wanted the king back.

▲ *General Franco, victor of the Civil War and right-wing dictator of Spain for almost 40 years.*

- **Complicating the picture** were Catalonians and Basques, who wanted to break away from Spain.

- **In February 1936**, elections put the Popular Front, formed by all the left-wing groups, in power.

- **In July 1936**, a wave of army revolts started in Morocco and threatened to topple the Popular Front. The Popular Front supporters armed themselves and a bitter civil war began, with terrible atrocities on both sides.

- **The forces of the Right** were called the Nationalists and were led by General Franco. They were supported by fascist (very right-wing) Germany and Italy.

- **The forces of the Left** were called the Republicans or Loyalists and were supported by Soviet Russia. Liberals from other countries, like the writer Laurie Lee, formed an International Brigade to fight for the Loyalists.

- **At first, Loyalists held** the northeast and the big cities, but they gradually fell back. In March 1939, Franco's forces captured Madrid, the last Loyalist stronghold.

- **Franco was dictator** of Spain until he died in 1975.

▲ *A recruiting poster for the fascist Falange party.*

The Long March

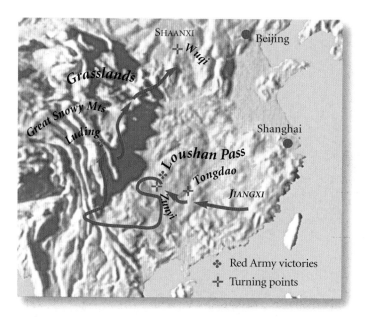

◄ *The heroic Long March of the Red Army – to escape the Nationalists – became Chinese legend.*

- **In 1912**, the last Chinese emperor, six-year-old Pu-Yi, gave up his throne in the face of rebellion and China became a republic, led by Sun Yat-sen.

- **When Sun died**, in 1925, leadership of his Kuomintang (Nationalist) party fell to Chiang Kai-shek, who allied with Communists to defeat warlords in the north.

- **In 1927**, Chiang Kai-shek turned on the Communists and forced their leaders to flee to the Jiangxi hills as he took control in Beijing.

- **By 1931**, the Communists had regrouped enough to set up a rival government in the south, called the Jiangxi soviet.

- **In 1934**, Chiang Kai-shek launched a massive attack on the Communist Red Army, forcing them to begin their famous Long March to the north to escape.

- **On the Long March**, the Red Army wound 10,000 km through the mountains, covering up to 100 km a day, until they reached Shaanxi in the north a year later.

- **Almost 95,000 of the 100,000** who set out on the Long March died of cold and hunger on the way. But, crucially, the Red Army survived.

- **During the March**, Mao Zedong became the Red Army leader.

- **Chiang was forced** to join with Mao to fight Japan in World War II, and Mao built up the Red Army forces.

- **After the war**, Mao drove the weakened Kuomintang party out and took control. Chiang Kai-shek fled to Taiwan.

▶ *Pu-Yi, the last emperor of China before rebellion led to the country becoming a republic.*

World War II

- **In World War II** (1939–1945) 17 million soldiers were killed – compared to ten million in World War I. Plus, twice as many civilians were killed, through starvation, bombings and massacres.

- **It was the first truly global war** – fought on the plains of Europe, in the jungles of Southeast Asia, on the deserts of Africa, among the islands of the Pacific, on (and under) the Atlantic Ocean, and in many other places.

- **It began** when Hitler's Germany invaded Poland on 1 September 1939. Great Britain thought the USSR would defend Poland but Hitler and Stalin made a pact. As Germany invaded Poland from the west, the USSR invaded from the east.

- **After a lull**, or 'Phoney War', in May–June 1940, the Germans quickly overran Norway and Denmark, then Luxembourg, the Netherlands, Belgium and France.

'Never in the field of human conflict have so many owed so much to so few' – Churchill on the British fighter pilots.

- **The British army** was trapped by the Channel coast, but the Germans held back, and 338,000 British troops got away from Dunkirk, France, on an armada of little boats.

▶ *Winston Churchill (1874–1965) was the British prime minister whose courage and inspiring speeches helped the British withstand the German threat.*

458

▶ *The bombing of Pearl Harbor by the Japanese forced the US to enter the war. Almost 4000 people were killed or injured by the attack, with the main targets being US war ships.*

- **By August 1940,** Germany launched air raids on England to prepare for an invasion. This was the Battle of Britain.

- **Fearing the USSR** would turn against him, Hitler launched a sudden invasion of the USSR on 22 June, 1941. The USA joined the war when Japan bombed its fleet without warning in Pearl Harbor, Hawaii, on 7 December, 1941.

- **Germany, Italy, Japan** and six other nations joined forces as the 'Axis'. Britain, the USA, USSR, China and 50 other nations were together called the Allies. In 1942, the Allies halted the Axis in Africa, invading Italy in 1943 and France in 1944. In 1945, the Allies drove into Germany from east and west. Germany surrendered on 7 May, 1945. The terrible Pacific conflict ended when the USA dropped atom bombs on the Japanese cities Hiroshima and Nagasaki. Japan surrendered on 2 September, 1945.

- **As the Allies** moved into Germany, they found the horror of Nazi death camps like Auschwitz and Buchenwald, where millions of Jews and others had been slaughtered by starvation and in gas chambers.

> **. . . FASCINATING FACT . . .**
> The key to the early German successes was the Blitzkrieg ('lightning war') – a rapid attack with tanks and aeroplanes.

India

- **Indian discontent** with British rule began to boil after the British killed 379 protestors at Amritsar, in 1920.

- **In 1921**, Mahatma Gandhi became the leader of a movement demanding independence for India.

- **Gandhi** led a series of non-violent protests against the British, such as boycotting British goods and refusing to pay taxes. He gained millions of supporters.

- **In 1930**, Gandhi marched to the sea to make salt from seawater in protest against a tax on salt.

- **In 1935**, the British gave India a new constitution that allowed Indians more power. For the Muslims, however, who were led by Mohammed Ali Jinnah, this was not enough.

- **Jinnah demanded** a new country for Muslims called Pakistan, separate from the Hindus.

- **In World War II**, Indians said they would only fight on the British side if they were given independence.

- **In 1942**, Gandhi launched his 'Quit India' campaign to get rid of the British, who then jailed Indian leaders.

- **In 1946**, Britain offered independence to all of India, but Muslims did not want to live under a Hindu majority and terrible riots broke out in Calcutta.

- **Indian and British leaders** agreed to partition (split) India and Pakistan. Pakistan became independent on 14 August, 1947, India the next day. 7.2 million Muslims immediately fled to Pakistan and 7.3 million Hindus and Sikhs to India.

▶ *The Indian government building in Delhi.*

461

Mao

- **Mao Zedong** (1893–1976) led China's struggle towards communism and was China's leader for 27 years.

- **Mao was born** in 1893 to a poor peasant family in Shaoshan in Hunan.

- **In 1921**, he and 11 others formed the Chinese Communist Party. As support grew, Mao taught peasants guerilla tactics. He led the Red Army on the Long March.

◀ *The 'Little Red Book', properly called* The Thoughts of Chairman Mao, *became the bible of communist China.*

- **In 1949, Mao led** the communist takeover of China and then ruled the country as chairman of the republic. Chinese people hoped communism would end poverty and oppression. 'We have stood up,' Mao said.

- **Mao spurred** peasants to turf out landlords and work together on collective farms. Peasants who had starved in the war ate again. Healthcare and education improved.

- **Mao's ideas** were stated in a little red book – *The Thoughts of Chairman Mao* – learned by heart by Chinese children.

- **In 1957**, Mao's 'Great Leap Forward' forced his people to work on communes to develop farming and industry. The upheaval brought famine as well as economic disaster.

- **In 1959**, Mao retired as chairman, but stayed in control.

- **In 1966**, Mao launched a 'Cultural Revolution' to purge China of corrupting foreign ideas. Led by Mao's wife Jiang Qing and friends (the Gang of Four), Mao's enemies were killed and scholars were tortured and imprisoned.

- **Chairman Mao** died in 1976 and the Gang of Four were driven out.

▶ *Mao's picture taking pride of place at the Forbidden City, Beijing – a walled medieval palace that was once home to China's long line of emperors.*

Gandhi

- **Mohandas Gandhi** (1869–1948) was the inspirational leader who led India's fight for independence in a remarkable campaign of non-violent protest.

- **Gandhi is often called** Mahatma, which means 'Great Soul'. He believed truth could only be known through tolerance and concern for others.

- **He was born** in Probandar in India. At 13, he married a girl of 13 called Kasturbai. They later had four children. At 19 he went to study law in London.

- **Gandhi went to work** as a lawyer in South Africa in 1893, but soon after arriving was thrown out of a railway carriage because of the colour of his skin. He then stayed in South Africa for 21 years to fight for Indian rights.

▶ *Gandhi always dressed with extreme simplicity, wearing just a plain robe and shorts, his feet bare or in sandals.*

▶ *A gathering of Indian Hindus. Gandhi campaigned to stop conflict between Hindus and Muslims.*

- **Gandhi emphasized** non-violent protest. By imposing hardship on himself and showing no anger or hatred, he believed he could persuade his opponents he was right. This method of action was called *Satyagraha*.

- **In 1915 Gandhi returned** to India, and after the Amritsar massacre led India's fight for independence.

- **In 1920**, Gandhi began a programme of hand-spinning and weaving that he believed would give Indians economic independence, so challenging the British.

- **Gandhi was jailed** again and again for his protests, both in South Africa and India, and spent seven years in jail.

- **Gandhi was assassinated** on 30 January, 1948, by a Hindu who hated his tolerance of Muslims and others.

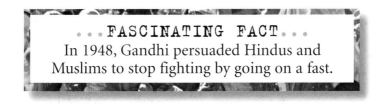

...FASCINATING FACT...
In 1948, Gandhi persuaded Hindus and
Muslims to stop fighting by going on a fast.

Israel

▲ *The Suez Canal, linking the Mediterranean and the Red Sea, was closed by Egypt during the 1967 war.*

- **In the 1920s**, Palestine was under British rule, and the British encouraged Jews to settle there.

- **In the aftermath** of the Holocaust, when Hitler killed six million Jews, most countries supported the idea of a homeland where Jews would not be persecuted.

- **In 1948**, the United Nations split Palestine between Arabs and Jews. Arabs saw this as a theft of Arab land.

- **Arabs immediately invaded Israel** (Jewish Palestine), but were defeated. Israel took over all of Palestine except the Gaza strip (to Egypt) and the West Bank (to Jordan).

- **In 1956–1957**, Arab Egypt took control of the Suez Canal.

- **In 1967**, Egypt closed the Gulf of Aqaba, Israel's only way to the Red Sea. Israel declared war on the Arab states.

- **Israel won the war** in just six days, and calls it the 'Six Day War'. Arabs call it the 'June War'. Afterwards, Israel controlled Sinai, the Gaza strip and the West Bank.

- **In 1973**, Egypt attacked the Israelis in Sinai, starting the Yom Kippur War. With US help, the Israelis repulsed them.

- **By the Camp David Accords** of 1978, Egypt recognized Israel's right to exist and Israel returned Sinai to Egypt. US president Jimmy Carter set up the agreement.

- **The PLO**, led by Yasser Arafat, began to fight for Palestinian independence after the Six Day War.

- **Israel has constructed settlements** in the West Bank, housing 400,000 Israelis.

- **The Gaza strip has been blockaded** by Israel since 2005–2007. However, the Palestinians have limited self rule in parts of the West Bank. Negotiations for a settlement have virtually ceased.

▼ *The mountainous, arid peninsula of Sinai has been fought over by Israel and Egypt for many years.*

The Cold War

- **The Cold War** was the rivalry between communist and non-communist countries after World War II – between the USSR and USA in particular.

- **It was called the Cold War** because the USSR and USA did not fight directly. But both supported countries that did, like the USA in Vietnam and the USSR in Korea.

- **The Iron Curtain** was the barrier between western Europe and communist eastern Europe.

- **The name Iron Curtain** was used by German propagandist Goebbels and adopted by Churchill.

- **The Berlin Wall** dividing communist East Berlin from the West was a powerful Cold War symbol. Dozens were shot trying to escape from the East over the wall.

◀ For many, the tearing down of the Berlin Wall, in 1989, marked the end of the Cold War. Berliners had a huge party on the ruins.

▶ *Fidel Castro, the prime minister of Cuba at the time of the 1962 missile crisis. The politics of Cuba's socialist revolutionary government was supported by the USSR and opposed by the USA.*

- **The Cold War** was fought using both propaganda and art, and by secret means such as spies and secret agents.

- **The USA and USSR** waged an arms race to build up nuclear bombs and missiles one step ahead of their rival.

- **Real war loomed** when US president Kennedy threatened the USSR as it attempted to build missile bases on the island of Cuba in 1962.

- **The Cold War** thawed after 1985, when Soviet leader Mikhail Gorbachev introduced reforms in the USSR and began to co-operate with the West.

- **In 1989, the Berlin Wall** came down. In 1989–1990, many eastern European countries broke away from Soviet control.

Scandinavia

- **In 1397**, Sweden, Norway and Denmark had joined together as one kingdom to combat the threat of German influence.

- **In 1523**, a Swedish noble called Gustavus Vasa took Sweden out of the Union. Under Gustavus Adolphus (ruled 1611–1632), and later Charles XII (ruled 1697–1718), Sweden became a powerful nation in its own right, and gained possession of Finland.

- **After the Napoleonic Wars**, Sweden lost Finland, but gained Norway from Denmark, which had sided with defeated France.

- **In the 1800s**, Norwegians began to revive national traditions – like the Viking language and 'Hardanger' fiddle music – and sought complete independence. This was finally granted in September 1905.

- **In World War II**, Norway tried to remain neutral, but Germany invaded.

◀ *Copenhagen's most famous landmark is the 1913 statue of the Little Mermaid, from the tale by Danish 19th-century children's writer, Hans Christian Andersen.*

▲ *The flag of the EU (European Union). Denmark joined the EU in 1973 and Sweden in 1995.*

- **The Germans** made a Norwegian who helped them, Vidkun Quisling, prime minister. Quisling is now a word for traitor.

- **Since 1932**, Sweden has been governed mostly by the socialist SDP, who have spread Sweden's high standard of living to all levels of society.

- **In 1966,** the National Insurance Act passed by Norway's Storting (parliament) gave Norwegians one of the world's best welfare systems.

- **In 1986**, Swedish PM Olof Palme was assassinated.

- **Although Sweden and Denmark** joined the European Union, Norwegians voted against joining in 1994.

Japan

- **In 1942**, Japanese conquests in World War II gave it a huge empire across Southeast Asia, but after it lost the decisive naval battle of Midway to the USA, the tide turned against Japan.

- **The final blow** for the Japanese was the devastating atomic bombs dropped on the cities of Hiroshima (6 August, 1945) and Nagasaki (9 August, 1945).

- **The Japanese accepted** the peace terms on 14 August, 1945, and surrendered to the USA on 2 September.

- **The surrender** brought a foreign occupying force to Japan, led by US general, Douglas MacArthur.

▲ *Emperor Hirohito (1901–1989) was the first Japanese emperor to give up his god-like status, ruling after 1945 as a figurehead only.*

- **MacArthur drew up** a new constitution for Japan. Under this, Emperor Hirohito lost all real power.

- **The Americans shared out** farmland, legalized unions and improved women's and children's rights.

- **The occupation force** left in 1952.

- **Led by the government**, Japan recovered from the ruin of the war and launched itself on an amazing industrial boom, which turned Japan into the world's healthiest economy in barely 25 years.

- **Japanese society** changed as people moved to the cities and the young began to behave independently.

- **In the 1980s**, the government was rocked by corruption scandals. The economy suffered too, as exports declined, and the country experienced a crisis of confidence.

- **An Asian financial crisis** in 1997 stalled the Japanese economy, which has seen relatively little growth since.

- **With an ageing population** and a falling birthrate, Japan's population is decreasing.

▲ *The devastating atomic blast at Hiroshima killed or wounded around 150,000 people.*

South Africa

▲ *Under the harsh rules of apartheid, blacks and whites were 'segregated' – kept apart from each other – in all kinds of public places and situations.*

- **In 1910**, four British colonies – Transvaal, Orange Free State, Cape Colony and Natal – joined to make the self-governing Union of South Africa.

- **White people** had almost complete power in the Union, while blacks had virtually no legal rights.

- **Mahatma Gandhi** campaigned for Indian rights in South Africa and had limited success.

- **Black South Africans set up** their own campaigning group in 1912, with the movement that was later called the ANC (African National Congress).

- **Afrikaners** – descended from the Dutch Boer people – began to fight for control. Their National Party made headway and in 1948 came to power. It enacted 'apartheid' laws to keep all the races firmly apart.

▶ *Nelson Mandela, South Africa's first black president. During his decades of imprisonment, Mandela provided a charismatic focus for ANC campaigns to end apartheid.*

- **The ANC** fought against apartheid – and especially against 'pass' laws that meant blacks had to carry passes.

- **In 1960**, police opened fire on protesting blacks at Sharpeville, killing 69. The government banned the ANC.

- **In the 1970s and 80s**, opposition to apartheid grew both in and outside South Africa, with many countries applying sanctions (trade restrictions).

- **In 1990**, President de Klerk released Nelson Mandela, an activist jailed since 1962, and repealed apartheid laws.

- **In 1994**, the ANC won the first open elections and Nelson Mandela became South Africa's first black president.

- **Under Mandela** (president 1994–1999), South Africa became a 'Rainbow Nation' in which different peoples cooperated. Court-like commissions investigated previous abuses of human rights and those guilty publicly sought forgiveness.

475

The United Nations

- **In the aftermath of World War I**, the great powers had set up a League of Nations – a forum for nations to come together, discuss world problems and so avoid war.

- **In 1942**, the Allies pledged to fight against the Axis powers with a statement called the Declaration by United Nations.

- **In 1944**, the same nations – including Britain, the USA, USSR and China – got together at Dumbarton Oaks in Washington D.C. to try and set up a peacekeeping organization.

- **The key to the Dumbarton Oaks plan** was a Security Council in which Britain, the USA, USSR and China would be permanent members.

- **In February 1945**, US president Roosevelt, British prime minister Churchill and Soviet leader Stalin met at Yalta in the Crimea and announced that a UN conference would meet in San Francisco. The three introduced the idea of them having a special veto (right to reject UN measures).

- **Fifty nations** met at San Francisco in April 1945 to draw up the Charter for the United Nations.

◀ *The UN flag flies over the UN's permanent headquarters in New York.*

- **Britain, the USA and USSR** gave themselves veto power over the Security Council, but the smaller nations gave the UN a General Assembly to help make it a global organization. France and China also have veto power.

- **The UN Charter** came into effect on 24 October, 1945.

- **In 1971**, the UN expelled Taiwan and admitted Communist China instead.

- **In recent years**, the UN peacekeeping force has been involved in keeping the peace in many places, including Haiti, the Congo, Kosovo, Sierra Leone and East Timor.

▼ *Churchill, Roosevelt and Stalin (from left) established the UN at their Yalta Conference, in 1945.*

Vietnam

- **From 1883**, Vietnam, along with Cambodia and Laos, was ruled by France as French Indochina.

- **As Germany invaded France** in World War II, Japan took over Vietnam.

- **When Japan was defeated**, in 1945, Vietnamese communists – the Vietminh, led by Ho Chi Minh – took over Vietnam.

- **British and Chinese troops** reclaimed Vietnam for the French, but the Vietminh fought back. The French set up a State of Vietnam under Emperor Bao Dai to oppose the Vietminh.

▲ *Ho Chi Minh, leader of the communist Vietminh.*

- **In 1954**, the warring parties agreed to split Vietnam into the North under Ho Chi Minh and the South under Bao Dai.

- **The Vietminh-backed Viet Cong** started a rebellion in the South. In 1965, the USA began to bomb North Vietnam, while the USSR and China supplied them with arms.

- **As fighting escalated**, Americans began to protest against US involvement and in 1973, the US withdrew.

- **In 1975**, the Viet Cong captured Saigon, the capital of the South, and the next year united North and South.

- **One million Vietnamese** left as refugees, but by 2000, Vietnam was developing quietly and some returned.

- **In the 21st century**, Vietnam's economy has expanded and the USA is now the country's leading trade partner.

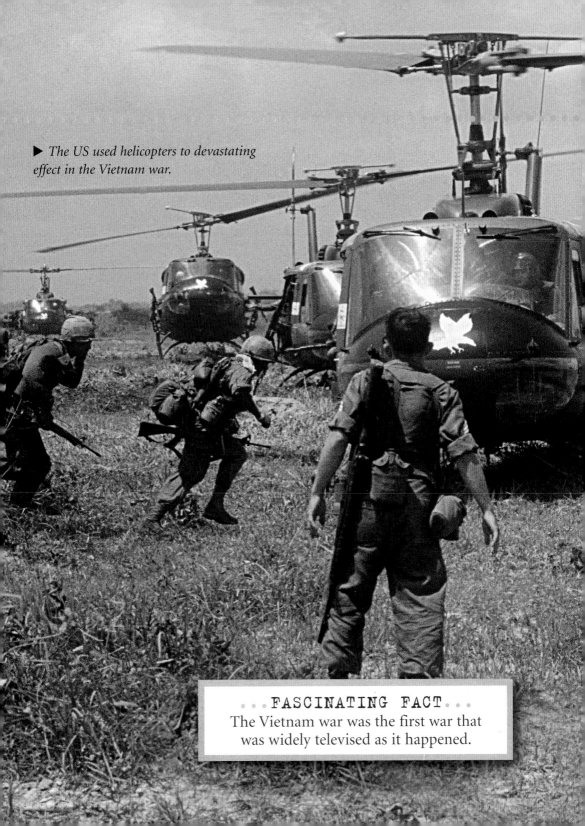

▶ *The US used helicopters to devastating effect in the Vietnam war.*

...FASCINATING FACT...
The Vietnam war was the first war that was widely televised as it happened.

Iraq and Iran

- **Iran used to be called** Persia, which, 2500 years ago, ruled over one of the great ancient empires.

- **The last shah** (king) of Iran was Muhammad Reza. Although backed by the USA, he was forced to flee the country in 1979 by Islamic extremists, led by the ayatollah (religious leader), Khomeini.

- **Iraq used to be called** Mesopotamia and was part of the Turkish Ottoman Empire until 1920 when it came under British control.

- **In 1930,** Iraq became independent as a kingdom but British influence was strong until the last king, Faisal II, was assassinated in 1958.

- **After years of wrangling,** Saddam Hussein became Iraqi president in 1979.

- **Saddam Hussein** was worried by the unsettling effects of the Islamic revolution in Iran and was also eager to seize disputed territory.

- **In September 1980,** Iraq invaded Iran to begin the eight-year-long Iran–Iraq War.

◀ *Ayatollah Khomeini – Iran's head of state from 1979 to 1989. He led a revolution in Iran that saw a return to very strict Islamic principles.*

- **The vicious war** devastated both countries and killed 1.5 million people. Iraq launched deadly bombing raids and Iran replied with missile attacks on Baghdad.

- **In 1988**, careful negotiations by the UN leader Perez de Cuéllar arranged a peace settlement.

- **In 1990**, Iraq invaded and annexed Kuwait.

- **In 1992**, in the Gulf War, a US-led multinational force expelled Iraqi forces from Kuwait.

- **In 2003**, accusing Saddam of possessing 'weapons of mass destruction', a US-led force invaded Iraq, ousting Saddam. The country collapsed in anarchy, as they fought each other and the foreign troops.

- **From 2003 to 2007**, large scale insurgency and terrorism claimed many thousands of Iraqi lives. Violence in Iraq continues on a smaller scale and foreign troops are withdrawing.

- **Saddam was captured in 2003**, tried in 2005–2006, and executed in 2006.

- **The collapse of Iraq** allowed Iran to become stronger and relations between Iran and the West greatly deteriorated.

- **Muslim clerics established** a dictatorship in Iran and elections in 2009 were rigged, leading to huge protests by ordinary Iranians.

- **Iran is accused** by America and the West of wanting to develop nuclear weapons.

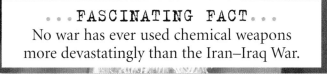

...FASCINATING FACT...
No war has ever used chemical weapons
more devastatingly than the Iran–Iraq War.

The break-up of the USSR

- **After Stalin died**, in 1953, many people were released from the Siberian prison camps, but the USSR, under its new leader Khrushchev, remained restrictive and secretive.

- **The KGB** was a secret police force. It dealt harshly with anyone who did not toe the communist line.

- **In the 1980s**, cracks began to appear in the communist machine.

- **In 1985**, Mikhail Gorbachev became Soviet leader and introduced policies of *perestroika* (economic reform), *glasnost* (government openness) and *demokratizatsiya* (increased democracy).

- **Gorbachev** also cut spending on arms, and improved relationships with the West.

- **In 1989**, a McDonalds restaurant opened in Moscow.

- **As people in the USSR** gained freedom, so people in communist eastern Europe demanded freedom. New democratic governments were elected in Hungary, Poland, Czechoslovakia, Romania and Bulgaria.

  - **The republics** within the USSR wanted independence too, and in 1991 the USSR was dissolved.

    - **Gorbachev's reforms** angered Communist Party leaders, who staged a coup and imprisoned Gorbachev, but he was freed and the coup was brought down by Boris Yeltsin, who became the first president of Russia (once the largest republic in the USSR).

◀ *Mikhail Gorbachev.*

- **Under Yeltsin**, the state industries of the Soviet era were gradually broken up and Russia seemed to be moving towards Western-style capitalism. But the collapse of the Communist Party structure led to chaos, lawlessness and economic problems. In 2000, the Russians elected Vladimir Putin as president, a strong leader who they hoped would see them out of the crisis.

- **Putin** (president 2000–2008 and PM since 2008) brought firm government but gradually restricted freedom. However, Russia grew more prosperous exporting oil and gas, and now much of Europe depends on Russian gas to keep warm.

▲ *The Kremlin, in Moscow, dates back to the 1100s and is a walled collection of palaces and churches. Home to the tsars, it then became the seat of USSR government.*

483

The European Union

- **The European Union** is an organization of 27 European countries, including France, Germany and the UK.

- **After World War II ended**, in 1945, Jean Monnet promoted the idea of uniting Europe economically and politically.

- **In 1952**, six countries formed the European Coal and Steel Community (ECSC), to trade in coal and steel.

- **The success of the ECSC** led the member countries to break down all trade barriers between them as part of the European Community (EC), in 1967.

- **From 1973 to 1981**, six new countries join the EC, including the UK.

- **In 1992**, the 12 EC members signed a treaty at Maastricht in the Netherlands to form the European Union (EU).

- **The EU added** cooperation on justice and police matters and cooperation in foreign and security affairs to the economic links of the EC. These three links are called the 'Three Pillars' of the EU.

- **The EU has five governing bodies**: the European Council, the Commission, Council of Ministers, Court of Justice and Parliament. The 27 Commissioners submit laws for the Council to make and put into effect. Parliament has very limited powers but is gaining more each year.

- **In 1999**, the EU launched the Euro, which is intended to become a single European currency.

- **The European Council**, which is made up of the heads of state or of government of each country, meets four times a year. Since 2009, it includes an official called the President of the European Council who represents the EU.

- **In 2009**, the last EU member approved the Lisbon Treaty, which simplified and streamlined the government of the EU.

▼ *The European Commission building in
Brussels. The Parliament is in Strasbourg.
The Court of Justice is in Luxembourg.*

Latin America

▶ *Activist Che Guevara played a major part in Cuba's revolution. Leaving Cuba for South America, he met an early death at the hands of political enemies and became an enduring hero, especially to young people in the 1960s and 1970s.*

- **In the 1950s**, many Latin American countries sought to break their dependence on single agricultural products such as sugar and beef by undertaking major industrialization programmes.

- **'Populist' alliances** between workers and industrialists came to the fore.

- **In Argentina**, Juan Perón came to power and tried to build up industry at the expense of agriculture.

- **Landowners** who were suffering from the emphasis on industry began to form alliances with the army. Army coups took place in Argentina (1955), Brazil (1964) and Chile (1973).

- **Many of the military regimes** in the region were secretly backed by foreign powers such as the USA.

- **In the 1960s**, some Latin American groups resorted to guerrilla warfare to bring down the military dictatorships.

- **In 1959**, an Argentinian communist called Che Guevara helped overthrow the dictator of Cuba and bring Fidel Castro to power.

- **In 1967**, Che Guevara was killed leading a guerilla band trying to overthrow the dictator of Bolivia.

- **Under the dictators**, opposition was suppressed and many people were tortured, imprisoned or 'disappeared', as 20,000 did in Argentina.

- **In the 1980s and 1990s**, economic failure brought down most Latin American dictators, including Pinochet in Chile (1990) and Galtieri in Argentina (1983).

- **Many of the Latin American nations** became democracies in the 1990s.

- **Brazil has become an economic giant**, but the destruction of its rainforests worries scientists and others.

◀ *Eva Perón, also known as Evita (1919–1952), was the wife of Argentinian leader Juan Perón. A former actress, she was loved by ordinary people and wielded great power in her husband's government.*

487

Index

F

factories 402
    Industrial Revolution 394, 395
    Russian Revolution 442, 443
    Victorian Age 432
Faeroes 276
Faisal I, king of Iraq *417*, 480
Falange party, Spain 454, *455*
famine 205
Faridun 104
farming **36–37**, *37*, 38, 147
    ancient Egypt 46
    Anglo-Saxons 240
    Aryans 80, 81
    Barbarians 226
    Britain 216
    China 54
    Ireland 188
    Iron Age 30
    Japan 178
    Meso America 76
    Mesopotamia 40
    Mexico 119
    migrations 44
    New Guinea 92
    North America 186
    revolution 392, 394
    Roman Empire 164, 228
    Semites 88
    Stone Age 26
    Vikings 252, *253*
Fasa 203
fascists, Spain 454, *455*
fashions, Egyptian 64
Father Apsu 52
Fatimah, caliph 246
February Revolution 443
Ferdinand II, emperor of Austria 372
Ferdinand, Franz 444
fermentation 147
feudal system 312
fiefs 302

figurines, Venus 27
Fiji 96
Finland 470
Fir Bolgs 215
Firdausi 102
fireworks *124*, *224*
fishing 64, 188, 252
Flanders 312
flints *16*, 26, 36, 188
flood stories 41, *41*, 204
Florence,
    Medicis 334, *335*
    Renaissance 329
    trade 312
Flores 18
Fon 201
food **146–147**, 280
football 125
Forbidden City, Beijing *61*, 322, *463*
Ford, Henry 430
forensic scientists 35
Forkbeard, Sweyn 282
Formorians 214
forts 226
forum 170, *170*
Fotheringay 363
Fountains Abbey, England 321
Fourier, Second Empire 440
France,
    Africa 423
    cave paintings 24, *25*
    Celts 210
    Charlemagne 270
    Charles Martel 132, 270
    Crimean War 427
    Cro-Magnon Man 22
    duke of Normandy 288
    European Union 484
    Gauls 196, *196*
    Germany 428
    Holy Roman Empire 264
    Hundred Years War 310
    Indochina 478

Industrial Revolution 394
Joan of Arc 324
Julius Caesar 190
Louis XIV 370
megaliths 32
monasteries 320, 321
Napoleonic Wars 406
philosophers 383
Prussia 405
Queen Mary 362
revolution 382, 408
Roman Empire *169*
Second Empire 440, 441
Sweden 470
Vikings 252, 253
War of Austrian Succession 404
World War I 444, 445, *445*
World War II 458, 459
Francis I, emperor 404, *405*
Francis, king of France 362
Franciscan monks *321*
Franco, General 454, *454*, 455
Frankish king 132
Franks 132, **196–197**, 264, 270
Franks, Battle of Tours 302
Franz Ferdinand, archduke *434*, 435
Fravashi 105
Frederick I, king of Prussia 405
Frederick II, king of Prussia 405
Frederick the Great *404*
French,
    British Empire 416
    Crusades 304
    India 386
    Italy 412, 413
    North America 388
    opium wars 437

French empire 398
French planters 378
French popes 314, *315*
French Revolution **390–391**, 398, 406
frescoes 69
Freya 261
Friedland 406
Frigg 261
Fronde, Louis XIV 370
Fu Su, China 130, 131
Fuad I, king of Egypt *417*
fuedal system **302–303**
Fujiwara rulers 344
Fujiwaras **238–239**, *239*
furnaces 31
Fyodor 361

G

Gabriel 167
Gades 149
Gaels 210
Gaia 150
Gaius, emperor 168
Galatia, Turkey 196
galleons *350*, 351
Gallia *169*
Gallipoli 445
Gallo-Romans 196
Galtieri 487
gambling 174
games 174
Gandhi, Mahatma 460, **464–465**, 474
Ganesha 84
Gang of Four 463
Ganges river, India 184, 192
Gaozu, emperor 56
Garibaldi 413, *413*
Gassire's Lute **202–203**
gatherers *147*
Gaul 190, **196–197**, 240
Gautama, Siddhartha 134, 135
Gayomart 102
Gaza Strip, Israel 466
Geb 66

Acknowledgements

The publishers would like to thank the following artists
who have contributed to this book:
Richard Berridge, Vanessa Card, Peter Dennis, Nicholas Forder, Chris Forsey,
Mike Foster, Terry Gabbey, Studio Galante, Sally Holmes, Richard Hook,
John James, Roger Kent, Aziz Khan, Angus McBride, Kevin Maddison,
Janos Marffy, Roger Payne, Terry Riley, Martin Sanders, Peter Sarson,
Rob Sheffield, Guy Smith, Nick Spender, Roger Stewart, Mike Taylor,
Rudi Vizi, Mike White, John Woodcock

The publishers would like to thank the following sources
for the use of their photographs:
CORBIS: Page 80 Lyndsey Hebberd; 236 Bass Museum of Art; 265 Archivo IcongraficoSA;
313 Michael Maslan Historic Photographs; 357 Philadelphia Museum of Art;
359 Asian Art and Archaeology Inc; 373 Macduff Everton;
383 Leonard de Selva; 408 Archivo IcongraficoSA; 436 Sean Sexton Collection;
455 Corbis; 461 Angelo Hornak; 479 Bettmann

All other pictures Corel; Digital STOCK; ILN; PhotoDisc